JAZZMEN

JAZZMEN

EDITED BY

FREDERIC RAMSEY, JR.

AND CHARLES EDWARD SMITH

WITH 32 PAGES OF ILLUSTRATIONS

NEW YORK

HARCOURT, BRACE AND COMPANY

Republished 1972
Scholarly Press, Inc., 22929 Industrial Drive East
St. Clair Shores, Michigan 48080

first edition

Library of Congress Cataloging in Publication Data

Ramsey, Frederic, 1915-   ed.
  Jazzmen.

  1. Jazz music. 2. Negro musicians.
3. Musicians, American. I. Smith, Charles Edward,
joint ed. II. Title.
ML3561.J3R3 1972   781.7'73   78-181233
ISBN 0-403-01654-1

"Now here is the list about that Jazz Playing. King Bolden and myself were the first men that began playing Jazz in the city of dear old New Orleans and his band had the whole of New Orleans Real Crazy and Running Wild behind it. Now that was all you could hear in New Orleans, that King Bolden's Band, and I was with him and that was between 1895 and 1896 and they did not have any dixie land Jazz Band in those days. Now here are the Bands that were in their prime in them days: Adam Olivier Band, John Robichaux, old Golden Rule, Bob Russell Band. Now that was all. And here is the thing that made King Bolden Band be the First Band that played Jazz. It was because it did not Read at all. I could fake like 500 myself; so you tell them that Bunk and King Bolden's Band was the first ones that started Jazz in the City or any place else. And now you are able to go now ahead with your Book."

FROM A LETTER TO THE EDITORS
BY WILLIE G. "BUNK" JOHNSON

CONTENTS

Introduction   xi

NEW ORLEANS

"Callin' our chillun home"   3

I   New Orleans Music   7
     by William Russell and Stephen W. Smith

II   White New Orleans   39
     by Charles Edward Smith

III   King Oliver and his Creole Jazz Band   59
     by Frederic Ramsey, Jr.

CHICAGO

"Every tub on its own bottom"   95

IV   Blues   101
     by E. Simms Campbell

V   Louis Armstrong   119
     by William Russell

VI   Bix Beiderbecke   143
     by Edward J. Nichols

VII   The Austin High School Gang   161
     by Charles Edward Smith

VIII   Boogie Woogie   183
     by William Russell

NEW YORK

"I'd rather drink muddy water, Lord"   209

IX   New York Turns on the Heat   213
     by Wilder Hobson

 X   The Five Pennies   221
     by Otis Ferguson

HOT JAZZ TODAY

"The world's jazz crazy, Lawdy, so am I"   245

  XI   Fifty-second Street   249
       by Wilder Hobson

 XII   Return to Chicago   255
       by Frederic Ramsey, Jr.

XIII   Land of Dreams   265
       by Charles Edward Smith

XIV   Hot Collecting   287
       by Stephen W. Smith

 XV   Consider the Critics   301
       by Roger Pryor Dodge

       Index   343

       Index of Music   355

ILLUSTRATIONS

NEW ORLEANS   32

    The Buddy Bolden Band—Laine's Band

    Basin Street Transom—"Down the Line"

    Baquet—Oliver—Keppard

    Henry Allen's Brass Band, Algiers, Louisiana

    The Original Superior Orchestra

    Joseph Petit at home

    Leon Rappolo—Band on riverboat *Sidney*

    Louis Armstrong, his mother and sister

    Roy Palmer, Sugar Johnny, Lawrence Dewey

    Ory's Band in California—Pop Foster

    The Original Creole Band

    King Oliver's Band in California, 1921

CHICAGO   128

    King Oliver's Creole Jazz Band

    King Oliver in the Plantation Café

    The Wolverines—Bix Beiderbecke

    The Old Sunset Café—Armstrong, Weatherford

    Louis Armstrong and his Hot Five

    Louis' Stompers—Dickerson's Orchestra

Husk O'Hare's Wolverines—Midway Garden
  Orchestra

Rappolo—Spanier—Teschmaker

Boogie Woogie pianists—Davenport—Yancey—
  Lofton

Bessie Smith

Johnny Dodds and Sidney Bechet

Fletcher Henderson—Luis Russell

HOT JAZZ TODAY   272

Duke Ellington and his Orchestra

Ella Fitzgerald

New Orleans, 1939

Willie Bunk Johnson

Jack Teagarden

Pete Johnson

Albert Ammons and Meade Lux Lewis

Hot Record Society holds a session

INTRODUCTION

IN PREPARING *Jazzmen* we have had a very definite purpose: to relate the story of jazz as it has unfolded about the
men who created it, the musicians themselves. To this story,
we have appended Roger Pryor Dodge's careful résumé of
the critical attitude which has developed along with jazz, and
Stephen Smith's remarks on the vagaries of hot record collecting, a hobby often coincidental with an interest in jazz
music.

But the center of the stage is reserved for two main groups
of musicians. The first group comprises the relatively small
company that made hot spots hotter in New Orleans of the
late nineteenth century. These were the men who "put jazz
on the map." Some of them are dead now, others are alive,
but forgotten and neglected. Like Willie "Bunk" Johnson,
they have had to forego former glories, abandon music, drive
a truck for $1.75 a day during the rice season, and starve the
rest of the time. As "Bunk" says, they must put their "nose
to the Grinding Stone," and forget about playing. More fortunate members of the pioneer group, some of them disciples
of "Bunk," like Louis Armstrong, are very much alive today,
still standing up in front of the lights and blowing on golden
trumpets presented by admiring friends.

From this first group of jazz pioneers, treated as a focal
point in the development of hot music, our story has gone
forward to a second group, which includes those who have
carried on the traditions of the pioneers and continued to
play jazz at its best. The forceful impact of Bessie Smith, the

"Empress of the Blues," upon the whole of jazz comes into our history at this point.

Far from being a history of things past, the story of *Jazzmen* has such continuity that past fuses with present. We cannot, as more esoteric members of the critical fraternity would have us do, overlook the present merely because it is here and now. The Boogie Woogie piano players had already developed a mature style in the early twenties, yet it waited until 1938 to find ready acceptance in the hot music field, and by such dispensers of musical taste as the arrangers. An inspired Sidney Bechet and a vigorous Louis Armstrong are also a part of this present which boasts a diversity of great, if scattered, talent.

This book represents a divergence of opinion, as an anthology should. It has been written by men selected for outstanding knowledge of particular subjects. Each man brings to his subject a thorough acquaintance with the music, and, generally speaking, with the men who play it. He brings to the writing of his material an enthusiasm born of a conviction that *Jazzmen* is a book that had to be written. We have retained discrepancies of opinion. Like most lively and healthy arts, jazz stirs up sharp critical differences, some of which appear contradictory, yet a surprising unanimity is found today among critics of hot music. Fortunately for jazz, fierce *discussion* is still the rule; as yet, standards haven't sifted down into dry dust, and no Academy of Jazz Music has been founded. Until this happens, hope remains for it. While retaining the contrasting opinions of each contributor, we have at the same time thrown the emphasis of the work upon the jazzmen. For it is the musicians, the creators of jazz, who have actually been most neglected while critical battles have been fought. We feel that their story, heretofore untold, is of major value. The article "New Orleans Music" implies what has long needed emphasis, that from any esthetic point of view the background of the blues, and consequently of jazz, has as much validity in its own field as any other form of art. In the course of time, the criticism of today will seem relatively unimportant. Already, source material obtained from the jazzmen themselves assumes much greater significance than it did ten or twenty years ago. This book has attempted to fill the gaps left by critics who, chiefly concerned with their appraisal of the music, have forgotten the musicians.

The method of research employed is worthy of notice. One or another of the authors has interviewed every living jazz musician who could contribute factual material. In some cases, their remarks were directly transcribed in shorthand; in others, careful notes were taken. The sum-total of information obtained in this manner was then typed and made available to all the contributors. Information from different sources was carefully collated and checked. A second series of interviews followed in order to clear up doubtful points. Each author prepared his contribution on the basis of this material; then a running text which continues the narrative from section to section was written. The search for this data has been an arduous but interesting one, taking us to the dives of Harlem, Chicago, and New Orleans, to the rice fields of Louisiana, to Storyville, the now legendary red-light district of New Orleans, to reform schools, even to the last stopping place of at least two jazz pioneers, a hospital for the insane.

Through it all we have tried to remember what the public would like to know about Buddy Bolden and Leon Rappolo and the rest of them. And we have decided that it would be pretty much what we ourselves found of interest. We asked Papa Laine for a story about Dave Perkins. Papa Laine said, "Well, I don't know any stories, but I'll tell you something that really happened." That's what we've tried to do in this book.

The editors owe a particular debt to the musicians whose names appear below. They have all generously contributed information previously unavailable from any sources, and throughout have encouraged and heartened us by their interest. Without their co-operation, this book could never have been written:

Henry Allen, Jr., Albert Ammons, Lillian Hardin Armstrong, Louis Armstrong, Isidore Barbarin, Paul Barbarin, Leonard Bechet, Sidney Bechet, "Sharkey" Bonano, Steve Brown, Tom Brown, Wellman Braud, Albert Brunies, Bill Challis, "Buddy" Christian, Lee Collins, Eddie Condon, Charles Cooke, William M. Cornish, "Cow Cow" Davenport, "Baby" Dodds, Johnny Dodds, Nat Dominique, Charles Elgar, "Duke" Ellington, George "Pop" Foster, "Bud" Freeman, Benny Goodman, Fred "Tubby" Hall, Otto Hardwick, Charlie Harris, Fletcher Henderson, J. C. Higginbotham, Earl Hines, Preston Jackson, James P. Johnson, Pete Johnson, Will M. Johnson, Captain Joseph Jones, Richard M. Jones, Rod Kless, Tommy Ladnier, Jack Laine, Jim Lannigan, Meade "Lux" Lewis, Steve Lewis, Joe Lindsay, "Cripple Clarence" Lofton, Bob Lyons, Jimmy MacPartland, Paul Mares, Joe Marsala, Marty Marsala, "Red" McKenzie, Ferdinand "Jelly Roll" Morton, "Big Eye" Louis Nelson, Jimmy Noone, Dave North, Manuel Perez, Alphonse J. Picou, J. Armand Piron, Luis Russell, "Pee Wee" Russell, Henry "Kid" Rena, Omer Simeon, "Zutty" Singleton, Ruby Smith, Francis "Muggsy" Spanier, Jess Stacy, Erskine Tate, "Pip" Villani, "Buck" Washington, George Wettling, Clarence Williams, Mayo Williams, and Jimmy Yancey.

Thanks are due to relatives of musicians who have generously provided us with additional research material: Mrs. Gladys B. Araumburo, Beatrice Armstrong, Mrs. Beiderbecke, Mrs. Rosa B. Graham, Joseph A. Johnson, Mrs. Victoria Johnson, Mrs. E. C. Rappolo, Mrs. Mary Rappolo, Mrs. Henry Rena, and Mrs. Marge Creath Singleton.

A special paragraph belongs to Willie "Bunk" Johnson for his invaluable contributions to this work, for his many letters that told us of "the city of dear old New Orleans" and the musicians who played in it. We found "Bunk" after a long, apparently hopeless search for a name that first appeared as legend only. A letter addressed in care of the postmaster of New Iberia, Louisiana, finally reached him. Then came a series of letters which told his story with remarkable freshness and clarity.

Finally, thanks are due to E. M. Ashcraft III, R. Park Breck, Sterling A. Brown, Albert Callahan, Larry Cunningham, Ernest Giardina, John Henry Hammond, Jr., Bud Hassler, David Kellum, Hoyte D. Kline, Alan Lomax, Franklyn Lyons, Paul Eduard Miller, Paul Morris, Roscoe Peacock, Dave Peyton and the Editors of the Chicago *Defender*, Dan Qualey, Herman Rosenberg, Francis Stanton and William Wagner for further information and assistance; and to Margaret Kidder, Mrs. Stephen W. Smith, and Alan Walker for checking data and helpful criticism.

F. R., JR.
C. E. S.

NEW ORLEANS

"Callin' our chillun home"

A FANTASTIC and wonderful city. A city with a hundred faces. The hard face for commerce and the soft face for making love. Scratching figures on the back of an envelope where the girl with the deep dark eyes waits on counter. Smell of burnt coffee and sound of ships. The deep face for a sad life and the pinched face for poverty. Marching, singing, laughing. The silver and copper laugh of the prostitute, and the toothless chuckle of the old man who remembers Buddy Bolden at Bogalusa.

Every writer makes his own city. The city of fine living and free spirit, woven into the dream of a poet. The city of brass bands and military marches, grand balls and rowdy lakefront parties. The city of Lulu White and Mahogany Hall, Josie Arlington and the palm tree growing crazily there in a vacant lot. The thin young man who drinks too much, looking at Congo Square, squeezing the last acrid sweetness out of sight and sound.

> Come on and hear
> Come on and hear

This is our city, not so far from Madame John's legacy but carrying with it another legacy, the dark human cargo of a Yankee slaver, the Marquis de Vaudreuil, raising a thin glass above a fringed cuff, drinking the drink and shattering the glass into tiny tinkling fragments. Bamboula and tinkling glass. Flat voices of invitation behind shuttered cribs. Canal Street murky yellow with night, her standards the Carnival colors, symbols of transient ownership, like a mistress smiling in turn at her lovers.

Up Rampart beyond Canal. That's Uptown. That's Bolden territory. Perdido by the gas works. Maybe there used to be a cypress swamp there but nobody remembers now. Everybody

remembers Bolden and his barber shop and his scandal sheet
and his ragtime band, playing a new music that didn't have a
name of its own. (They say the word for it came from Chicago
"down around 22nd"; they say it came from an Elizabethan
slang word meaning hit it hard and from an American slang
word meaning it don't mean a thing but it costs real money
around 22nd.)

Don't look for the eagle on the Eagle Saloon. And don't
look for Masonic Hall because it's a vacant lot. But listen
hard some night, listen hard at the corner of Rampart and
Perdido and you'll hear a whacky horn playing an uptown rag,
way out and way off, filling out the tune. That would be King
Bolden, calling his children.

If you want to know why Ragtime (the first) wasn't jazz,
and why uptown rags weren't just a new ragtime but had to
wait for a trip up the river to get a name out of the barrel,
well, listen to that horn. There's a little of it in Louis and in
Joe Oliver and in Bunk. Maybe if you listen close there's a
little of it here, between the covers of a book. Maybe if you
listen hard (standing on the corner of Rampart and Perdido
where the old Eagle sign blew down one night) you'll see
what Bunk meant when he played that way, and what Louis
meant when he played that way, and what Buddy Bolden
meant when he said, "You can't play without the king."

Maybe you'd go down Perdido where there aren't any side-
walks, even today, and where the battered houses squat in patterns of poverty, with a hedge or a flower or a puny palm tree
out front, trying to say what poverty can't say . . .

I knows how to write!

And maybe you don't think this has much to do with jazz,
or the city we'd like to build for you. But if you want to go
with the saints to the funeral (to a slow march) you want to
know where he lived and died, don't you, and what he was
up against because his skin was black or white or maybe a

shade between? You want to know why he came from the beat side of town (but wasn't beat) to play down in Storyville where they wanted the blues slow and mean and the rags fast and dirty, to play for a gangster out at Pontchartrain (the big shot from Chicago who threw the dough around), to play in the brass bands Carnival Day and on the wagons Sunday night.

Maybe you'll turn back, see the slave ships unload their flesh-and-blood cargo, see the trickle from the plantation country . . . free bewildered black skin, coffee skin, saffron skin, coming to the hard city of commerce, soft city of song, martial city of music, dream city of silver and copper laughter. And you'll find the answer, you'll know why it began just there, not somewhere else.

You have to think of New Orleans the band city or it will be hard to understand why it couldn't have happened on the levee at Memphis, on the waterfront of Savannah, or on the Gulf Coast with the deep, sobbing blues. You think of the band city, the opera, the funerals and the balls, you think of the Creole Negroes:

"Jazz came from uptown."

"It was that raggedy uptown stuff."

Elsewhere they forgot the music that they had brought with them, and they forgot the words. In Carolina all that would be left would be the blues and a children's nonsense game with some words that might have come over in the hold of a Yankee clipper or might have been made up out of the sharp phonetics of children at play.

In New Orleans you could still hear the bamboula on Congo Square when Buddy Bolden cut his first chorus on cornet. You could still hear the bamboula and you couldn't see a note of written music. Whatever he learned he put away when he started off on the real tune. It was something like Bunk:

If you put down what Bunk played he would say,
do you think I'm a fool, I can't play that!

Cajun or Creole, black or white, the others heard. They heard because their lives were part of that life, and because the music didn't draw a color line. White or black or a shade between, they listened hard when the Bolden Band pointed its horns towards Lincoln Park, because that was the King.

Old Willy Cornish said the crowd would be over there, with Robichaux, and Bolden's Band would start right out like the killers they were. You could see a glow on his very dark cheek and the soft voice seemed to come from back there, wherever his eyes were. He said that was

callin' our chillun home.

C. E. S.

I

NEW ORLEANS MUSIC

BY WILLIAM RUSSELL
AND STEPHEN W. SMITH

EARLY IN the nineteenth century, soon after the Louisiana Purchase, slaves were allowed for the first time to assemble for social and recreational diversion. The most popular meeting place was a large open field at Orleans and Rampart, known as Congo Square. In earlier times the space had been a ceremonial ground of the Oumas Indians. Today, landscaped with palm trees, it forms a part of the municipal grounds called Beauregard Square. The Negroes, however, still speak of the place as Congo Square, in memory of the days when it was an open, dusty field, its grass worn bare by the stomping and shuffling of hundreds of restless bare feet. A century ago, slaves met there every Saturday and Sunday night to perform the tribal and sexual dances which they had brought with them from the Congo.

Before the Civil War the Congo Dances were one of the unusual sights of New Orleans to which tourists were always taken. At times almost as many white spectators as dancers gathered for the festive occasions. That the Negroes had not forgotten their dances, even after years of repression and exile from their native Africa, is attested by descriptive accounts of the times. Gaily dressed in their finest, many of the men with anklets of jingles, the Negroes rallied at the first roll of the bamboulas, large tom-toms constructed from casks covered with cowhide and beaten with two long beef bones. Galvanized by the steady, hypnotic rumble of drums, the frenzied crowd was transported to Guinea, their traditional homeland. The men, prancing, stomping and shouting, "Dansez Bamboula! Badoum! Badoum!" weaved around the women, who, swaying as their bare feet massaged the earth, intoned age-old chants. The shrieks of children around the edge of the square, as they mimicked the dancers, mingled with the cries of vendors of ginger-cakes, sweetmeats, and brilliant-hued liquors.

Though discontinued during the war, the Congo Dances were again performed after the emancipation and were not entirely abandoned even two decades later, when a correspondent of the New York World reported:

A dry-goods box and an old pork barrel formed the orchestra. These were beaten with sticks or bones, used like drumsticks so as to keep up a continuous rattle, while some old men and women chanted a song that appeared to me to be purely African in its many vowelled syllabification. . . . In the dance, the women did not move their feet from the ground. They only writhed their bodies and swayed in undulatory motions from ankles to waist. . . . The men leaped and performed feats of gymnastic dancing. . . . Small bells were attached to their ankles. . . . Owing to the noise I could not even attempt to catch the words of the song. I asked several old women to recite them to me, but they only laughed and shook their heads. In their patois they told me—"no use, you could never understand it. C'est le Congo!"

Voodoo incantations, brought over on slave ships, were the foundation for religious chants and songs of consolation of those who felt the weight of the "Black Man's Burden" and the sting of their master's lash. By nature the Negroes were no less happy than other people. But mirth and laughter find little expression in the song of a people long depressed with thoughts of exile, slavery, and oppression. Music born under such conditions can only express a spirit of resignation touched with yearnings. Thus, the primitive African chants, some consisting apparently only of incessant moans, became the basis of the blues.

Before emancipation, the musical instruments of the slaves had to be mainly home-made affairs. The drums were at first hollowed out of logs. After covering one end with skin, the drums were beaten with bare hands. The term "bamboula dance" came from the name of the smallest drum which was originally fashioned from a tube of bamboo. Other instruments were rattles, such as a pair of bones used as castanets, and the jaw bones of asses. When the latter were left out in the sun to dry, the teeth loosened and rattled when struck. Other instruments of African origin were a crudely formed banjo and a type of marimbula similar to that now used in Cuba.

In New Orleans after the Civil War, Negroes began to use more and more the usual wind and string instruments of the whites. Such instruments were already widely used by the Creole Negroes, most of whom, though skilled in written music, were not so close to the blues background. The latter were improvisational in character. Soon Negro groups, having learned to play by ear, were engaged to play for dances and by 1880 were found on some of the packets on the Mississippi River. On the boats the Negroes worked as porters, barbers, and waiters during the day and entertained the passengers with music at night.

Historians point out that few of these early musicians could read music; that they were "fake" players. This is a highly significant fact when one considers how the music of the jazz band evolved and reached maturity during the last years of the nineteenth century. Although naturally influenced by the music of their former masters, the Negroes retained much of the African material in their playing. The leader of the first great orchestra, Buddy Bolden, was already in his teens before the Congo Dances were discontinued. The Negroes were accustomed to endless repetition of short motifs and were not bothered by the brevity of form in the white man's popular song. Nor did they worry about the trite character of the melodies, for being unaccustomed to read music, they quickly altered the tune anyway.

With the New Orleans Negro, improvisation was an essential part of musical skill, as is the case with every extra-European musician. In all cultures except that of Europe, where for a century improvisation has been a lost art, creative performance is a requisite. Thus, where there was no premium on exact repetition and hide-bound imitation, only those with the urge to express themselves and an innate power of invention took up music. When a musician could play only what he *felt*, those without feeling never even got started and mediocre talents soon fell by the wayside. It is important to note that the greatest talent went into dance orchestras, the *only* field open for those with professional musical ambitions.

The fact that these men were not primarily note readers also explains, when collective improvisation was attempted, the origin of the characteristic New Orleans polyphony, which in its more complex manifestations became a dissonant counterpoint that antedated Schoenberg.

The young New Orleans aspirant, having no teacher to show him the supposed limitations of his instrument, went ahead by himself and frequently hit upon new paths and opened up undreamed-of possibilities. In classical music the wind instruments had always lagged behind in their development. Especially the brasses were subordinated to the strings. But the freedom of the New Orleans musician from any restraining tradition and supervision enabled him to develop on most of the instruments not only new technical resources but an appropriate and unique jazz style. Incidentally, the remarkable technical equipment of many of the instrumentalists can be explained partly by the abundance of time on their hands.

So when Buddy Bolden, the barber of Franklin Street, gathered his orchestra together in the back room of his shop to try over a few new tunes for a special dance at Tin Type Hall, it was no ordinary group of musicians. Nor was Buddy an ordinary cornetist. In his day, he was entirely without competition, both in his ability as a musician and his hold upon the public. The power of his sonorous tone has never been equaled. When Buddy Bolden played in the pecan grove over in Gretna, he could be heard across the river throughout uptown New Orleans. Nor was Bolden just a musician. He was an "all-around" man. In addition to running his barber shop, he edited and published *The Cricket*, a scandal sheet as full of gossip as New Orleans had always been of corruption and vice. Buddy was able to scoop the field with the stories brought in by his friend, a "spider," also employed by the New Orleans police.

Before the Spanish-American War, Bolden had already played himself into the hearts of the uptown Negroes. By the turn of the century his following was so large that his band could not fill all the engagements. Soon "Kid" Bolden became "King" Bolden.

When he wasn't playing out at picnics during the day, Buddy could probably be found blowing his horn at Miss Cole's Lawn Parties. Miss Cole's was an open-air dance pavilion up on Josephine Street. At night, he might work at any of a dozen places, at private parties, although his music was too "barrel-house" for the most refined tastes. The nature of this music may be inferred from Herbert Asbury's description of these taverns in his book, *The French Quarter*:

As its name implies, the barrel-house was strictly a drinking-place, and no lower guzzle-shop was ever operated in the United States. It usually occupied a long, narrow room, with a row of racked barrels on one side, and on the other a table on which were a large number of heavy glass tumblers, or a sort of bin filled with earthenware mugs. For five cents a customer was permitted to fill a mug or tumbler at the spigot of any of the barrels, but if he failed to refill almost immediately he was promptly ejected. If he drank until his capacity was reached, he was dragged into the alley, or, in some places, into a back room. In either event, he was robbed, and if he was unlucky enough to land in the alley, sneak thieves usually stripped him of his clothing as well as of the few coins which he might have in his pockets. Most of these dives served only brandy, Irish whisky, and wine, and the liquors which masqueraded under these names were as false as the hearts of the proprietors.

From barrel-houses and honky-tonks came many of the descriptive words which were applied to the music played in them; such as "gully-low," meaning, as its name implies, low as a ditch or "gully," hence "low-down," and "gut-bucket," referring originally to the bucket which caught drippings, or "gutterings" from the barrels, later to the unrestrained brand of music that was played by small bands in the dives.

More often Bolden played at one of the dance halls in the Negro district, such as Perseverance Hall, downtown on Villere Street, or Tin Type Hall, uptown on Liberty. George, the janitor of Perseverance, rented the hall on condition that the clubs who used it would hire the Bolden Band. Some of the clubs they played for were The Buzzards, Mysterious Babies, and the Fourth District Carnival Club. In the daytime, Tin Type Hall was used as a sort of morgue, for here the hustlers and roustabouts were always laid out when they were killed. The hustlers, gamblers, and race track followers were often hard-working musicians in their off seasons, or when luck turned and they needed a little ready cash. At night, however, the Tin Type trembled with life and activity, especially when Bolden was "socking it out." The "high class" or "dicty" people didn't go to such low-down affairs as the Tin Type dances. At about twelve o'clock, when the ball was getting right, the more respectable Negroes who did attend went home. Then Bolden played a number called *Don't Go 'Way Nobody*, and the dancing got rough. When the orchestra settled down to the slow blues, the music was mean and dirty, as Tin Type roared full blast.

The blues were played much slower than today and the orchestra would really "moan it out." Buddy, who liked to hear the shuffling of feet as a background to his music, would yell out to his orchestra:

> 'Way down, 'way down low
> So I can hear those whores
> Drag their feet across the floor.

And with the final exhortation: "Oh you bitches, shake your asses," he cracked down on the blues.

Among the blues Buddy had to play every night were *Careless Love Blues* and *219 Took My Babe Away*. There were several original tunes by Bolden, such as *Emancipation Day* and a number inspired by some "low-life" women who had worked on a boat with the band. The words of the song, which later became his "theme" song, went:

> I thought I heard Buddy Bolden say,
> "Funky-butt, funky-butt, take it away."

Two of the rags they played were *Idaho* and *Joyce 76*. The Bolden Band changed the notes and time values around: "when we got going good they'd cross three times at once," was the way Willy Cornish described what happened.

Later Bolden moved his barber shop farther up Franklin Street to St. Andrews, near the Garden district, and played regularly at Johnson Park. On still nights, Buddy's cornet could be heard for miles, from the river back to Lake Pontchartrain.

A short distance from Johnson Park was Lincoln Park, where John Robichaux's Orchestra often played. Some nights, when the time came for Buddy Bolden to start, there wasn't anybody in Johnson Park. So Buddy, saying, "It's time to call my chillun home," stuck his horn through a hole in the fence and the people came rushing. Soon Lincoln Park was emptied.

Bolden's Band was of the rough-and-ready school, without the polish of the note readers, such as the veteran Claiborne William's Band, or the sweetness of Robichaux's Orchestra. It was usually a small bunch of from five to seven men. Buddy used William Warner or Frank Lewis, or sometimes both, on clarinet. Warner had a C clarinet, while Lewis played the usual B Flat instrument. Willy Cornish, the only member of the original band living today, played a piston (valve) trombone. For a mute, Cornish used an empty bottle. Bolden, who almost always played with an open horn, sometimes used a rubber plunger, water glass, half a cocoanut shell, derby hat, a piece of cloth, or his hand, for muted effects. Bolden, as a rule, played everything in the key of B Flat. The rhythm section, as usual in early New Orleans, had no piano, and consisted of Jeff Mumford, guitar, James Johnson, bass, and drummer Cornelius Tillman, or McMurray with his old single-head drum and its bright red snares.

Bolden's Band played for a while at Nancy Hanks' Saloon, on Customhouse Street, down in the red-light district. They used to sell fireworks out in front which, on one occasion, set the place on fire. At times, this joint got too rough for even the Bolden Band.

Carnival time always saw New Orleans in its most festive mood. It was also the busiest time for musicians. Everyone was needed in the street parades which celebrated Mardi Gras. There was at least one parade a day for the week before Mardi Gras, and on the final Tuesday, there were usually five or six. Each parade employed about fourteen bands, with a total of more than two hundred musicians. There were six gay weeks of masked balls. During the final week, balconies were decorated and maskers danced in the specially lighted streets. The parades, during the final week of pageantry, always started at Calliope Street and St. Charles Avenue, and after going up Canal, Royal, and Orleans, ended at the site of the old Congo

Square where, in the case of evening parades, the event was climaxed with a masquerade ball. In the old days, the spectacular parades, lighted by hundreds of torches, were elaborately staged. At times the realism went beyond the bounds of staging, when, for instance, the Indians, hired to put on a battle, acted with such fervor and ferocity that several of their number were killed.

King Bolden got his share of jobs in the carnival balls, as well as the parades. It was during an early celebration that the legendary riot at Longshoremen's Hall took place. Buddy was always a prime favorite with the ladies. This suited Buddy well, for he was as immoderate in his appetite for women as for hard liquor and hot music. Women carried instruments when the men marched. When a girl carried a fellow's instrument, it was "really somethin'!" It meant "lay off," she was the main girl. But Buddy Bolden never had to worry. He was never known to march down the street with only one woman. Often he could be seen coming along with three; one carrying his instrument, one his coat, another his hat—all three satisfied. Inside at dances, the girls rushed around him in the best matinée-idol tradition, handing him nickels and dimes tied in their handkerchiefs. Buddy took the money and threw the handkerchiefs away. A story persists that one night at Longshoremen's, also known as the Teamsters and Loaders Hall, Buddy's feminine admirers were unusually demonstrative. A few of them began fighting over Buddy and soon, with some of the men in the crowd taking sides, the battle became a free-for-all.

The tougher the dance the more raggedy was the playing. But, like other New Orleans bands of the late nineteenth century, the Bolden Band knew quadrilles, polkas, and other traditional dances. Those who could read, like Willy Cornish, helped to acquaint the band with these tunes, as with the Scott Joplin rags. Many of the halls and parks in which they played are still in use today as may be seen from the list supplied by Bunk Johnson:

Here are the names of the dance halls:

> Oddfellowers Hall
> Love and Charity Hall
> Come Clean
> Big Easy
> The Big 4
> Number 12 Hall
> Lincoln Park
> Johnson Park
> Fair Ground.

All these except the Fair Ground were uptown.
Here are the dance halls downtown (Creole section):

> Economy Hall
> Hopes Hall
> Fron-zi-me Hall
> Perseverance Hall
> New Hall
> Independent Hall.

Now during that time prades and funerals were great at hiring brass bands. Here are the brass bands I played with:

> The old Teao
> Charlie Dablayes Brass Band
> The Diamond Stone Brass Band
> The Old Columbis Brass Band
> Frank Welsh Brass Band
> The Old Excelsior Brass Band.
> And so many other of the old days.

Now these are the names of the brass bands I played in later years:

> The Algiers and Pacific Brass Band
> Kid Allen's father Brass Band
> Frank Duson Eagle Brass Band
> George Mc Cullons Brass Band.
> And so many no names brass bands.

The bands were for prades, funerals, Labor day prades, carnival prades, and Club prades such as Bulls Club and other clubs of that kind.

In later years there were several changes in King Bolden's Band. Around the corner from the Odd Fellows' Hall, at Perdido and Rampart, there was a regular "gin barbershop" where musicians were accustomed to hang out while waiting to get calls for jobs. Here Bolden picked up Bob Lyons, the bass player, and Frankie Dusen, his trombonist. Others were Sam Dutrey, clarinet, Jimmie Palao, violin, and Henry Baltimore or "Zino," drums. His guitar player was Brock Mumford, around whom Buddy wrote a little song, The Old Cow Died and Old Brock Cried. On this number the whole band sang the vocal chorus. Today, in the corner building at Rampart and Perdido, where the Eagle Saloon stood for years, Bob Lyons runs a shoeshine stand. When interviewed recently, Lyons said:

"Tell 'em Bob is settin' pretty. Tell 'em I feel good as a monkey."

Buddy used to hang around a saloon on Gravier and Rampart, run by "a guy named Mustache." He called it "my office." But he was never very businesslike. When it came to paying the men, he always had a check but he never got it cashed. When the men cornered him, he'd tell them to go to his office and stay there until he came.

"If you want anything to drink, tell Mustache I said to give you a good hot Tom and Jerry. I'll be there in about ten minutes."

He never got there. So one night the fellows "framed him up." They put him out of the band. That night they were playing at the Masonic Hall, one of the rougher spots on the tough side of town. They replaced Bolden with a fellow called Edward Clem, who had been a member of a rival band, that of Charlie Galloway. When Bolden got in, the band was playing and he looked up and saw Clem, and said to Frankie Dusen, the assistant leader:

"What's the matter, Dusen, we gonna use two cornets to-night?"

Dusen said: "No."

"What're you gonna do with the King, Dusen?"

Dusen replied: "You can go back home."

"You mean to tell me you're gonna put me out of my own band? I got you from Algiers when nobody would have you, Dusen."

"That makes no difference, I'm the King now."

So Bolden said: "Well, I'll shove on back to Mustache's and take it easy."

But a dance was never anything around New Orleans without King Bolden. Whenever he opened up the window at the Masonic or Globe Hall and stuck his old cornet out and blew, people came from far and wide to hear him.

Finally the day came when Buddy Bolden marched in his last procession. For years he had been mentally and physically overtaxed. Under the stress of excitement, his mind snapped and he went on a rampage during a Labor Day parade. Down in New Orleans, there are those who say that women killed Buddy Bolden, but wiser heads know it was also overwork, that at last Buddy had played himself out. The king of them all was committed to the East Louisiana State Hospital on June 5, 1907, where, listed as a barber, his reputation as cornetist was promptly forgotten, and he was known only as one of several Boldens from New Orleans. He died there in 1931.

Freddie Keppard, a much younger musician than Bolden, played violin in a primitive style known as "alley fiddle." But he wanted a more forceful instrument. He took up cornet and soon became the "hottest thing" in New Orleans. Although Keppard never learned to read a note and played in the most robust and rough manner, he was associated early in his career with the more finished Creole musicians in the downtown section. He played in the Olympia Band, which had been a rival of Buddy Bolden's Band. The earliest clarinetist of the Olympia was Picou, who first played the celebrated clarinet part of *High Society*. Taken from the piccolo part of a standard march used in all New Orleans street parades, *High Society* became a test piece which forever afterwards all aspiring clarinetists had to "cut" before they could get a job. Picou composed many of the New Orleans classics, including *Muskrat Ramble*, *Snake Rag*, *Alligator Hop*, and *Olympia Rag*. Later, the clarinet in the Olympia Band was played by "Big Eye" Louis Nelson, whose C clarinet inspired many of the younger players, including Jimmy Noone, Sidney Bechet, and Johnny Dodds. A little on the French side in appearance, genial in a quiet way, Louis became a changed person when he put a clarinet to his lips. He had a big tone and while he played in the fluid style characteristic of New Orleans, he brought to it a broad inventiveness. As with Bechet, he had a vibrato that was in keeping with his sweeping crescendos, and just a touch of blue quality. While he played he seemed oblivious of the smoke-filled room and of the dancers. He sat hunched forward, his clarinet pointed towards the floor.

The drummer of the Olympia was "Ratty" John Vean, who shook all over, each part of his body geared to a different rhythm. Vean was the first to introduce the four-beat bass drum part, the bass drum being played by his right foot, the other leg being free to vibrate with the speed of a trip-hammer. Meanwhile, both hands performed incredible feats of virtuosity on the head of the snare drum, the rim, and various traps. His head, motivated by a two beat rhythm, protruded and withdrew like a turtle's from its shell, while his stomach whirled spasmodically with a rapidity which would make a dervish dizzy. The trouble with "Old Man" Vean, was that, aside from being oversexed, he went to sleep on the job after a few drinks and then the Olympians had to do without any drumming. A little later, Louis Cottrelle took over the rhythm. He was also called "Old Man" Cottrelle, and because of his sound, legitimate methods and knowledge of rudiments, was known as the father of New Orleans drumming. He was the inspiration and instructor of many of the younger drummers. Finally, Ernest Trapiana became the drummer of the Olympia.

Joseph Petit not only played valve trombone, he was the manager of the Olympia. In later days the slide trombone was played by Zue Robinson for a while. Zue, one of the most picturesque characters of New Orleans music, was a real rambler who could never stay put very long. When he first started, he was so bad they sent him home. But such a sturdy individualist as this relative of Buddy Bolden's could not be stopped so easily. After a year of "woodshedding," he suddenly came back and "went crazy on his trombone." He played with unbelievable ease sensational stuff which would be impossible for many present-day trombonists. Personally, Zue was independent and irresponsible, and has been described by some of his fellow workers as "the most spiteful man in the world." Years ahead of his time, Zue was unquestionably one of the first great modern trombonists. He had a far-reaching influence in setting the jazz style for slide trombones.

Keppard and others from the Olympia formed the nucleus of the Original Creole Band, the first important group to leave New Orleans. Organized by Bill Johnson, they started on a series of vaudeville tours as early as 1911. Bill Johnson was one of the earliest string bass players. One time, when playing up in Shreveport, his bow broke; so he had to pluck the strings the rest of the night. The effect was so novel and added so much more swing and flexibility to his playing, that he took to slapping his bass entirely thereafter. Johnson's brother, Dink, who fooled around with piano sometimes, was the drummer of the Creole Band. The guitar of Norwood

Williams filled out the rhythm section. The early bands usually had a violin, and the Original Creoles used Jimmie Palao, who had played with the Olympians and Buddy Bolden. Eddie Venson was the trombonist, and George Baquet, another member of the Olympia Band, the clarinetist. Baquet was also an expert legitimate musician, with a finished technique. In the brass bands, he usually played an E Flat instrument. On the funeral marches his tone, full of sweetness and sadness, could be heard wailing high above the other parts.

Since he was the only one able to read music in the Creole Band, Baquet usually had to carry the melody in a fairly straight manner, down low. Keppard meanwhile embellished the tune with intricate passage work, utilizing his remarkable range. Keppard, without having too perfect an execution, did have the greatest range of any cornetist of his time. He had such imagination in invention that other cornetists found his figurations impossible to copy. At times Keppard played so low he sounded like a trombone. On the other hand, he was the first to exploit the high range, going even above high E. As strong as Samson, he was noted for his powerful tone. When he was on tour with the Creole Band, the patrons in the front rows of the theatres always got up after the first number and moved back. But at times Keppard could play so softly he could be heard only a few feet away. In later years he took on a lot of weight, becoming almost as broad as he was tall. He drank fabulous quantities of liquor. During the Prohibition era, he carried a water bottle strapped under his arm, but not for water. Once when the leader of an orchestra with which he had been hired to play reminded him that drinking on the job was not allowed, Freddie picked up his cornet and bottle and packed up to leave, but was prevailed upon to stay. King Keppard, as he too was called, never lost the power to swing and to arouse unbridled enthusiasm. He could get people so excited that they stood up and yelled.

Nothing stopped Keppard; if he came up against a new

number he'd never heard and couldn't read, he usually developed valve trouble. But all the time that he was fooling around with his horn, blowing the spit out, taking the valves apart and licking them, Keppard was all ears, learning the new tune. If anyone started to bawl him out, he said: "Go on, you play your part, I'll catch up." When the next chorus came around, there was Freddie, with his horn pointed up high as it always was, socking it out with his rough, sure tone, with a vibrato so fast and ferocious that he seemed to be tearing the horn to pieces. On an old classic, such as *Panama*, his pet tune, he was 'way ahead of everyone. Keppard usually played just a few notes, perhaps two or three to the bar, but they were all strictly barrelhouse. With his remarkable range, he could do everything, and was playing music thirty years ago which would sound modern today.

Although Keppard was in and out of New Orleans, much of his time from 1913 to 1918 was spent in touring with the Original Creole Band throughout the country, from Maine to California and from the Mason Dixon line to the Great Lakes. The Creole Band appeared mainly in vaudeville but had an extended run at the Winter Garden in New York. They opened the road for other bands which later came up from the South. Everywhere they played the old New Orleans stand-by tunes and also other favorites of theirs, such as *Steamboat Blues*, *Roustabout Shuffle*, and Scott Joplin's *Pepper Rag*. Early in 1916 the Victor Phonograph Company approached the Original Creoles with an offer to record. Keppard thought it over, and said:

"Nothin' doin', boys. We won't put our stuff on records for everybody to steal."

He persuaded the other fellows to turn down the recording offer. A few months later, Victor signed Nick La Rocca's group, which under the name of the Original Dixieland Jazz Band went on to fame and fortune.

In 1917 Baquet remained in New York, so Jimmy Noone

came up and joined the band when they reached Detroit. Six months later, in Chicago, the Original Creole Band broke up, storing the scenery from their vaudeville act in a warehouse down on 31st Street.

After Buddy Bolden had been taken away, several members of his band, including Lyons, Brock, and Dusen, formed the Eagle Band. They were called "the Boys in Brown" because of their brown military uniforms. On their caps was printed "Eagle Band," and Dusen had his marked "Eagle Band Manager." At first they had a very good cornetist by the name of Ned, but he soon burnt himself out. Then Bunk Johnson came along, a rather small man who wore his cap far back on his head and was a veritable giant when he picked up a cornet. Of all musicians, Bunk was the ideal successor to the throne of King Bolden. Bunk put on long pants to go out with the Bolden Band. In Bunk's very first band, the leader always "smacked the cornet out of Bunk's mouth" when he didn't play the right notes, no matter where they were playing.

It may seem paradoxical that Bunk, who hailed from the tough uptown section near the river, called the Irish Channel, had the most refined taste and finished execution of all cornetists. He had an unprecedented sense of swing and feeling for the low-down blues and gutbucket style, yet a tone unrivaled in its beauty. It was not as loud as others, nor was his range remarkable. He was not a "high note" man; he rarely went above A. Bunk had, however, an unusually fast technique, and the musicianship that enabled him to fit into any type of organization. He was noted for his ability to improvise second cornet parts. But he was second to none in his power to swing a band along with him. "Every one looked up to Bunk," as one old-timer said, and no wonder, with a tone of such unusual warmth and beauty of vibrato. Bunk never cared to read. When a leader once wrote down some of the music Bunk had played and stuck it up for him to do again, Bunk said:

"Do you think I'm a fool? I can't play that."

Bunk describes his early musical training in the following words:

We will begin, first thing is where I was born. I was born in the city of dear old New Orleans some years ago on December the 27th, 1879. I was born uptown on Laurel Street between Peters Ave. and Octivia St., so now all of you know just where my home is. When I was seven years I started to taking music lessons. After one year I was doing so good that Prof. Wallace he then told me to tell my mother to come over to the school because he would like very much to have a good talk with her. I did just as he told me and my mother went over to the school and seen him. He told her that he could make a real cornetist out of me if she would get me a cornet just good enough to take lessons on and when I became good on the old one then she could get me a real cheap brass cornet. Now me and my old cornet, when my mother got it, night and day I puffed on it and when I did get the slite of it, Oh boy, I really went. Then my mother saw just what headway I was making with the old cornet. Then she told me, "Son, mama saw a cheap cornet and a new one and as you are doing so good I got to get it for you if you will be a good boy." Now I was that and my dear mother got it for me.

My Prof. was a Mexican; his name was Mr. Wallace Cutchey. He told me that I had a long way to go and a short time to make it in. Boy I got busy and I really made the grade. When I became the age of fifteen years old I was good to go and I really have been going ever since. Now for faking and playing by head I was hard to beat.

The first band I played with was Adam Olivier's and it played by music; that was in the year of 1894. My friend Tony Jackson started playing piano with Olivier's Band. I stayed with them about one year until I got a good chance to get with King Bolden. Bolden heard me play with Olivier's Band. Then he wanted me to jump Olivier's and come with him because he had the most work and the biggest name in New Orleans. It was the town's talk, King Bolden Band.

So I told Mr. Olivier that I think I could do better with King

Bolden so he told me to suit myself and so I did and went on
with King Bolden in the year of 1895. When I started playing
with him Bolden was a married man and two children. He must
of been between 25 or 30 years old at that time. Now here are
the men in the band when I went in to it: Cornelius Tilman,
drummer, Willy Cornish, trombone, Bolden, cornet, Bunk, cornet,
Willie Warner, clarinet, Mumford, guitar, and Jimmie Johnson,
bass. That was the old Bolden band when I went in to it. They
were all men; I was the only young one in the Band, in short
pants.

The picture you have of Bolden's first band was taken just before I started playing with his large band. In those days he only
carried a five piece band. In the late years Bolden's five piece band
became so great in the city of New Orleans that he had to make
his band bigger by putting in drums and cornet which made it a
seven piece band.

I stayed with Bolden until 1898 and then I left and started to
playing with Bob Russell Band. I did not stay very long with it
because they could not play very much. I went back to Bolden
and when I started playing the second time he had taken Frank
Duson in the band in place of Willy Cornish. I stayed about seven
months and then I left and went on the road for two years with
P. G. Loral and then I came in and started playing with first one
band and then another. That was the year of 1900. I went to
playing with a little band in Tom Anderson Dance Hall.

In later years, before he finally left New Orleans to settle
in the western part of the state, Bunk played occasionally with
John Robichaux's Orchestra. Robichaux's was for years the
class "name band" of New Orleans and was in demand for
all the better parties. It played for socials of the whites and
had the most desirable spots in the city, the Grunewald (now
the Roosevelt) and Antoine's. They played all styles of music
and everything from quadrilles to rags. Monday night Robichaux gave balls in uptown New Orleans, at the Masonic
Hall, also known as the Odd Fellows' Hall.

Bunk, however, reached the zenith of his career between
1911 and 1914, when he played regularly with the Eagle Band.
It was Bunk who got Sidney Bechet to join this band:

Now Sidney Bechet was just starting on clarinet and Leonard Bechet, trombone, and Sidney Desvigne was just starting cornet and Joe Bechet, guitar. I know they had a little band named the "Silver Bell." So there was nothing else for me to do but break into the "Silver Bell." I went to Sidney Bechet mother's house and asked her to let him play clarinet with me in the Eagle Band. She told me yes but here is what I would have to do. "You'll have to bring Sidney home after he is through playing each and every job, that would be the only way that I can let him go in your care if you promise me that you will do that."

Every Saturday night at the Masonic Hall was Eagle Band night. The Saturday night mob on South Rampart wasn't an especially high class bunch and they liked their music hot. And that was the only way the Eagle Band knew how to "serve it up," so they were easily the most popular uptown band.

A handbill advertising an Eagle dance had this heading:

The Eagle Boys fly high
And never lose a feather
If you miss this dance
You'll have the blues forever.

In the daytime Bunk put on his brown uniform and his Eagle hat and led the band in all their parades. New Orleans could always find an excuse for a parade, not only during Carnival, but for every national holiday, Jackson Day, Emancipation Day, and election campaigns. The most unusual of all were the funeral processions, under the auspices of the lodges, clubs, and societies. Everyone in New Orleans belonged to some secret order or society. When the member died, he had to have a band. "He was nothin' if he didn't have a band!" The societies used one side of their aprons for parades and the other for funerals. When the church bells tolled out mournfully, a couple of the brethren down on Rampart Street paused to remark:

"What's that I hear, twelve o'clock in the daytime—church bells ringin'?"

"Man, you don' hear no church bells ringin' twelve o'clock in the day!"

"Yes, indeed, somebody must be dead."

"Ain' nobody dead. Somebody must be dead drunk."

"No, I think there's a funeral."

"Why, looky here, I see there *is* a funeral."

"I b'lieve I hear that trambone moan."

With a slow pausing tread, the procession marched to the graveyard. With the exception of a few older downtown cemeteries that had their whitewashed tombs above ground, graveyards were usually a couple of miles "up or back o' town." Most of the cemeteries, such as Cypress Grove, St. Joseph's, and Lafayette, had plots for the burial of Negroes. On the way out to the graveyard, the band played in dead-march time, with muffled drums, soft and somber dirges, including *Free As a Bird, When the Saints Go Marching On, Nearer My God to Thee*, and real funeral marches. But Zutty Singleton says that once the body was interred: "The mourning got over quick. Right out of the graveyard, the drummer would throw on the snares, roll the drums, get the cats together and light out. The cornet would give a few notes, and then about three blocks from the graveyard they would cut loose."

They came back playing *High Society* and *King Porter Stomp*, but first of all they swung out on *Didn't He Ramble, He Rambled Round the Town till the Butcher Cut Him Down*.

The funerals and parades always had a "second line" which consisted of the kids who danced along behind. The bands had a way of strutting, of swinging their bodies, and of turning corners in spectacular fashion, and the boys who marched along on the sidewalk with them mimicked every action. When the big band "went crazy" after the funeral, the kids cut up with their primitive version of the "Susie Q" and

danced the "shudders." With their leader, the boys joined in
the general tumult as they shimmied along, and sang, yelled,
and clapped. Many had tin flageolets or home-made whistles
cut from stalks of reed on which they played the tune. Only
the tough kids joined the second line. Their mothers did not
approve; if they ever caught the kids, they jerked them out of
the parade. A few of these future jazzmen were actually helpful. These were the water boys, who carried buckets of water
to refresh the tired marchers whose lips were parched after a
hot march under the boiling sun.

The Eagle Band and others were often a feature of the picnics held during the summer months. The oldest resort established was Milneburg out on Lake Pontchartrain, near the old
lighthouse and Spanish Fort. The many good times at the picnics there in the old days were immortalized in the *Milneburg
Joys*, a classic stomp played by all New Orleans bands. A
casino near the Fort and various amusement concessions were
added about 1900. For years these offered lucrative employment to musicians. The lake front has since been filled in and
today none of these buildings remain.

In later years West End became the most popular summer
resort. On the lake, by the New Basin Canal, West End has
a charming park for picnics. It also has several night clubs.
Just across the canal, in the western section of West End, is
a small settlement known as "Bucktown," which was at one
time a wide-open spot.

On Sunday afternoons, Washington Park, uptown on Car-
rollton Avenue, was a popular meeting place for bands. Here
at the ball games and balloon ascensions, bands fought it out
until one emerged the victor. But the real battles occurred
when two bands, out advertising in their wagons, locked
wheels on some important corner. In New Orleans it was customary to advertise amusement events such as prize fights,
river excursions, and dances by having the band ride through
the streets on a large furniture wagon and play at the main

corners. They put the entire band, guitar, bass, and all, in the wagon, and the back end, the "tail gate," was reserved for the trombone. There he could sit, with his feet dangling over the edge, and slip his slide up and down without any danger of poking another player.

Frequently, when there were two dances the same night, and the bands ran into one another, there was an honest-to-goodness cutting contest. They hitched on or locked wheels, so that neither band could escape, and went to it, blasting at each other until one band, exhausted, called for mercy. Meanwhile, everyone, young and old, gathered from blocks around to shout encouragement and approval for his favorite. The band which received the loudest cheers was the winner and drew the crowd to its dance that night. Any downtown band which ventured across Canal Street was looking for trouble. If the Eagle Band ever caught up with them in their own uptown home territory it was just too bad. As one Creole said:

"Get out of that neighborhood if you see the Eagle Band coming."

Downtown, some of the Creole bands, the "Frenchmen," as they were called, had their following. The Imperial and Armand Piron's were among the most popular downtown bands. The leader of the Imperial was Emanuel Perez, one of the best cornetists in New Orleans. He was an excellent reader and teacher, and could hold his own with any legitimate or symphony man. Perez's first job, at the age of seventeen, had been with Robichaux's Orchestra when they were playing at Antoine's famous restaurant in 1895. Three years later, he became a member of the Imperial Band with Picou, Peter Bocage, and Buddie Johnson, trombonist. When Emanuel finished a night's work, he didn't stay around for a single drink. He always said, "Good night, boys, see you tomorrow night," and took every cent of his two dollars home. He saved his money and was later able to retire to a grocery business.

The Eagle Band stuck to a small instrumentation for marching, as well as for inside dance work, but ordinarily brass bands such as the Onward with Joe Oliver, the Tuxedo with Buddy Petit, and the Excelsior with Henry Allen, Sr., Lorenzo and Louis Tio, used from twelve to eighteen men. Some bands used three or four cornets, including, possibly, one small E Flat cornet, an alto horn or two, a couple of trombones, a baritone, two to four clarinets, with one an E Flat instrument. A few bands had tubas, and all had bass and snare drums. Black Benny, famous as a bass drummer, was a familiar sight at parades, where his spectacular two-handed beating attracted many a follower. Some of the men, especially the ones from downtown, could read music well enough to play the standard marches such as those of Sousa. But many a player would have had to quit if the man marching beside him had stopped playing.

Some of the most popular dance tunes of early New Orleans were the Scott Joplin numbers, such as *Maple Leaf Rag* and *Climax Rag*. *Tiger Rag* was also known as *Number Two Rag*, which came from an old French quadrille, *La Marseillaise*. *Barnyard Blues*, first played by Keppard, *Cannon Ball Rag*, and *Rubber Plant*, were other favorites. The prevalence of "rags" among the selections is no indication that the old-timers didn't really swing their music. Originally, some of the rags had been played in a fast, jerky fashion by the pianist entertainers, but the orchestras slowed them down to fox-trot tempo or made them into stomps. Then there were always the blues, some, such as "the shags," of the meanest sort. The folk and work songs of the Negroes added their influence; for example, *Good-by Bag, I Know You've Gone* came from the song sung by the mill workers as they emptied the rice bags. *Lift 'Em Up Joe* was taken by Joe Oliver from a song of the railroad hands as they raised the rails.

For dance jobs practically every New Orleans group used seven pieces. The cornet, playing the melody most of the

time, was considered the leader. The clarinet played a faster
moving part, usually of legato runs and arpeggios, and filled
in at the end of phrases with characteristic "breaks." The
trombone, which at times supported the others with a sort of
rhythmic bass, also took its own counter-melody in the best
style of New Orleans music, and supplied a moving melodic
line, or "slides," when the other parts were stationary. The
use of a violin in a hot band is difficult to understand except
as a relic of European influence. Jelly Roll Morton is entirely
right when he says:

"Violinists weren't known to play anything illegitimate,
even in New Orleans."

The rhythm sections consisted of drums, guitar, and string
bass. The absence of pianos in New Orleans orchestras could
be explained, in part, by the difficulty of fitting them into the
wagons so often used for street advertising.

The pianists did, however, find their place in Storyville, the
world renowned red-light district of New Orleans. Named
after the alderman who drew up the ordinance creating it in
1897, Storyville consisted of a dozen square blocks back of the
French Quarter. Its principal thoroughfares were Iberville,
Bienville, Liberty, Franklin, and, most celebrated of all, Basin
Street. For two hundred years, half of the time under French
and Spanish rule, New Orleans had been known for its gaiety
and tolerance of human failings, its political corruption, crime,
and vice. With the founding of the restricted district, Storyville soon became the most glamorous, as well as the most
notorious center of legalized vice in history. It was for twenty
years the showplace and scandal of New Orleans. Visitors from
all over the world thronged the "tenderloin" nightly, especially
during Carnival time.

Storyville was bossed by Tom Anderson, whose "city hall"
was his main saloon, the Arlington Annex. Anderson published
and sold, for twenty-five cents a copy, the Blue Book, a direc-
tory and guide of the sporting district, which listed the names

and addresses of all prostitutes and entertainers. There were ads with extravagant claims, and illustrations of all the main houses of pleasure. Some of these, such as Josie Arlington's five-dollar house on Basin Street, were gaily tinseled palaces, full of gaudy tapestries, heavy plush-covered sofas, laces, leopard-skin rugs, gilt statuary, mirrors, and cut-glass chandeliers. In every parlor was a piano, and often there was music by a string trio, since the brothels did not favor loud bands. In addition to the musicians, there were dancers and singers.

Ann Cook, one of the very first blues singers, worked for Countess Willie Piazza, under whose roof a Central American revolution had been plotted. Piazza's *maison joie*, which specialized in Octoroons, also had the distinction of being the first bordello to hire a pianist to entertain the customers. He was a riot and was known quite appropriately as John the Baptist. At a later date Tony Jackson was the featured pianist-entertainer and made a big hit with his song, *I've Got Elgin Movements in My Hips with Twenty Years Guarantee*. Tony left New Orleans about 1908 and traveled throughout the tenderloin circuit, later winning national fame as a singer and pianist in New York.

Down in the same block on Basin Street was Mahogany Hall, run by Lulu White. She was called the "Diamond Queen," and her mirror-room and beautiful Octoroons were known across the continent. At Lulu's, the pianists at various times were Al Carrel, Richard M. Jones, and Clarence Williams, who celebrated Lulu White's establishment in the tune *Mahogany Hall Stomp*.

Tom Anderson's Annex usually employed a string trio with piano, guitar, and violin. Among the first to play there was Jelly Roll Morton. Jelly Roll, who has been called the "Dizzy Dean of music," blew in from Gulfport. Inspired by King Porter, a pianist from Mobile, he wrote the *King Porter Stomp* and a number of other tunes such as *Milneburg Joys*, originally called the *Pee Hole Blues*, which became part of the

Kid Bolden's Band before 1895
Standing, Jimmie Johnson, Buddy Bolden, Willy Cornish (valve trombone), Willy Warner
Seated, Brock Mumford, Frank Lewis   *photo from Willy Cornish*

Jack Laine's Reliance Band in 1910
Standing, Manuel Mello, Alcide Nunez, Leonce Mello, Alfred Laine, Tim Harris, Mike Stevens
Seated, Jack Laine

Right, Dave Perkins and Jack Laine   *photo from Jack Laine*

Basin Street Transom

Souvenir postcard of Storyville from Tom Anderson's bartender, Albert Callahan

George Baquet

"Another one that left New Orleans with the Creole Ragtime Band year 1911, took Chicago by storm."

photo from Sidney Desvigne

Picture of Joe Oliver taken on Canal Street before he left New Orleans

photo from Victoria Johnson

The Real Old Jazz Fred Keppard Cornet Player with Creole Ragtime Band left New Orleans year 1911 for Chicago he was a member of the Old Olympia Band."

Henry Allen's Brass Band, Algiers, La.

Standing, Jack Carey, unknown, Collins, Palao, August Rousseau, Joe Howard, Oscar Celestin, Henry Allen
Seated, Jiles, unknown

When this picture was taken, "Play Jack Carey," meant "Play Tiger Rag." Joe Howard taught Louis Armstrong to read, while Louis was "back o' Jones."

The Original Superior Orchestra

Standing, Buddie Johnson, Willie Bunk Johnson, Big Eye Louis Nelson,
Billy Marrero
Seated, Walter Brundy, Peter Bocage, Richard Payne

Describing the band as it was when he joined it, Bunk says: "The Old
Imperial Band never did like the Superior Band much because wherever
they played we would close them down on the street. We would run
them. That's the way the Superior Band treated the Imperial Band. That's
what caused the hatred. They were good sight readers but we had them
some."

Joseph Petit at home, Creole Section

photo from Sidney Desvigne

"After a while Leon lost interest in the violin because he couldn't march with it in street parades."

Band on riverboat *Sidney*

Fifth from left, Perez; extreme right, Jimmie Johnson of the Buddy Bolden Band

In the spring of 1920 when Louis came home from playing on the river-boat he took his mother and his sister Beatrice to a studio and this picture was taken.

When in 1914 Roy Palmer, Sugar Johnny, Lawrence Dewey and their
New Orleans Band toured the country they took the riverboat atmosphere
with them, even to the good ship *Lady Lee*. This picture was taken August
12, 1915, in a Chicago theatre.

Kid Ory's Band

Mutt Carey, cornet, Fred
Washington, piano, Bud Scott,
banjo, two reeds, and Pop
Foster, string bass and tuba

One of the early bands to hit
the West Coast, they were
billed as "Kid Ory's Seven
Pods of Pepper, with Ory's
Creole trombone," or as
"Ory's Brown Skinned Band."

Tubas were big and noisy but
Pop Foster, like Jimmie Johnson of the Bolden Band, preferred string bass.

LET US DO YOUR PLAYING

THE FAMOUS

CREOLE ORCHESTRA from NEW ORLEANS, La

For Balls, Parties and Picnics

REASONABLE PRICES TO EVERYONE

W. M. JOHNSON,	JIMMIE PALAO
Manager and Bass Violinist.	Leader and Violinist
FREDDIE KEPPARD, Cornet	W. M. Williams, Guitar
GEORGE BAQUET, Clarinet	EDDIE VENSON, Trombone
D. JOHNSON, Drummer	

Give us two Days' Notice,   401 Central Ave.   Phone M. 1405

"The Original Creole Band came to Chicago in 1911 at the Grand Theatre. Keppard and all there, and Bill Williams, made a hit and brought on jealousy of the Northern brothers. Creole brothers down South heard of their success and, one by one, came to the land of free and plenty dollars."—Chicago *Defender.*

photo and card from W. M. Johnson

King Oliver's Creole Jazz Band toured the West Coast in 1921.

"Joe wore overalls and Lilly had on a gingham dress."

standard New Orleans repertory. He left New Orleans a little later than Tony Jackson, traveled up the river and spent several years in Chicago and California before going East.

In 1910 there were almost two hundred houses of pleasure in Storyville, including the fifty cent cribs, bare one-room holes, which lined the streets. Also in the district were nine cabarets, many "dance schools," innumerable honky-tonks, barrel-houses, and gambling joints.

One of the first cabarets established was the 101 Ranch, on Franklin Street, originally a low dive and hangout for river roustabouts, gamblers, and cutthroats. But about 1910, Billy Phillips decided to put some class in his joint. He hired an orchestra and entertainers, raised the prices, and fixed the odds in the gambling games a little more in favor of the house. For the next seven years, some of New Orleans' hottest musicians played here, including Joe Oliver, Perez, Baquet, Bechet, Roy Palmer, and "Pop" Foster. Here could be seen future members of the New Orleans Rhythm Kings, the Original Dixieland Jazz Band, and the Halfway House gang, whose first impressions of hot were received while listening to the older Negro musicians.

Peter Lala's cabaret, on Iberville Street, was one of the most popular and famous. Known also as the 25 Club, it was a favorite meeting place of musicians. After their night's work, they met their girls, many of whom worked as entertainers and hostesses elsewhere in Storyville. About dawn a few pianists dropped in and started a cutting contest, and perhaps someone who could read would play over a new tune for the band so they could learn it. By the time the band played it over a few times, its composer would probably never recognize the tune. Possibly the best "all-star" orchestra to play in New Orleans during that period was at Pete Lala's, consisting of such men as Joe Oliver, Lorenzo Tio, Zue Robinson, and Henry Zino. Later, trombonist Kid Ory had charge of Pete's band and when Oliver left for Chicago, Louis Armstrong came in.

The fanciest decorated resort was the Tuxedo Dance Hall, across from the 101 Ranch. After the killing of Billy Phillips in the Tuxedo, the police clamped down on Storyville. A few places closed up and some cut the size of their orchestras, as the district quieted down for a few weeks. At the Tuxedo, Keppard, when he had to reduce the number of men to cut expenses, fired the guitar, bass, and violin, and hired Buddy Christian to play piano. At other times, Celestin and Bob Frank had bands at the Tuxedo and, later on, a new clarinetist, Johnny Dodds, worked there.

There were many other clubs, always opening and closing, with ever-changing orchestras. Some of the better known were: Rice's, where Perez and clarinetist Lawrence Dewey once played; Frank Early's, with Buddie Petit and Jimmy Noone in the band; and Eddie Grociele's, where Piron had a band with Big Eye Louis. Big Eye, who had worked at Jack White's, a cabaret under a tent on Iberville Street, was possibly the first to try a piano in an orchestra. The pianist's name was Black Pete; he couldn't play a single tune, but could chord along and fill in the rhythm in place of the strings.

The early taxi-dancehalls, called "dancing schools" in New Orleans, were gyp joints then as they are today. The girls lined up in the middle of the floor and danced only when someone bought a drink. A bottle of beer rather than a ticket was good for a dance with one of the girls. The girl selected got five cents on each sale of a twenty-five cent drink. As soon as the music started, the waiter grabbed the bottle, even though the unlucky customer had taken only a sip. The orchestra had to pause between dances to allow the men a long time to buy drinks. If they played too often and too long they were fired.

A colorful part of Storyville life was found in the honky-tonks and barrel-houses. The old 28 Club, run by Kyser, was a typical "tonk," jammed every night with river rowdies, card sharks, roughnecks, pimps, and all varieties of male parasites. Drunks whose money had been spent or stolen were thrown out into the alley. All the good old crooked gambling games were played: faro, three-card monte, shell, craps, and banco. Drinks were cheap, but if a customer wanted to keep a place at the bar, his glass had to be filled often. And if anyone sat down at the piano in the 28 Club, he knew he'd better not play anything else but the blues. In these dives they dragged out the blues with a slow beat and fierce intensity. Apparently there were hundreds of Negroes who could sit down and play and sing the low-down blues. They made up the words to fit their mood and the occasion, but invariably pianists knew only one tune. If someone yelled, "Play somethin' else!", he played the same blues a little faster, and the entire tonk, satisfied, shook in a quicker tempo.

One night a week, as a special added attraction, the 28 Club put on a "ham kick." A ham was hung up high and the contest was won by the girl who could kick highest. Many, having had a few drinks, fell down and rolled around on the floor. This was all part of the fun.

Another stimulus to trade was the featured "pig-ankle" night, when handouts of ankles and pigfeet were given to the patrons. Bessie Smith must have been thinking of New Orleans' low life when, many years later, she shouted the words of her song *Gimme a Pigfoot*:

> Check all your razors and your guns,
> We're gonna be wrastlin' when the wagon comes.
> Gimme a pigfoot and a bottle o' beer,
> Send me, Gate, I don't care.
> Gimme a reefer and a gang o' gin,
> Slay me 'cause I'm in my sin.

Storyville was kind to hot music. With a dozen bands, many trios, and other musicians employed every night, it is little wonder that jazz first sprang up and flourished in New Orleans. But it was a tough life for the musicians. Hours were "eight until," and the pay ranged from $1.00 to $2.50 a night. Many spots gave them a chance to make a little more by permitting one of the musicians to come down off the balcony to pass the hat. With America's entrance into the World War, the handwriting was seen on the wall, for the Secretary of the Navy ordered the suppression of all open prostitution. A city ordinance was passed and with a rapid exodus of harlots, Storyville came to an official end in November, 1917. The brothels were closed and furniture, mirrors, and fittings were sold. Countess Willie Piazza's famed white piano, badly out of tune, brought at auction one dollar and twenty-five cents.

Then the musicians really had the *Basin Street Blues* and began to look for new fields of employment. New Orleans jazz spread fan-like up the Mississippi Valley, from coast to coast, and throughout the world. The Original Creole Band had already left years before. Dink Johnson, their drummer, had settled in California and organized his Louisiana Six. He was soon joined by Kid Ory's Brown Skinned Jazz Band, with cornetist Mutt Carey. As early as 1913, Bunk, Clarence Williams, Zino, and Sidney Bechet had carried New Orleans jazz to Texas. A little later such stars as Perez, Tig Chambers, Tio, Atkins, Cottrelle, and Dominique, journeyed to Chicago. In 1914, "Sugar" Johnny, an erratic but sensational cornetist, took north another Creole Band, with Lawrence Dewey, Roy Palmer, Herbert Lindsay, and Louis Keppard. In Chicago, he added "Tubby" Hall, Sidney Bechet, Lil Hardin, and Wellman Braud.

The Mississippi riverboats carried jazz not only up the river to Memphis, St. Louis, and Davenport, but to cities on the tributaries, such as Kansas City and Omaha on the Missouri, and the Ohio River towns as far as Pittsburgh. Fate Marable, leader of many great bands on the riverboats, settled in St. Louis, where Charlie Creath soon organized another fine band, with the late Tommy Ladnier, "Pop" Foster, and Zutty Singleton.

Changing industrial conditions brought an inevitable shift of Negro population to the manufacturing centers of the North. This aided in the dissemination of hot jazz, but the principal reason for the scattering of the New Orleans jazz-men is found in the fall of Storyville. As Lizzie Green, in *Good Time Flat Blues*, bemoaned:

> *I can't keep open, I'm gonna close up shack.*
> *The chief of police done tore my playhouse down;*
> *No use in grievin', I'm gonna leave this town.*

II

WHITE NEW ORLEANS

BY CHARLES EDWARD SMITH

BY JACK LAINE'S time, New Orleans music was taking shape. When the old-timers talk about white bands, it's about Jack Laine's Ragtime Band. Some of them, now venerable and white-haired, speak of Jack Laine as "the old man." There were white bands before him, brass to march by and strings for dancing, but it wasn't "Dixieland." Many years before, a bank in New Orleans had issued a ten-dollar bill with the word *dix* printed in large letters on one side. From this, the words "Dixie" or "Dixieland" meant New Orleans, long before the word was used as a general name for the South. This designation, in its original sense, gave a name to hot jazz played by New Orleans musicians. Today, it is applied more specifically to improvised hot music as played by small five- or six-piece orchestras, and usually implies that they are white, although the term is used loosely. The white "Dixieland" style was first developed by the small combinations of musicians who played with Laine.

Jack Laine was born in 1873 and began to play an alto horn as soon as he was old enough to tote one around. Like almost every kid in New Orleans he wanted to play an instrument and play it well enough to march with the brass bands during Mardi Gras. He realized this ambition long before he was twenty. The most exciting day for Jack was the day before Carnival. At present it's just another day of the Mardi Gras week, a long round of elaborate parades with floats to satiate the tourist trade, and bare-legged girls stepping jauntily before the bands. It wasn't that way in Papa Laine's time. The crowds were there, of course. Canal Street was packed, temporary reviewing stands put up at intervals, from the waterfront to Rampart Street. But the day before Carnival was then the occasion for the military parade, biggest event of the year for the brass bands—and for the shiny-eyed kids who wanted some day to grow up and play in them.

It didn't take Jack long to become a full-fledged musician, playing alto horn and sometimes playing drums. They used bands in those preradio days for every conceivable event, at Lucy Tanner's resort, picnics at Kramer's lot across the wide curve of the Mississippi in Algiers, Milneburg on the lake front, prize fights, race track, house parties; they were beginning to use them in the fabulous houses of the part of town that was soon to be called Storyville.

In the eighteenth century, before the Spanish rule of Count Alexander O'Reilly, the city was famous for its brilliant dances. Early in the next century the French Opera was founded and when in 1864 under the "carpetbag" legislature Bandmaster Patrick Sarsfield Gilmore assembled the city's military bands, trumpet and drum corps in Lafayette Square for a concert, the number of musicians was said to total five hundred.

Improvised music, introduced into New Orleans white music through the influence of uptown Negroes, had by the latter part of the nineteenth century become as traditional for some groups of white musicians as had brass band music. Though the music itself might give the clue, many people are unaware that the majority of early ragtime musicians also played in brass bands. They played by note for marches and played by note at some of the more sedate balls, but had plenty of opportunity to play "ear music" at house parties, at the race track, and in "the district." Previously, whole families had played written music and in some instances, like that of the Rappolo family, they were merely carrying on a tradition brought with them from the mother country. But with many of the Italian and German families, as with the Creole Negroes, it was shocking to see a younger generation neglecting its reading, not reading at all in some extreme cases, and in many others just reading enough to get by.

The first band in which Jack Laine played had a Rappolo on clarinet. Laine doesn't recall now what his first name was, or his relationship to the famous Rappolo of the New Orleans Rhythm Kings, but he does remember how good he was. In the band there was a cornet, an alto horn, a key trombone, clarinet, and drums, but no piano, even when they played for dances. For parties and dances they added a guitar, string bass, and violin, while for marches they often had more brass than that indicated.

Most old-timers, like Ernest Giardina, remark that jazz "probably came from the Negroes," and some qualify this by saying that it came from uptown, where so many of the strictly New Orleans tunes had their origin. A few hold out for themselves, saying *they* and *they alone* created jazz music, but such claims need hardly be taken seriously today when overwhelming proofs as to jazz backgrounds have come to light. On the other hand, it should be emphasized that white New Orleans contributed its own background to jazz, and since this background was different from that of the Negro, "Dixieland" music was bound to show differences.

Although personnel varied from time to time the men who constituted Jack Laine's Ragtime Band, as given by Jack himself, were: Jack Laine, leader and drums; Achille Baquet, clarinet; Lawrence Vega, cornet; Dave Perkins, trombone; Willy Guitar, string bass; and Morton Abraham, guitar.

As a dance band, Jack Laine's Ragtime Band played in the days when the crowd was more likely to call for a quadrille or a polka than they were to ask for a rag. But one of the favorites of the Laine Band was Joplin's *Shadow Rag*. The rags caught on. Rehearsed until improvisation fused with written music learned by ear, it made a solid contrapuntal core that changed white New Orleans, almost overnight, from traditional round dances to white imitations of Negro shags and trots. It was fitting, if a shade ironical to the do-or-die "Dixielanders" who claim that jazz came from the whites or the later "Original Dixieland Jazz Band" that there were in that granddaddy of all Dixieland combinations, two light-skinned, blue-eyed Negroes. These were the clarinet player, Achille Baquet, and the trombone player, Dave Perkins.

Around 1900 there were plenty of jobs in New Orleans and the best of them went to Laine's men, because they were the only white men in the city who knew the jazz vernacular. In the summer at Milneburg, a mecca for New Orleanians from the moist heat that blanketed the city, bands played at houses and on pavilions. At Carnival time jobs piled up, five and six a day. There wasn't time to go home, so they took on a second home and a second mother between jobs. Mother Laine let them sleep wherever there was space, on cots, on chairs, even on the rug. For two hours she saw that they weren't disturbed. Then they went on to another job.

To prepare for a night's job they got together for rehearsal in the afternoon. In their repertoire were several uptown rags. *Tiger Rag* they called *Praline*, after the candy made with maple sugar, pecans, and sometimes cocoanut shreds—because it was a raggy tune. *Livery Stable Blues* was *Meat Ball*. Playing the tunes time after time they stamped them with their own personalities. There were readers in the band, Dave Perkins among them, but you didn't have to read on the rags; once the tune was set you played it.

The boys played together, New Orleans style, but they didn't jam. Not for the dances, anyway. Rehearsals were idea-sessions. Alcide "Yellow" Nunez, who was in Jack Laine's first

Reliance Brass Band, often played with them. He was good at ideas, as was Vega. Perkins, in Jack's words, "was wonderful at it." But none of the boys were slouches; Jack was a good idea man himself. They ran in breaks and fitted parts together in a kind of improvised counterpoint, playing the tune over and over. One of the breaks was Achille Baquet's famous "well-in-a-bucket." They worked on different tunes until it was time to go to the job. Spot variations were rare. On the job they played what they'd rehearsed in the afternoon, note for note.

They did not play in a smooth tempo like that of the New Orleans Rhythm Kings. It was so staccato it would sound jerky to modern ears, yet syncopation was its dominant feature. To "rag" a tune was to syncopate it. And though brass bands did not syncopate, their marches had a scintillating quality that could not be found in band music anywhere else. Maybe it was because the boys doubled in ragtime. Maybe it was because it was New Orleans.

Jack Laine's first brass band was the Reliance Brass Band and Orchestra. This was only the first of several. Jack had as many as three brass bands at once, with a few dance bands thrown in for good measure. About 1905 he had his own minstrels and led a circus band in which Yellow Nunez and Dave Perkins both played. In the first Reliance were: Alcide Nunez, clarinet; Johnny Lala, cornet; Manuel Marlow, cornet and leader; Jules Casoff, trombone; Mike Stevens, small drum; and Jack Laine, bass drum.

Almost all of the early white New Orleans musicians played in Laine's bands. There were, of course, a few exceptions. Leon Rappolo never played for him but the Brunies boys did and so did "Stale Bread" Lacoume. Alfred Laine, a son of the old man, had a band with Henry Ragas on piano, Eddie Edwards on trombone, Johnny Lala on cornet, Abraham on string bass, Irving Lusher on guitar, and sometimes Richard Brunies on cornet. Another band out of the Laine fold, Ernest Giardina's

Ragtime Band, played at the Tonti Social Club about 1908 or 1909. This band, which also played at Quarella's Pavilion at Milneburg, had Giardina on violin, Ragas on piano, Edwards on trombone, Achille Baquet on clarinet, Lawrence Vega on cornet, and Tony Sbarbaro on drums. Other musicians sometimes played with the band but this was typical of its personnel. Like so many musicians who got their first jobs with Papa Laine, Giardina credits Jack with the first band to play Dixieland style.

Most New Orleans musicians, white or colored, used only superlatives in talking about Vega. Jack Laine described him as "a master on cornet." It wasn't simply that he had a warm tone and excellent rhythm, qualities rare enough in themselves. What put him at the top with the few really excellent cornet players of the city was that he played creatively, rounding out a tune with original variations and adapting style and tonal quality to the tune played. When Vega played cornet there wasn't another white man in the city who could touch him.

Dave Perkins was not merely a good foundation trombone. His tone was rich and full. He could give the band long notes to build on or play melodic stuff in a style that he'd begun to learn years before on key trombone. The beat came from the three-piece rhythm section that constituted half the band. Abraham, the little Mexican guitar player, could play rhythm or make the strings talk like a piano on slow blues. Jack was all over the drums and Willy Guitar, who by freak coincidence lived on Music Street, had a typical doghouse sense of humor. People who didn't give a hang about the music sugar'd the band just to look at Willy's grimaces. He was one of the first in a long line of pantomimic bass players and, incidentally, one of the first to slap and finger the strings. Achille Baquet's clarinet had a clear, liquid tone; the phrasing had a clean edge. Nunez's tone had in it a very blue quality.

Some of these musicians played in "the district." Almost all of them played on the wagons Sunday nights, ballyhooing for a prize fight, a dance, or a commercial product. When Ruskin's cigar came out, they had one of the Laine bands out advertising it. The boys wore slick new uniforms and Johnny Fischer tore his on the wire taping of a case of cigars. "We remembered that," Jack said, "because the cigar company paid for a new uniform."

Around 1910, there were a number of bands in the city, trying to play the new music and some of them making a good job of it. Without trying to fix them as to date, Giardina recalled Johnny Fischer's, Schilling's, Nunez's, Brown's, Massarini's, Bill Gallaty's. Sooner or later most of the men who made up these bands played with Jack Laine or in one of his bands.

Dave Perkins played several times with Buddy Bolden and other Negro bands yet for years his secret was well kept. On trolley cars he stood on the rear platform so that he would not be faced with the choice of taking a Jim Crow seat toward the back of the car or sitting up front with the whites. Square and short, with blue eyes, a small mustache and a good shock of hair, Dave was nice-looking, more American than Latin in appearance. They still talk about the white girl who was in love with him. This developed into a serious affair. When it came to an end, as seemed inevitable, Dave didn't change much outwardly. Maybe he drank a little more than usual. Then he was brought down by a prolonged illness, but by this time most of his friends had deserted him. He was taken care of by a Negro woman he'd known since childhood. She saw that he had something to eat, nursed him back to health. When he was well again, Dave married her. The white local took away his union card, by that gesture ending the first period of Dixieland music.

The Jack Laine era produced a "crying" clarinet player whose name was Monty Korn. It produced the anomaly—in a city where whites and Negroes rarely played together—of Negro musicians in the town's best white band. It produced so many jobs during Carnival that Jack Laine's pay-off was often as much as $2000. It produced bands that were to venture North, West, East, and abroad, spreading the fame of Dixieland music. The first of these bands out of Papa Laine's informal school was Tom Brown's Band from Dixieland.

The story of Brown's Band from Dixieland properly begins in 1913. In that year Frisco & McDermott, a vaudeville act, played the Young Men's Gymnastic Club of New Orleans. The music for the dance team was furnished by Tom Brown's Band. Frisco, who was a talent scout as well as an adept at holding the burning end of a cigar in his mouth, talked about the band when he got back to Chicago. Presently they got offers which they could not accept because of local contracts. In June, 1915, however, they could and did take a job at the Lamb's Café in Chicago. On that job, the first northward thrust of "Dixieland," were:

Tom Brown, leader and trombone; Ray Lopez, cornet; Gus Mueller, clarinet; Arnold Loyocano, bass and piano; and William Lambert, drums.

They didn't have union clearance on that first Chicago job. According to Tom Brown it was an attempt by union officials to lowrate them that gave jazz its name. Jazz, or jass as it was then spelled, was a familiar word around 22nd Street where the red lights glowed, but it wasn't used about music. The story has it that the statement that jazz music was being played at Lamb's Café was a whispering campaign, the purpose of which was to smear the band. Whatever its purpose, it had the effect of popularizing the band. People were curious to know what "jass" music was, and they came in droves to find out. Presently the new sign out front read: "Added attraction—Brown's Dixieland Jass Band, Direct from New Orleans, Best Dance Music in Chicago."

In New Orleans Tom Brown had had Blind Clarence on

clarinet. He was a good clarinet player who could knock off the right stuff. But Blind Clarence liked to drink. Whenever he went on one of his periodic sprees he cursed everyone out. There are always plenty of brawls in the band business—its history is full of smashed heads and broken promises. Playing the street corners and playing in "the district" wasn't Sunday School, yet the men got along. Blind Clarence didn't, so he had to go. Larry Shields had been the next clarinet to play with Brown in New Orleans. So when Brown heard of an opening for a clarinet in Bert Kelly's Orchestra in White City, the Chicago resort, he sent home for Shields. Larry came North but he didn't get along in the White City band. Tom says it was because Larry didn't play their style, because he wasn't at home in anything but a Dixieland band. At any rate, they swapped clarinets. Mueller went to the White City band, Shields to the strictly Crescent City outfit of Tom Brown.

Early in 1916 Harry James went to New Orleans to find a Dixieland combination for Chicago's Booster Club. He went straight to the 102 Ranch, on Crozat Street in the heart of Storyville. Someone in Chicago may have told him how to find the place but it couldn't have been difficult. The *Blue Book*, Tom Anderson's guide, listed it along with the illuminating lists of "landladies" and "new arrivals." It had been called the 101 Ranch until 1913. In that year Billy Phillips, the owner, was killed by "Gyp the Blood." The new owner changed the name to 102.

The 102 featured a three-piece combination of clarinet, piano and drums. Alcide Nunez, nicknamed "Yellow" for his complexion, played clarinet. The man at the piano, Henry Ragas, had light eyes, soft, sensitive features. And Johnny Stein, who stayed in New Orleans when the band went North, was on drums. James told Nunez to get more men, so as to make it like Brown's Band.

The band that came North consisted of Nunez, Ragas, Tony Sbarbaro on drums, Eddie Edwards on trombone, and

Dominick James La Rocca on cornet. In the flush of their first success Nunez, after whom the band was first named, sent back a postcard photo of the boys to Papa Laine. On the card was the name Dixie Land Jass Band and a message reading:

This is the band that clean up Chi. Ill. and run all the other boys back home. Jack, you no that, what the use of bringing up again? And when we come back home this Band will be Jack Laine's Band, that what all us boys said to each other. All saying that the old man was good to all the boys and they can't forget you. Well Jack I heard that you are big and fat as ever and was good to hear that. from Kid Yellow. Best wishes to family.

There was nothing wrong with the spirit of this message but it wasn't quite true. All the other boys hadn't run back home. Brown's Band went to New York for a run of eleven weeks at the Century Theatre. After that it played vaudeville, the musicians dressing up like rustics for the sake of showmanship. They were billed as the "Five Rubes" and talented Larry Shields, in a world that wasn't quite jazz-crazy enough to take it straight, played the role of the "silly kid."

The Brown Band went home before returning to Chicago in the fall of that same year. When they got back to Chicago another swap was effected. This time Larry Shields replaced Nunez in the Dixie Land Jass Band, Nunez going to Brown. In November, 1916, Sam Salvin came to Tom Brown with the offer of a New York job. Tom's band had broken up but he told Salvin about the Dixie Land Jass Band playing on North Clark Street and managed by Eddie Edwards.

The rest is musical history. The Original Dixieland Jazz Band opened at Reisenweber's, off Columbus Circle in New York City. The patrons had to be told that the new music was "jass" and that it could be danced to. Once they caught on, the floor was crowded, the "sugar can" filled with lavish tips. The management slapped on a cover charge, Victor and Aeolian recorded the band, and they got as much as $1000 a night to play at private parties. "Dixieland" music had arrived. For the next few years the band and its music were to be sensational.

And what about the band and its music? In New Orleans some had been, as La Rocca explained, "fakers" who played by ear. Some had other professions. Yet none were, strictly speaking, musical amateurs. All had played in New Orleans bands. Even La Rocca had been in one of the last bands organized by Jack Laine. It was La Rocca, too, the ride man on cornet, who liked to lead. Edwards, quiet and sensible, was business manager. He worked out contracts and kept the books in order. Sbarbaro was enthusiastic, impulsive; Ragas sensitive. Shields, who no longer had to play the silly kid, was a mature musician, respected by all.

The music of the Original Dixieland Jazz Band was collective improvisation very similar to that of Jack Laine's Ragtime Band. The tempo was more like that of ragtime than what is recognized today as jazz tempo. Therefore, when modern bands play "Dixieland style" they refer to the spirit, but not the letter, of that style. Proof of this is found on Victor recordings made by the band. On these records it is possible to hear the Original Dixieland Jazz Band as they played in 1917 and the same band augmented twenty years later (1937) playing the same numbers. The ragtime tempo is so unfamiliar to our ears that the first impulse is to laugh it off as "corn," especially since on many of the early discs the "novelty" was laid on thick. Yet when the mind has overcome these elements it is possible to listen to playing that was certainly authentic New Orleans music.

It is largely because of tempo that critics of hot music refer to the Dixieland Band of 1917 as lacking swing. Added to the staccato tempo was a tendency to hit hard and fast so that the effect upon the ear was often less one of syncopation than it was one of rhythmic variety. Of course, there was syncopation. It was very evident in the piano style of Ragas on blues, for

instance, and in the liquid improvisations of Shields on clarinet. On the recording of *Lazy Daddy*, Sbarbaro's incessant,
buoyant rhythm, laying down four beats in a bar, seems to
float the melody. La Rocca's cornet had a somewhat bland
tone, foil to the limpid quality of Shields' playing. He had
what might be described as a "sock" style, "blowing in"
phrases with little bursts of sound and riding the melody while
Shields soared above it and Edwards laid the foundation. It
had military and brass band quality, as had the tunes themselves, and it had rare talent in the person of Larry Shields.
Incidentally, on recordings the band balance so favorable to
Shields' clarinet was achieved by having La Rocca stand about
twenty feet away from the crude recording apparatus.

The clear vibrant tone and careful phrasing that marked
Shields' playing made an unforgettable impression on jazz
music. His improvisations were imaginative and, like the best
choruses, melodically definitive. Almost every clarinet player,
from Rappolo on, plays Shields' chorus of *Tiger Rag* note for
note. Like Picou's chorus of *High Society*, it is considered the
only way it should be played. Even in adapting the tune to
cornet, Bix Beiderbecke followed the pattern sketched by
Shields, using many of his breaks.

While the Dixieland Band was having its momentous success in New York, other bands followed in its wake. Emmett
Hardy, who played with the Brunies boys, came up to Chicago
with Paul Mares on the first northward venture of the New
Orleans Rhythm Kings. Hardy, according to those who knew
his playing, was more like Vega than any other New Orleans
cornet player. His playing had punch, a rhythmic "attack"
similar to that Vega had learned from the great Negro trumpeters, and it had originality. But while Hardy played on riverboats, where Bix first heard him, he did not come to Friars'
Inn until the Dixieland Band had gone abroad. A band that
followed the Dixieland to Chicago was that of George
"Happy" Schilling with Johnny Fischer on clarinet, Arnold

Loyocano on piano, Happy on trombone. To New York came the Louisiana Five, with Yellow Nunez and Alfred Laine.

Before the Dixieland Band went to London their popularity had become something of an ordeal. Ragas, particularly, was affected. Drinking had become a habit with him, and this, along with the strenuous round of parties and engagements, undermined his health. A month before the band was to sail to England, Ragas died in his room in a dingy hotel around the corner from Reisenweber's.

It was a personal tragedy to the members of the Dixieland Band and it was also a business tragedy. La Rocca said, "I don't know how many pianists we tried before we found one who couldn't read music." Finally, they took J. Russell Robinson who, despite his understanding of written music, was able to play along with the Dixielanders. It was while he was with the band that they brought out *Margie* and *Singin' the Blues*.

Eddie Edwards didn't care to go abroad and the London engagements were filled by another New Orleans trombone player, Emil Christian. The band aroused a storm of controversial opinion and continued to celebrate a phenomenal success. The hair splitting was over the question of whether jazz was music or musical anarchy. Nick La Rocca, in a widely published interview, admitted that it was "revolution in 4-4 time."

On its return to America the band continued to tour. But meanwhile the Negro bands and through them two bands of young talented musicians—the New Orleans Rhythm Kings and the Wolverines—had had a perceptible influence on the tempo of American dance music. The music of the Dixieland Band changed. In the early twenties the band, with radically altered personnel, recorded *Toddlin' Blues*. It was in true fox-trot tempo.

Get Out of Here and Go on Home—that's what they called *Tiger Rag* in "the district." It sounds funny now, with all the big houses torn down or fallen into disrepair. Take Lulu White's. The name is there in cut glass but the windows are boarded up and where you can look through there's not a sign of the overstuffed furniture. The girls are gone, too, those girls of various shapes, sizes and colors to whom she was "landlady." "Down the Line" meant Basin Street, but today it's only a blues song. There isn't any line any more and Stale Bread Lacoume peddles programs at the race track.

You can search Basin Street up and down and you won't find The Function. Nor will the natives enlighten you, unless you come across someone like Albert Callahan. Callahan was Tom Anderson's bartender. He has a weathered face, a long bulbous nose and gray eyes that have seen the world and what goes on in it. He knew The Function, where the musicians had sessions of hot music. Most of the sporting houses had string trios, or just a blues piano player, he explained. It was in the cabarets that you heard the hot bands.

Leon Joseph Rappolo came down to "the district" when he was a kid, to hear Louis Armstrong play. Seeing him enter, Louis would catch his eye, crook thumb and index finger at him. He was right, too. Rappolo was no fool.

Stale Bread played in the district but only when he'd learned to play legitimate musical instruments. A lot of nonsense has been talked about Stale Bread and his Spasm Band. Jazz didn't come from toy instruments, no matter how quaint or colorful these street corner bands sound to the tourist trade. A great many New Orleans musicians did begin their careers on something conjured out of odds and ends that made sound. Rapp's was a one-string violin, made with a cigar box. Stale Bread himself didn't play a toy instrument but he did make a business of what others confined to the back yard.

In 1896 Stale Bread got together his first band, years before Rappolo was born. He himself played zither but the line-up is so raggle-taggle that it might as well be listed:

Stale Bread (Emile August Lacoume, Sr.), zither; Cajun

(Willie Bussey), harmonica; Whiskey (Emile Benrod), bass constructed from half-barrel, strung with clothes-line wire and played with cypress-stick bow; Warm Gravy (Cleve Craven), four-string, cheese-box banjo; Slew-foot Pete (Albert Montluzin), soap box cut down to make a four-string guitar.

With these crude instruments the boys dished out home cooking for Doc Malney's Minstrel Show. They continued playing, one job following another, until 1901. In that year Stale Bread went blind from an eye infection. By 1903 he was back in the music business and the band was practically legitimate:

Stale Bread (Lacoume), zither and piano; Dolly (Charles Carey), string bass; Dude (Jimmy Lacoume), banjo; Sonny (?), guitar & mandolin; Sweet Potato (Harry Carey), tambourine & cornet.

Within a few years Stale Bread was playing on riverboats, sometimes with Lawrence Vega, of whom he commented, "he was a real musician." One job was on Basin Street at Toro's, with Harold Peterson on drums. Years later, when he played at the Halfway House with the Brunies and Rappolo, Stale Bread played banjo. He liked people to think of him as a musician, not as a blind man playing music. He wore dark glasses and most of the time no one seemed to notice it. The boys didn't read music, anyway.

Abbie Brunies recalled vividly the first job he and George had, both in knee pants and both playing cornet. It was for a Mardi Gras parade on Canal Street. The thrill of marching for the first time, and playing in a band, their own band, stayed with them years later when they'd played thousands of jobs. Abbie carries a photograph of that first job with him and keeps it near his music stand with a couple of other pictures, all of them bands with Rappolo.

Because there is only one Rappolo. It's a large Sicilian family he comes from, Leon a common family name and Leon Joseph far from being rare, but there is only one Rappolo.

Even the Rappolos admit that. He was born Leon Joseph Rappolo, March 16, 1902, in Lutcher, Louisiana, where his father, a concert musician, led bands and taught music.

Leon's father disapproved of the childish contraption made of a cigar box and a piece of wire. It was true that Grandfather Leon Rappolo had been a famous clarinet player in Sicily. True, too, that there were many successful musicians in the Rappolo family. But in New Orleans, music no longer seemed a profitable following. The profession was overcrowded and the musicians who played on the fringe, who had taken over the Negro style of playing and had jobs in Storyville,—these were looked upon as fakers. The culture that years before had supported the French Opera, snubbed the new music. Newspapers, incensed at its popularity, denounced it in their editorial columns. All in all, music appeared to be on the decline. But Leon's father was himself a musician. When Leon was ten and about to enter the Rugby Academy, his father presented him with a real violin.

Professor Carrie, a Negro, gave him his first lessons. But the pupil was impatient. He soon realized that he couldn't march in a brass band with a violin. From then on his interest in the violin decreased, his study lagged. He began to cast longing eyes on his father's clarinet. It wasn't just that a clarinet was almost synonymous with the name Rappolo. To a ten-year-old there was something much more important than that. It was the fact that you could play clarinet in a brass band, and march in a parade. The clarinet was father's, and not to be touched. Leon learned snare drum. But he kept looking at the clarinet, wanting to play it. Finally he got up his courage, blew through the reed a few times, choosing occasions when his father was not at home.

Mrs. Rappolo might have stopped him. She didn't. She could see how much he loved to play. Very soon, despite the care with which Leon's two pretty sisters and his mother kept the secret, his father discovered Leon playing his clarinet. He did the only thing left to do. He sent Leon to Professor Sonta Guriffe and asked him to teach his boy how to finger and how to read music. Professor Guriffe said he would teach him for nothing. It was, he told Leon's father and mother, an honor to teach a Rappolo. When Professor Guriffe put it this way, there was no idea of ragtime in his mind. The Rappolos were legitimate musicians. The grandfather after whom Leon was named still played clarinet at the age of 92, but it was concert clarinet. With Leon the emphasis was to shift to jazz. Fano, a third cousin, now plays jazz clarinet.

Leon grew up with the Brunies boys and played with them and their friends. Often he played on the clarinet of Eddie Cherie, who knew the ragtime technique and could show him how to play it. Eddie Cherie, like Dave Perkins, was part Negro. None of the boys who played in Abbie Brunies' little band knew it at the time. Eddie was good and none of them got curious about him. He could play the whole chorus of *High Society*, the way Picou played it, never crowding the notes for want of breath and never losing the easy, apparently unconscious rhythm. Sometimes the boys would sneak down to Storyville and listen to the bands.

At the age of fourteen Leon ran away from home to play in a pit band with Bee Palmer's act on the Orpheum Circuit. He couldn't read very well but he'd already learned to play a New Orleans clarinet. His father had the police stop him at Hattiesburg, Mississippi. Even if the boy had to be a musician, he was too young to go away from home. Shortly after that Leon went into the Halfway House with Albert Brunies, and his father didn't object. He could see how things were. When he was off the job, Leon would keep blowing the clarinet or strum on the guitar, learning to pick out solo parts. Years later Melrose heard him playing in a hotel room, wanted to record the guitar. Just solos. Leon didn't speak Sicilian and couldn't sing any of the folk songs that were popular among the Italian population in New Orleans.

Leon was seventeen when the New Orleans Rhythm Kings were organized. In this band was the nucleus of the personnel that a few years later went into the Friars' Inn. Before going to Chicago, the band made a trip to Mobile and, after that, one to Texas.

The New Orleans Rhythm Kings were young when they came to the Friars' Inn. About them have arisen stories, some true, some fanciful, but all fitting into a logical pattern. Rappolo, caught up in a whirl of marijuana and bright life, faded out of the picture while still young. He was playing at the Halfway House with Abbie Brunies before he left New Orleans. When he came back, he played there again, and Abbie took care of him very much like a brother, because Leon was sick then, sick and perhaps doomed to life in a sanitarium. He now plays saxophone in the hospital band. The story that a big "name" band leader gave him a clarinet is not true. Rappolo's best clarinet is at the bottom of Lake Pontchartrain, where he threw it one night, and his second best clarinet his mother keeps for him.

Paul Mares came to Chicago in 1920. They had wanted Abbie Brunies for a job and he couldn't go, so they sent Paul. They got George Brunies about the same time. They worked the Strekfus line, played a job at Fox Lake, Wisconsin. Rapp came North in time to work with them at the Cascades Ballroom, where the piano was a tone and a half off. They went from there to Friars' Inn which, as one of the musicians described it, was the hangout of the big money people; you had to spend money there. Nevertheless, it was a "cheap" joint. The number they were hired on was *Wabash Blues*. Personnel varied from time to time. Jack Pettis played saxophone, Elmer Schoebel played piano. String bass was played first by Arnold Loyocano, then by Steve Brown, last by Chink Martin. Ben Pollack followed Frank Snyder on drums. Stitzel came in on piano, Lew Black on banjo (also Bob Gillette), and Don

Murray played tenor saxophone for the recording of *Angry*. Others played briefly with the band.

The most important white band after the Dixieland—certainly closer to the jazz spirit than any other white band of its time—the New Orleans Rhythm Kings have been amply rerecorded. Jazz followers of today can hear Rappolo and the New Orleans Rhythm Kings through the releases of the Hot Record Society and through the English Brunswick releases.

Abbie Brunies and his brother George, who shifted to trombone to provide the foundation for the New Orleans Rhythm Kings, played in many of Papa Laine's outfits when they were kids. Bands such as the Reliance. Carnival. Dance. Milneburg. Halfway House. Storyville. They listened to bands like that of Joe Oliver and something of it went into the way they played. Thus the Dixieland school of Papa Laine was once more freshened with the discoveries of Negro improvisers. It was, in fact, no longer Dixieland.

Because the musicians in New Orleans started out early in life, the city was flooded with child prodigies. Out of these a few were really gifted and were to leave their mark on jazz development. The Rhythm Kings were to make important contributions for they were in themselves creative and technically uninhibited, as the Dixielanders had been before them. To acknowledge the influences that contributed to their music is not to deny its originality. No music is without antecedent. The Negro himself, coming to America, traded his own instruments for those identified with western music, assimilated in his folk music the strains of English and Continental folk song, assimilated the Spanish-American music which was already a mixture of Negro, Spanish, and Indian. To ignore these influences, and the backgrounds from which they spring, is to fail to grasp the significance of the music itself.

Albert Callahan was bartender in the place where George Brunies first worked in "the district." Brunies was small, and a little chubby. Maybe he didn't quite swagger, but he put up a brave show of confidence. When the band started, the manager kept looking at the chubby boy. Finally he came up to Callahan, frowned, and jerked his head toward the band.

"They sent a schoolboy!"

Callahan blew on a glass until it fogged, then polished it with a dry cloth. He squinted his eyes and looked up, but without lifting his head from the job he was doing, he said: "That's a good schoolboy you got there; he's a musician!"

If Storyville hadn't closed, a lot of the musicians would have stayed on in New Orleans. As it was, they had to go. When Josephus Daniels, Secretary of the Navy under Wilson, asked municipalities to clamp down on all forms of vice, it meant the end of Storyville, just as filling in the lakefront at Pontchartrain had meant the end of Milneburg. A local ordinance put the Indian sign on Storyville on October 10, 1917.

That night in the sporting houses liquor splashed like water. Big parties were given "on the line," and, for the first time in the history of that mercenary kingdom, everything was on the house. A light breeze gently stirred the fronds of Josie Arlington's palm tree. Somewhere close by there was the sound of a girl having a crying jag. The air was soft and yellow and warm, the way it is in New Orleans, and from the open doors of sporting houses and cabarets came the sounds of bands playing. As the evening wore on the musicians came out of the houses, one band after another, and formed into line—"the best damned brass band parade that New Orleans ever had." Slowly it marched down the streets, Iberville, Conti, Customhouse. And as it made its solemn stand it played Nearer My God to Thee—plaintively, like the brass band on the way to the graveyard. On Franklin Street, prostitutes moved out of the long-shuttered cribs, mattresses on their shoulders. The brasses moaned, while the clarinets sung shrilly above them. And over on Basin Street where the pretty quadroons gave America one of its popular blues, a red light flickered faintly and went out.

III

KING OLIVER AND HIS CREOLE JAZZ BAND

BY FREDERIC RAMSEY, JR.

IN 1885, thirty-two years before the last mattress had been carried out of the cribs of Storyville into the clean air and the last hymn had been sung, Joseph Oliver was born in a house on Dryades Street. He was raised in the Garden District; his first years were marked by a series of moving-days which took his family from Dryades to Eighth Street, from Eighth Street to First, then to Second between Saratoga and Franklin, finally to Nashville and Coliseum Avenue, where his mother died, in 1900. This left Joe under the care of his half-sister, Victoria Davis, who had nursed him when he was a baby. It was while they were living on Second Street that a man persuaded the family to let Joe play in a children's brass band he was forming. At this time, Buddy Bolden's Band was in its prime, and Bunk Johnson was "puffing on his cornet" in a way that made everyone "real crazy." Bunk remembers that first band in which Joe Oliver played. He says:

Now here is the name of the man who started Joe out on cornet, Mr. Kenchen. I do not know what year Mr. Kenchen started his young band but as close as I can remember, it was about 1899 or 1900 I might be wrong but that's as near as I can get to it, now I think that was just about the time Mr. Kenchen started his young brass band uptown, learning them how to read music. Now Joe was a poor cornet player a long time. . . .

Joe's family says he was "slow to learn music," but that he wasn't really "poor a long time." Then they tell of the time the Kenchen band played at a birthday party given for Joe's year-old niece. It was a swell affair, with the band in good form. When they heard Joe play on that day, they knew that he was learning how to handle a cornet. After they had played, the boys finished up a fine birthday cake that Joe's sister had baked and trimmed with burning candles.

The "young brass band" became so accomplished that Mr. Kenchen decided it was time to go on tour. Families of the fifteen- and sixteen-year-old musicians objected, but were over-ruled by the boys themselves, who were itching to go. They set off on a riverboat, and landed at Baton Rouge. Then rumors came drifting back down the river about their adven-tures, making the families frantic with worry. No definite news was received, but there was one persistent story about a fight they had with a gang of river bullies. It was said Joe had a bad forehead-wound caused by "a lick on the haid" delivered by a wicked broomstick wielded by the enemy. Confirmation of this came when Joe arrived in New Orleans with a scar over one eye which stayed with him throughout his life. After the trip, Joe settled down to less exciting work. He found a job as butler for a family of white people. Bunk tells about it:

Walter Brundy and I, we used to go up to Second and Magazine where he was working on the premises, and I used to help Joe a great deal in his cornet playing. The music that Joe had was too hard for him to play. I would make Brundy talk to him, and I would steal it and bring it to our band and we would play it. Now here is the first orchestra Joe played with, that was the old Eagle Band. Now here is the name of the men who were in it when Joe got in the band: James Philip, drummer; Frank Duson, trombone, Joe Oliver, cornet; Frank Lewis, clarinet; Alcide Frank Vilion; Brock Mumford, guitar; Bob Lyons, bass. If I am not wrong, Joe played with them about two years to my knowing.

His employers must have understood Joe's interest in music. Whenever he wanted to play, they accepted his substitute, a young boy whom he trained as butler. Playing with the Eagle Band, which was composed of older men for the most part, was hard on Joe. They sent him home from his first job with them, he "played so loud and so bad," according to one of the men who heard him on that day. The trouble with the Eagle Band was that it "flew high," and disregarded the written notes. Joe hadn't played this kind of music before, but it wasn't hard to work into it, for he had a natural feeling for this style. Soon he became known for a variation he played on the old hymn, *Sing On;* someone always requested it at any one of the many funerals and picnics held by the clubs and associations to which he belonged. Bunk was playing blues and stomps for all he was worth; Joe listened to Bunk, and came out a little later with a stomp of his own, called *Dippermouth.* Whenever a crowd caught sight of Joe Oliver in a street band, they "clapped and hollered at him" until he eased their minds with some choruses of *Dippermouth.* Bunk Johnson continues:

Now here is where Joe got well; when he crossed Canal Street and became a member of the Onward Brass Band with Manuel Perez, then he got real good and has been going ever since.

In the Onward Band, then later in his own band, Joe added a little more to his growing reputation. For the Oliver Band was the best brass band, the one that attracted the biggest army of kids, the one that always came last; for they had to clear the streets for Oliver when he came marching up under the hot summer sun, his cornet glistening while he played.

Like most enterprising musicians of that period, Perez, besides leading his own Onward Band, had a job in Storyville, at Rice's Hall. So it wasn't long before Joe Oliver "crossed Canal Street" as all the others had done. When he did cross, he found himself in a district that was working full time, wide

open night and day, entirely different from his own respectable home territory. Some time went by before he got "real
good." But there were so many dance halls and cabarets in
and around "the district," such as the 101 Ranch, Parker's,
Fewclothes's, Tom Anderson's, Odd Fellows' Hall, Hope Hall,
and Economy Hall which needed musicians, that a young man
like Joe who wanted to play all the time just couldn't miss.
But first he had to prove his talent to these men who played
in Storyville, for their ears were used to Bolden, to Bunk,
Keppard, and Perez; these were the ones they talked about,
the ones they admired. Joe was playing with a small band at
the Aberdeen Brothers', a cabaret on the corner of Bienville
and Marais Streets. With him were Big Eye Louis, clarinet;
Deedee Chandler, drums; Richard Jones, piano. Jones says
something got into Joe one night as he sat quietly in the
corner and listened to the musicians who were praising Keppard and Perez. He was infuriated by their tiresome adulation;
didn't they know that Joe Oliver could play a cornet, too? So
he came forth from his silence, strode to the piano, and said,
"Jones, beat it out in B Flat." Jones began to beat, and Joe
began to blow. The notes tore out clear as a bell, crisp and
clean. He played as he never had before, filling the little dance
hall with low, throbbing blues. Jones backed him with a slow,
steady beat. With this rhythm behind him, Joe walked straight
through the hall, out onto the sidewalk. There was no mistak-
ing what he meant when he pointed his cornet, first towards
Pete Lala's, where Keppard played, then directly across the
street, to where Perez was working. A few hot blasts brought
crowds out of both joints; they saw Joe Oliver on the sidewalk,
playing as if he would blow down every house on the street.
Soon every rathole and crib down the line was deserted by its
patrons, who came running up to Joe, bewitched by his cornet.
When the last joint had poured out its crew, he turned around
and led the crowd into Aberdeen's, where he walked to the
stand, breathless, excited, and opened his mouth wide to let

out the big, important words that were boiling in his head. But all he could say was, "There! that'll show 'em!"

After that night, they never called him anything but "King" Oliver. He moved fast, once he was on the way; soon he was leading the band at Lala's Cabaret. It was one of the best in New Orleans, with Lorenzo Tio, clarinet; Zue Robinson, trombone; Buddy Christian, piano; Zino, drums; and Oliver, cornet. Lala's was a landmark to all who came to Storyville; the lights that shone forth on warm summer nights from the corner of Marais and Iberville Streets drew crowds of tourists, just as the street lamp above drew moths and gnats. Inside the low, smoky room, the musicians sweated for their bread, delivering "gully-low" stomps and blues, the kind that the respectable "dicty" people pretended to hate, but yelled for as soon as they had a few drinks under their belts. When the dawn lights came up and the street lights began to flicker, when the last drunk had been swept out of the place, the jazzmen of Storyville came out of their dance halls and walked over to Pete Lala's. There they hung their hats, dug out their instruments, and blew in the dawn. When they had finished, they picked up their things and went slowly home through the silent rows of shuttered cribs and gingerbread palaces. At this hour, Marais Street smelled like a fetid marsh, as the musty odor of the good time flats rose and mingled with the morning mist.

By the time a war decree closed the pleasure domes run by the ladies of Basin Street, Joe Oliver had a name, he was a famous cornetist, a "King." Nevertheless, he had to find a place to play in, a dive where he could earn his living. For King Oliver, as well as for many another New Orleans musician, Chicago was the answer.

Chicagoans who lived by day first saw Joe Oliver when he was playing in a cart under the El pillars of the Loop. The city was keyed high with war-time tension, teeming with parades. Joe and his friends had volunteered to play for a campaign to sell Liberty Bonds. They hired a cart, climbed into it and put on a "New Orleans Jazz Jam" on Wabash Street for the crowds that swarmed through the Loop. The "tail gate" trombone was something new to Chicagoans, something they didn't forget. They began to inquire about this band, and to seek it out in its home territory on the South Side. For Chicagoans who lived by night, the band was not such a novelty; they had already discovered Joe playing in two South Side night spots.

The story of how Joe Oliver got two jobs at the same time is one of rivalry between members of two famous New Orleans bands. The whole thing began when the Original Creole Band, a group of jazz pioneers that had left New Orleans in 1911, had balked at having to play a new, long series of road engagements. They wanted a place to sit down in, some cabaret that would keep them from the grind of one-night stands. Bill Johnson, their string bass player, angled for such a job, and was successful in obtaining an offer of steady work at the Royal Gardens Café, to become effective when and if he could recruit a band. With this promise behind him, he called on Jimmy Noone, clarinet; Eddie Venson, trombone; Paul Barbarin, drums; and Lottie Taylor, pianist. That was good, but not quite good enough to make the grade. They had to have a cornetist, a really first-rate one, because there was a group of New Orleans musicians over at the Dreamland Café that mustn't get a chance to cut their stuff. Then they thought of Joe Oliver, who seemed right for the job. So they sent off a telegram, knowing that if King Joe came up, they needn't worry about anyone else. Unfortunately, as soon as the word leaked out that he was on his way, the gang at the Dreamland decided that they wanted Joe, too. Sugar Johnny, their cornetist, had burned himself out with liquor and ladies. So Lawrence Dewey, the leader, hatched a plot to bring Oliver into his band. On the day Oliver arrived, he and Sidney Bechet, an old friend of Joe's, would meet him at the station and make a big fuss over him; as a result of this display of friendship, Joe would just naturally join their band in the Dreamland. The final details were in order the night before Joe's arrival. Lawrence didn't gamble on the chance that Sidney *might* get out of bed in time to meet an early morning train; he persuaded Bechet to spend the night in his home, where he could be sure to wake him in time. The dawn of the next day found them both up, anxiously hurrying over to the station to carry out their plan. They received a rude shock when they came up on the platform. For there, standing half-asleep behind one of the pillars, was Eddie Venson, of the Royal Gardens faction. Quickly, they ducked out of sight behind another pillar, pretending they had never seen Eddie Venson, or anyone like him. Just as they did this, the train pulled in. Each faction moved swiftly forward, no longer able to dodge behind pillars. The two groups met at King Oliver, who was neutral ground, at least for the time being.

"Why, hullo, Venson, where did you come from?"

" 'Morning, Dewey, didn't count on meetin' you here!"

Joe didn't know what that meant, but he found out. Both the Dreamland and the Royal Gardens needed a "King" on cornet, and there was only one to go around. This called for serious deliberation; so they all went to the nearest bar for a drink. Their solution, which had a lasting effect upon the course of Chicago jazz, was profoundly simple. Joe joined both bands.

Officially, Venson won his point, for he had completed an orchestra, with the King as his cornetist. And this group did open shortly after in the Royal Gardens. Yet Oliver doubled at the Dreamland with Dewey and his New Orleans Jazz Band.

Other cornet players had come to Chicago before Joe, but they all had to take a back seat as his reputation spread out from the South Side. Freddie Keppard dropped in at the Royal Gardens to see how the new orchestra was getting along.

A battle of cornets followed, a duel that was a triumph for Oliver. It was agreed, in the words of Richard M. Jones, that "Joe Oliver beat the socks off Keppard when he got to Chicago."

Every week brought a new triumph for Oliver.

This was the time of Chicago's high-tide post-war fever; of crowds that flocked down to hear the amazing Creole Jazz Band that was setting the tempo of the South Side; of the *Royal Garden Blues*, first composed and played by this orchestra in the building that is now a Government flop-house; of Prohibition that was no prohibition; of house-rent parties that started early and broke up late, perhaps the next day, perhaps the day after. It was great to be a cheerful, successful cornetist from 'way down the river, when it was just right if you could loaf all day long, then go to work and blow the insides out of the Royal Gardens while the dancers yelled for more and more and more. With all this excitement around him, Joe remained the same mild, kind-hearted person he had been in New Orleans, and held on to the simple things he had always liked. His only excesses were in the way of food; for breakfast, he ate huge portions of hominy, washed down with a large pitcher of water. At lunchtime, he took a crack at his favorite meal: half-a-dozen hamburgers and a quart of milk. Once a man saw him putting away one of these lunches, and bet that he couldn't eat a dozen pies at one sitting. Joe took him up, side-bets were placed, and he began. He didn't crack a smile until the eleventh pie, then paused to look at the surrounding circle of eyes that were getting bigger and bigger; at this, the stranger was sure of victory. But the twelfth pie went down on the next round. The chagrined loser was astounded. Between meals, Joe liked to play pool, while Sundays always found him out at the ball park with the children he invariably took with him.

Two years of this life, mixed with the work at the Dreamland and the Royal Gardens, rolled by; then in 1920, an offer came from the Dreamland. If he could organize his own band, he could play there all the time, and give up the work at the Royal Gardens. So he recruited his players. One of the first persons he chose was the pianist Lil Hardin, a bright young girl who had come up from Memphis in 1917 to continue musical studies begun at Fiske University, and had been side-tracked into jazz, almost without realizing what had happened. Lil had been playing with the old Dreamland orchestra. Besides "Lilly," as the boys called her, Joe took on Honoré Dutrey, trombone; Minor Hall, drums; Ed Garland, bass. Noone struck out on his own, leaving them without a clarinet. A few nights later, a new face appeared in the Dreamland when a serious-looking young man came strolling over to the stand where the members of the band were sitting, and began to undo the newspaper wrapping from a long bundle under his arm. When he came to the last layer of paper, Johnny Dodds took out a shiny, black, B Flat clarinet, smiled shyly as King Joe shook his hand and asked him how he'd liked the train ride from New Orleans to Chicago.

This new orchestra came into the Dreamland every night at 9:30; by 10 o'clock, King Oliver and his Creole Jazz Band were going fast and hard. They didn't stop until 1 A.M., when they packed instruments and moved seven blocks down the street to the Pekin Café. The rambling hulk of the old Pekin Theatre had been a respectable place, once; but it was re-modeled into a night-club, with a large, comfortable bar on the ground floor and a cabaret in the room overhead. The down-grade days of the Pekin Theatre were up-grade for the Pekin Café, with a large gangster patronage that wasn't squeamish about spending money. They gave out their best in brawls that shook the floors and left the glassware in shattered bits. Bathtub booze was easy to get; the fights it inspired meant anything from relatively harmless gin-bottle tossing to gunplay. No one ever thought of restraining these outpourings of feeling.

Perhaps the members of the Creole Jazz Band wanted to get away from the bullet-laden atmosphere of the Pekin, perhaps they felt a need for a different brand of excitement; whatever their reasons, the end of May, 1921, saw the little group heading for California.

The contract with the Pergola Dancing Pavilion of San Francisco called for a seven-piece orchestra, consisting of Joe Oliver, Honoré Dutrey, John Dodds, Lillian Hardin, Minor Hall, Edward Garland, and James Palao: "said band shall play continuously, dance music as played in so-called 'nickel dances,' as directed by the party of the first part, between 8 and 12 P.M." The contract covered a six-month period extending from June, 1921, to December. At the end of this time, Lil returned to Chicago for a vacation from nickel dances. Minor Hall left, too, because he and Joe hadn't been able to get along very well. If anyone fell out with the King, it was up to that person to get out at the same time; that is how Joe kept discipline in his small, close-knit unit. "This is a matter of business," he once wrote, "I mean I wants you to be a band man, and a band man only, and do all you can for the welfare of the band in the line of playing your best at all times." When Hall left, Joe asked Baby Dodds, Johnny's brother, if he wouldn't like to give up his work on the steamboat *St. Paul* and play with the Creole Band. Joe never had any trouble replacing a player who left, because he was on top; any one of a number of his New Orleans friends was always glad of a chance to join him.

The band swept on to Los Angeles with a full complement of Dodds brothers. There, Jelly Roll Morton asked the group to join him for a night at the Wayside Park. Los Angeles cakewalkers had never heard anything like the music of the Creole Jazz Band before; they flocked to hear the strange, compelling sounds that came from the familiar bandstand, while word of the new triumph filtered back to the *Defender*, Chicago's Negro newspaper:

King Oliver set Los Angeles on fire. He was offered all kinds of inducements to stay, and the highest salary ever offered anyone. All Los Angeles says he's the greatest, and some hot babies have been here the past year.

But "the highest salary ever offered anyone" wasn't enough to keep the men away from Chicago. They came back after an absence of a year, and moved straight into the Lincoln Gardens Café. This was nothing but the old Royal Gardens with a fresh coat of paint and a new name.

At this time, Chicagoans who knew their jazz were unanimous in their opinion that King Oliver was the greatest cornetist ever to play in Chicago. There was only one challenge ever put up to this fact. That was a rumor, a story about a young fellow called Louis Armstrong. When King Oliver left New Orleans, he had seen to it that "little Louis" succeeded him as cornetist at Lala's Cabaret. Now they said that Louis was doing more than just "making good" on King Joe's old job. That seemed to be a fine thing to Joe. He was proud of Louis, and of what he had done for him. Let him come to Chicago, then, and they could give the town an idea of what two cornetists from New Orleans could do. So a wire went to Louis; it caught him in mid-afternoon of a hot July day, just as he had finished marching with the Tuxedo Band for a funeral. Louis didn't have to be persuaded; he was in a hurry to get to Chicago. When he arrived at the Lincoln Gardens, Louis made all the stories that had preceded him come true.

The home of the Lincoln Gardens Café was a tall, thin building, with scrolls cut in the stone of the sharply peaked gable where it lapped onto the second story. The façade of the two top floors bulged with lumpish balconies that looked dourly down on 31st Street through swollen, bay-window eyes. Underneath these eyes, two round, ugly arches drooped over the entrance to the ground floor. Once inside those arches, weary wanderers through Chicago's night life received a shock that stiffened their backs, as the low-down voice of the bayou came blasting forth at them from the horns of Joe Oliver and Louis Armstrong.

For this cry from the faraway swampland tore at faint hearts as they passed through the dark, narrow hall. The entrance-hall led into a large, dimly lighted room whose edges faded off under a balcony built out from the second story. The dancers on the floor bounced with rhythm as the cornet team polished off a break.

There were no waltzes played at the Lincoln Gardens; the customers liked the Bunny-hug, the Charleston, the Black Bottom. A stomp ended; a minute's silence broke in on the din, then Joe tooted a few notes down low to the orchestra, stomped his feet to give the beat, turned around, and they were off on a new piece, first impatient for a release from the stiffness of the opening bars, then relieved to be tearing through fast and loud in their own way. Lil Hardin hit hard on her four beats to a measure, while the deep beat of Bill Johnson's string bass and the clearly defined foundation of Baby Dodds' drum and high-toned, biting cymbal filled out the "bounce" and kept the others sweeping forward. This motion led to a climax, a point beyond which the breathless pace of the music seemed doomed to fall, unless something would intervene. Then Joe and Louis stepped out, and one of their "breaks" came rolling out of the two short horns, fiercely and flawlessly.

These breaks puzzled audiences that crowded around the stand at the Lincoln Gardens. No one understood how Joe and Louis could play together without looking at each other, or without written music at all, yet run through a break and not clash on a single note. They never did discover how this happened. They watched the team while it was in action, and failed to see any signals. It was a mystery. But it was easy for Louis and "Papa Joe."

A chorus or two before they rose to play, Joe leaned over

to Louis and half-sang, half-whispered the tune of the next break in his ear. When the time came, he nodded to Louis, and they cracked it out without a miss. As for knowing when the time had come, that was something you couldn't write down, it had to be felt. This stunt required two men with remarkably keen ears. That's what Jelly Roll Morton means when he talks about King Oliver:

My God, what a memory that man had. I used to play a piano chorus, something like King Porter or Tomcat, and Oliver would take the thing and remember every note. You can't find men like that today.

There wasn't much music on the stands, just a few scribbled-over sheets with no titles at the top. Joe had them torn off, because he didn't want the other musicians who came to listen to know what his men were playing. The white band at the Friars' Inn had already put one over on him. These men had carefully listened to the way the Creole brethren played the *Jazzin' Babies Blues*, then recorded it as an original tune of their own. Their only "original" contribution was the title, *Tin Roof Blues*.

However, the thing that counted more than the melody with King Oliver's men was their way of playing in and around it in duels of expression. This form of improvisation stimulated intensity of expression from each player. Today, it is almost a lost art, buried in large dance orchestras of technically proficient readers who cling desperately to a written score. The Creole Band never worried much about scores, it didn't have to, with musicians who knew how much to contribute in the way of solos, and when to stop. Each had a true feeling for the right notes at the right time. There was not so much interest in showing off individual talent, as in creating well-balanced ensemble music, and the powerful effect that inevitably comes from such playing. It was here that Johnny Dodds played an important part in holding the music together. The clear notes of his clarinet sang against the pattern set by the others at one moment, then blended with it, providing a splendid background for solos. His tone was full, complemented by perfect control in the upper register, a stumbling-block for most clarinetists.

Another contributor to the unusual strength of the ensemble work was Honoré Dutrey, the trombone player. Dutrey freed the trombone from the requirements set for it as a foundation instrument that backed up the rhythm section with an "oompah" that rivaled the tuba, and in so doing, added a powerful voice to the Creole Jazz Band. With King Oliver playing first cornet and Louis Armstrong second, no more voices were needed. The rhythm section could be counted on for a clear, forceful beat unmarred by any display of purely technical virtuosity. The band gained from the absence of saxophones, for the players of this instrument could hardly be said to have developed a hot style at that time. It is no wonder, then, that this Creole Jazz Band left a clear impression on the minds of all who heard it, as can be seen by a note published years later in the Chicago *Defender:*

King Oliver, whose name today brings pleasant memories, was located at the Lincoln Gardens Café and Dance Hall. With his little six-piece band he startled white musicians. From all over the city they would gather to hear King Joe blow those weird, soulful tunes. He was really a profitable asset to the place. Later on, he brought Louis Armstrong, a green-looking country boy with big forehead, thin lips and robust physique. This newcomer brought us an entirely different style of playing than King Joe had given us. He was younger, had more power of delivery, and could send his stuff out with a knack.

Fortunately, the period during which the "newcomer" was "sending his stuff out with a knack" was one of great activity in the recording studios. King Oliver and his orchestra waxed their initial set of records for the Paramount Company, but these sides were not the first to go on sale. The first to be

released were made while the band was touring through southern Indiana, and had dropped in for a few days of recording
at the studios of the Starr Piano Company in Richmond.
They cut a total of ten sides, one right after the other. There
was nothing but a horn for the men to play into, for this was
before the days of electrical recording. Even under the best of
circumstances, it was difficult for the engineers to get a proper
balance of instruments, as may be seen from the instruction
sheet which they gave the musicians:

We start work by making a short test which is immediately played
back to the performer from the wax and from that we begin to
judge positions and tone and arrangement of music and everything that is necessary to make a good record. After the faults have
been found we try another test wax and still another, etc.—if necessary will use one hundred test waxes in a date although this would
be almost a physical impossibility—however, when we have played
back a wax that sounds perfect, we begin to make a master—we
make three masters of each number tested out.

When the King Oliver Jazz Band cut loose in the small
studio on the warm April day chosen for the session, it nearly
smashed the recording machinery on the first test. So the engineers had to do some quick figuring over "positions and
tone and arrangement of music" before the date could proceed. They saved the day by moving the real threats to their
machinery, Joe and Louis, twenty feet away from the horn.
Under these conditions, Louis Armstrong recorded a solo for
the first time in his life, exactly as it can be heard today by
anyone lucky enough to possess a copy of the Gennett *Chimes
Blues.*

In June, 1923, the Spikes Brothers announced that they
had copies of this record for sale in their Los Angeles store.
As soon as the market quickened with the demands made
throughout the United States for these records, the Paramount Company proceeded to press its masters. The Okeh
Company then anounced in the *Defender:*

King Oliver's Jazz Orchestra, Chicago's big favorites, make first Okeh records. For years, King Oliver's Band has served up jazz to thousands at the Lincoln Gardens, Chicago's dazzling cabaret, but man alive, can't these boys play it, say it in true blues harmony. Why, they are the ones who put jazz on the map.

The Columbia Phonograph Company was next, with four new sides and the claim that "Nobody ever heard music like these boys can play it."

But after February, 1924, the only way to hear music "like these boys can play it" was to purchase the records made in the previous year. For the band "that put jazz on the map" was completely broken up shortly after the last Columbia recording session. Many reasons have been given for this split at a time when the band was in its prime. Some say that the regular members of the band complained bitterly because Joe arranged for a second recording session with Gennett, but used different musicians for the date. Yet when the records were issued, the company was still using the name "King Oliver's Creole Jazz Band," which the original group had made famous. It was said, too, that Oliver could no longer play with his former force. Joe felt this, himself. It came home to him every time that Louis Armstrong put a cornet to his strong lips and blew with all the wind his young lungs could force through the mouthpiece. At 24, Louis could put the freshness and vigor of youth into his playing. Joe Oliver had been 24 years old in 1909. He realized this, and as there was no resentment in his nature, he was proud of his second cornetist. When Louis arrived in Chicago, Joe had talked about him with Lil Hardin, and opened her eyes to the ability of the "green-looking country boy." Louis called Oliver "Papa Joe" because of the kind treatment he received from him. When other musicians talked about Armstrong, and asked Joe what he could do with a second cornetist who was going ahead so quickly, Joe smiled quietly and said: "As long as he's in my band, he won't hurt me." He was right. As long as

Louis' youth and strength worked for him every night, he had nothing to fear.

Possibly the others in King Oliver's Orchestra felt that he wasn't giving Armstrong a chance to forge ahead, possibly they were tired of playing under one man for so long. Whatever their reasons, when Oliver wanted to go on a tour through Ohio, Michigan, and Pennsylvania early in 1924, the Dodds brothers and Dutrey voted to stay behind to fill the job left open at the Lincoln Gardens when Oliver left. Louis and Lil Hardin stuck with Joe and made the trip. For his tour, Joe added new players, including Buddy Christian, banjo; John Lindsay, bass; Albert Nicholas, clarinet; and Rudy Jackson, clarinet and saxophone. Jackson later joined "Duke" Ellington. This was the first large orchestra Oliver ever had.

When he returned to Chicago in June, the Dodds-Dutrey combination moved out of the Lincoln Gardens into The Stables, where it stayed for several years. At this time, Armstrong left King Joe. This was something that had been brewing for months. In February, Lil and Louis had been married. Lil was ambitious for her husband, and had obtained an offer for him from Ollie Powers, who promised to give Louis more money, and a chance to play first cornet. Louis made the shift, leaving Joe terribly disturbed. As Lil stayed on with Oliver, she was subjected to many worried inquiries. Whenever Lil told him that Armstrong was doing very well, he grunted, pretended he didn't care, then said, "What does Louis think he's gonna do there, all by himself, without us? He'll find out, he'll have to come back." But Louis Armstrong never had to come back.

When Fall came, business was not what it had once been at the Lincoln Gardens, and the management decided to stay open for the three best nights of the week, Wednesday, Saturday and Sunday, but to close the rest of the time. So on September 6, 1924, the *Defender* carried a notice Joe had inserted:

AT LIBERTY. The celebrated KING OLIVER'S JAZZ BAND 8 men playing 15 instruments. Open for engagements in or out of Chicago. Joseph Oliver, 3033 South State Street, Chicago.

Before this date, Joe had never had particularly good luck. But by sticking close to his idea of being "a band man, and a band man only," he had managed to reach the top of his profession, and to gather together an orchestra that deserved all the fame and money that came to it. Henceforth, he was trailed by misfortunes which dogged him and pulled him down. This never stopped him; he went on trying to organize one band after another, sometimes meeting with fair success, only to have someone else come along and draw the musicians in his orchestra away from him. Whenever everything seemed to be going fairly well, there was sure to be some particularly unfair blow from an unexpected source. At times it must have seemed that regardless of how hard he tried, the cards were stacked against him. Yet he was so cheerful during his misfortunes that few people ever suspected what was happening.

The first discouraging set-back occurred while he was trying to recruit a new band. The Lincoln Gardens planned to bring in the crowds again with a "bigger and better" interior, to be shown at a gala "opening" to be held on Christmas Eve. Luis Russell, Paul Barbarin, Albert Nicholas, and Barney Bigard were with Charlie Cook at Harmon's Dreamland Casino; they agreed to play with Joe when the opening at the Gardens materialized. The Gardens opened on Christmas Eve, but someone was careless, a fire flamed up, and before the evening was over, the interior was completely gutted.

This left every musician to shift for himself. Joe found work as featured soloist with Peyton's Symphonic Syncopators, at the Plantation Café, where he was billed as "the world's greatest jazz cornetist." It was all right to be a featured soloist, but it wasn't like having a band of your own. The other musicians teased him about his work under another man. Peyton, who was quite friendly to Joe, nevertheless couldn't refrain from stressing his unaccustomed position as leader of an orchestra that Joe Oliver played in. One night when Joe had finished a set and was preparing to light a cigarette on the stand, Peyton came over to him and said, "Hey, Joe, you can't smoke here in my band, you know. If you want to smoke, you have to go outside while you're workin' for me." The "world's greatest jazz cornetist" slowly rose and went out to finish his cigarette.

Happily, the "symphonic" days didn't last long. At the end of February, 1925, the Symphonic Syncopators left the Plantation, and Joe was able to secure the men he had wanted for so many months. Luis Russell, piano; Cobb, bass; Scott, banjo; Barbarin, drums, made a strong rhythm section; Nicholas and Bigard were an excellent reed team, while Ory played the kind of "tail gate" trombone Joe always liked to have beside him. This band became so popular that outside offers began to come in. They played in May for a dance at Crane College. In August, Faggen, an Eastern manager, wanted Oliver to bring his band to the Rosemont Dance Hall, "a beautiful ballroom in Brooklyn, playing the leading attractions of the country."

In April, 1926, the Vocalion Company contracted for a series of recordings. "All of them are red-hot, and they'll come out soon," was the way the Defender described the test pressings. They came out soon, but they weren't all red-hot. The Dixie Syncopators was a large orchestra; it could not play the swiftly moving, well-integrated jazz that comes from smaller groups. With the possible exception of Sugar Foot Stomp, the sweeping phrases, breaks, and ensemble passages with which the early Creole Jazz Band had so astounded its audiences do not come forth from the grooves of these records. Yet Joe was fairly well pleased with them, as may be seen from a letter he wrote to Buddie Petit in May:

Dear Sir:
I recieve your letter which was quite a surprise to hear from you. At the same time, I was glad to get a line from you. I'm always glad to hear from my old friends and know that they are doing fine. Yes, I'm in the big windy city, and doing pretty good for an old man. Only trying to hold my end with the youngsters, that's all. You ask me about Louis eh? Well, he work across the street from me, but I seldom see him. Have you heard my late record *Snag It* on the Vocalion record? It isn't a very good recording, as they released the wrong number. See we make three master records and they select the best one of the three to put on sale. My luck were they picked the worst one. At that the record is selling like hot pies.

If you've got a real good blues, have someone to write it just as you play them and send them to me, we can make some jack on them. Now, have the blues wrote down just as you can play them, it's the originality that counts. By the way, what become of Bunk? I would like very much to hear from him. Well, I won't take up any more of your time. I will close hope to hear from you real soon.

Sincerely yours Jos. Oliver

With Louis playing at the old Sunset Café, 35th Street could boast of having two "Kings of Hot Jazz on the Cornet" in the same block, with a fire department waiting around the corner to rush in and cool things off when the music became too hot. At least, that's what they claimed in the *Defender*. This same sheet then assumed the solemn duty of warning all musicians against the day when jazz would be on the way out. "They're getting ready for the grey-haired days," Dave Peyton thundered, "at last the boys are beginning to see the handwriting on the wall. Luis Russell and Bob Schoffner of King Oliver's Band are studying musical theory."

Peyton's reputation as a prophet must have increased considerably when in January, 1927, Schoffner received a short, specific note:

Dear Sir and Bro:
I wish to inform you that two weeks from the above date you will be available for any engagement you may secure, as your serv-

ices will be no longer required with King Oliver's Dixie Syncopators. Kindly accept this as a legal two weeks notice. Wish you luck and success.

Fraternally yours,
Joseph Oliver

Peyton was right, too, when he talked about the "grey-haired days." Musicians were hard hit, not by old age, but by their own depression, which came two years before the business crisis. Republicans were still very sure there really was a chicken in every pot and a car in every garage, but somehow this didn't apply to musicians. The nation-wide installation of talking movie machinery was putting them out of work, and nothing was being done about it.

Even the relatively good position of the men at the Plantation was far from ideal. The contract called for work during the week from 9:30 P.M. to 4:30 A.M., and on Saturday nights the hours were even longer. Joe found it difficult to hold his men. Albert Nicholas and Darnell Howard threatened to go to China to follow Teddy Weatherford, who had discovered that American sailors far from home were willing to pay good money to hear hot jazz. Joe wrote to New York and asked Rudy Jackson if he and Buster Bailey wouldn't come on to Chicago and work for him. They never came.

In spite of his heavy schedule at the Plantation, Joe decided to enter the field of music publishing. A notice in the Defender of April, 1926, said that "King Oliver, writer of Snag It, can be seen in his office at the Plantation from 2 to 4:30 every afternoon." Joe had always shown an interest in writing down melodies as he heard them sung or played in the South. He often adapted traditional blues themes and songs for his orchestra to play. Later, when some of these early themes were recorded by the Creole Jazz Band, he and Lil Hardin arranged them, obtained a copyright, and they were then published. The title to these melodies was never really clear, as many of them had been sung in Texas, on the

Gulf Coast and in the South generally, long before jazz bands developed in New Orleans. Yet it is true that Joe Oliver took as important a part in spreading the influence of these blues as anyone, certainly as much as the other notators who claim priority in this field. A proof of the validity of his early work is to be had in the frequency with which some of the themes he first introduced keep recurring. Five years after he had copyrighted and recorded a melody entitled *Camp Meeting Blues*, Oliver was very surprised to hear a record by Duke Ellington's Orchestra, *Creole Love Call*, which was built around the theme of the older *Camp Meeting Blues*. Looking at the label, he saw that Ellington, Miley, and Rudy Jackson were listed as composers, but his own name was omitted. The same thing happened later when a group of white musicians made a record which they titled, appropriately enough under the circumstances, *Apologies*, for apologies were certainly due to Oliver for use of his *Dippermouth* theme. Yet the name of the composer-arranger on this label simply reads "Mezzrow." Later still, the Bob Crosby Orchestra released a record, *Dixieland Shuffle*, which is closely patterned after the earlier version the Creole Jazz Band made for the Okeh Company, *Riverside Blues*. Again, Oliver's name is absent. In this way his name has been unnecessarily blotted out and forgotten. This is a not unusual occurrence in jazz, where it is hard to pin down the source of any melody, and where melodies are more often heard as improvised by individual players, and not as written.

While holding office hours at the Plantation, Joe composed another tune, *Doctor Jazz*, which he advertised in Chicago by hiring a cart, placing his band in it, and playing the new tune wherever a crowd gathered. This was probably the last time a New Orleans band played in a wagon. Late in January, 1927, the doors of the Plantation Café were closed. Joe sent out several letters, all similar to the one below, which was addressed to a booker in Cleveland, Ohio:

Dear Sir:

I have been located at the Plantation Cafe since I played the week engagement for you at the South Main Garden. At present the Plantation has closed for a period of six weeks for remodeling. I am at leasure should you or any of your clients have anything to offer I would highly appreciate any favor you can render.

I have eleven men, a red hot singing and jazz combination as well as playing all the standard and special arrangements. Hoping an early reply.

Respectfully yours,
Joseph Oliver

This letter-writing campaign produced a nibble from the "Jean Goldkette Orchestras and Attractions, Inc.," who wrote asking him to hold the first week in May open for bookings. Oliver answered, "My intention is not to renew my contract with the Plantation Cafe so I will be available for any other engagement that you might have will meet my approval." He was still dictating his own terms. Then Faggen, who had not forgotten the orchestra, wrote and offered Joe a two-week engagement in Harlem's Savoy Ballroom, to begin May 9. Then the Goldkette Attractions booked a tour to St. Louis and Detroit. Everything was set, Joe and his men were ready to go on the road to New York. Before he left, he played for his friend Peyton, who has recorded what he heard on this last night:

There is but one King Oliver, the Supreme Sultan of Jazz. When he played *Oh, How I Miss You Tonight*, he cried and moaned on his $500 trumpet of gold. Encore'd four times, he was a sensation. He's the biggest man in the orchestra world.

With this send-off, King Oliver, his orchestra, and his "$500 trumpet of gold" left for Missouri, where Joe got a wire from Faggen asking him why he had not sent any advance publicity material. He answered it with a night letter:

Just receive wire, out of town at time of its arrival. All writeups and Photos destroyed in Plantation Cafe fire (stop) Can have cut forward you from St. Louis if desired (stop) Inform me what band we will alternate with so I can get line on stuff to use (stop) Will do utmost to make my two weeks a success.

Oliver needn't have worried about the "stuff to use," for the Dixie Syncopators were recognized by all who went to the "block-long" dance hall as the biggest thing "in the orchestra world."

For the engagement at the Savoy, Joe had sent down to Algiers, Louisiana, for Henry Allen, Jr., son of the bandmaster of the Allen Brass Band. He had added Pop Foster, string bass, to his rhythm section, and had done away with the bass horn which never sounded quite right to any jazz musician who had been brought up in New Orleans. For the first two weeks of their stay in New York, Foster and Allen lived with Joe at the home of his sister Victoria, now Mrs. Johnson. The orchestra did so well at the Savoy that an offer came from the Cotton Club for a long-term contract similar to the one Oliver had had at the Plantation. But the pay was too little for King Oliver, who was fresh from Chicago, where he was "Supreme Sultan" and could name a good price. However, the sum seemed just right to another orchestra leader, a young fellow named Ellington from Washington, D. C., who was glad to move into the Cotton Club after the Kentucky Club, where his Washingtonians had been playing.

This left Oliver to pick up as many dates in and around New York as he could. When he turned down the Cotton Club, he probably hadn't fully understood that odd dates were the only alternative, that good jobs in New York were rare, that the predepression figures he had become used to in Chicago were nothing but a faraway dream that no one would ever realize again. When he came into New York, it had looked as if he could pick and choose from the offers that were made. Yet when offers did come, the price always seemed too low. One thing was certain to Joe; they were below the union scale, which he had always paid his men. He didn't want to risk taking work that was paid "below scale," because he had a feeling that if unions or managers ever punished anyone for violation of contracts, he would be the one most heavily penalized, regardless of the heavy guilt of others. He held out too long, and lost. There was nothing left but one-night stands, such as the one he played at Dexter Park, called "Plantation Night in Brooklyn, a night's reception," where "to protect our patrons from the unruly element, we will refuse admittance to all undesirables. Don't try to push—you won't be able to shove: here's a dance you will love." He played at Quogue, at Newark, then there was a night in Asbury Park, where dancers were told to "have your fun, or go to the door and get your dough." The men were restless for lack of steady work. Ory returned to Chicago before the Dexter Park extravaganza, and Paul Barbarin went back to New Orleans to play with Piron's orchestra. Then, Luis Russell found work at a place called The Nest, and Oliver's band quietly dropped away from him one by one to join Luis Russell. Even Barbarin came back from New Orleans to play for Russell.

Oliver kept going in spite of the hard times that were pinching him, and held eleven men together long enough to arrange for a recording date with Brunswick. When this was over, he went back to Chicago for a short visit. He wrote a letter to Peyton on his return to New York:

I cannot begin to express my appreciation for making the trip it was a real pleasure for me to be with the old gang again, yet, I longed for the "bright lights" of New York.

I am sure it will interest you to know that I have just signed a nice little contract with the Victor. Brunswick, of course, hated to lose me but was kind enough to wish me success with the Victor. Russell's band is still hitting a la Babe Ruth. . . .

The Victor contract helped. It was easier to hold the musicians when there was money floating around. Joe made several attempts to improve the personnel of his band by writing his New Orleans friends and asking them to join him, as he had done so often before. Early in 1930, he wrote Bunk Johnson, who was barnstorming in Electra, Texas:

Dear Bunk:

I receive your letter, was glad to hear from and know you are enjoying God's best blessing which is good health. This leave me well. Well pal, I've got you some, I'm a grand father now. But, I'm sure you will be kind enough to admit that I'm a few years younger then you are. I know you remember when I use to come around and listen to you play Ha! Ha! Now Bunk, it's your fault you are still down there working for nothing. I had two good jobs for you. I did all I could to locate you but failed. I even tried to get some fellow by the name of Guy Kelly, I heard he was very good. Looks like those guys are afraid to leave the South. Now Bunk you must keep in touch with me because I can't tell just when some thing good will turn up. If I know how and where to reach you it will mean a wonderful break for you. In the mean time I will send you a few numbers to arrange. I can give you some extra change as a side line. Have you got any good blues? if so send them to me and I will make them bring you some real money. When making my arrangements, always write the cornet a real low down solo a la Bunk, remember how you use to drive the blues down? Oh! boy. . . . I never hear from those fellows in New Orleans they never write me. Old Billie Marrero's son John is here, I don't even see him often. Louis Armstrong is out of the City. He is some cornet player now Bunk. That bird can hit F and G with ease. I haven't heard from Walter Brundy in some time. I receive one letter from him and no more, although I answered his letter soon as I received same. Bunk this is strange. I made a record yesterday with Lizzie Miles we were talking about the old gang, and your name came up. How is your wife and children? Hope they are all well. I will get out first thing Monday and see if I can find some kind of job for you. But don't do the same thing over. . . . I too, would like to see you, so we could sit down and talk about old times. Remember Second and Magazine when Walter Brundy would talk to me while you steal my music? Ha! Ha! I often think about those days. . . . Looking to hear from you real soon. I remain with kind regards.

Very truly yours, Jos. Oliver.

But Bunk didn't want to leave the South any more than the other musicians there who were sticking to what little work they had. He probably knew how the situation had changed for Joe Oliver, and preferred to stay in the deep South where he could still "drive the blues down." In general, music was becoming more and more "sweet" as the axis of influence on popular taste was shifted to Hollywood. Large orchestras were canned and shipped to small movie houses, where musicians who had played locally were dismissed. Joe received a letter from a friend in Shreveport who told him what was happening:

My Esteemed Friend
Joe King Oliver:
Your letter was indeed a surprise you can't imagine my delight on hearing from you. Well I have had charge of the orchestra at the Star Theatre for two years but I think the talking pictures will freeze me out this season as it has done to lots of other unfortunate musicians. Your letter could not have come at a more opportune time as I think you can help me or give me the right dope on my new adventure. My wife and I have entered the field of Song writing and I know you can tell me just what to do to have them Published or sold. . . .
I have been told you sent for Tio is he with you. I will always remember you as the inspiration of Louis. Few People know that but some day I am going to write the *Defender* telling the world that you was the inspiration of Louis.
Write soon and give the Low Down. Your Life Long Friend,
A. W. Kimball

Joe did his best to help his friends; he lent them money, he helped them to publish their songs, and he encouraged young musicians in Harlem who wanted to form bands of their own. He wrote to Lee Collins in New Orleans:

Dear Friend Lee:
At this very late date I wish to acknowledge receipt of your letter and apologize for my seeming neglect by not answering sooner. My reason was caused by the many recording dates which

I have had recently and you know what it mean, keeping a bunch of musicians in line.

I was mighty pleased to hear from you, and note with particular interest the progress you've made since I saw you last. Keep up the good work, you will hit the gold some day. . . .

I hope this will find you well. I am feeling great since I've taken off about thirty-five pounds, I am now down to two twenty-five, will try to hold it there, for I feel much better. Things in the music line are about the same here as down there—very dull. I am looking forward to seeing you in the near future. Regards to all the boys. Let me hear from you real soon.

> With kindest regards, I am
> Very truly yours,
> Joseph Oliver

But the time had come when Joe couldn't help his friends very much. He needed help himself. As soon as the Victor recording dates were finished, and there was no more money to hand out, Joe entered the hardest part of his life. There was nothing left for him but disappointment brought on by each new stroke of bad luck. The moment that he "took a tumble," as he said in a later letter, his followers deserted him.

The orchestra played in Newark; Joe was paid with a rubber check, and the men in the band harassed him for the money. Agents exacted ruinous commissions for their bookings. In 1931, he was induced to take a band on tour through the South. Once he was away from New York, his name had no influence. The orchestra never went very far South; it was stranded for a while in Erie, Pennsylvania, until Joe's sister sent enough money to start the band on its way again. Then Joe went to Huntington, West Virginia, where he stayed for nearly four years, leading an orchestra which worked in the surrounding country, driving about in a bus he bought for this purpose. His peculiar luck hit him again; he was forced to write an agent in Bowling Green, Kentucky:

I deeply regret the necessity of advising you that we will be unable to fill the engagement February 14th. I was very unfortunate in having the block in the motor of my bus split because of freezing, which will necessitate the cost of a new motor at a very considerable expense.

Also a great number of promoters to whom I appealed for advance money, (not exceeding $15.00 each), in order to raise a sufficient sum to enable me to make various dates as scheduled, failed to respond, thereby causing me great embarrassment, and under the circumstances, compelling me to cancel a number of engagements.

It hurts me grievously to dissapoint you and the public, yet, I would rather order the date positively cancelled at this early date than to take a chance on being able to make it, and then, perhaps, be compelled to advise you differently when it would be too late to recall the advertisements.

Trusting that my misfortune may incur no ill will, I wish to remain

Very sincerely yours,
    King Oliver

When misfortune descended upon Joe, it came not only once, but many times. He was able to fix the frozen block, only to have the bus wrecked in an accident that took place a month later. He spent the rest of 1935 trying to make up for the damages to his bus. Then his teeth began to bother him; before he could afford to do anything about it, a bad case of pyorrhea developed, and he lost them all. A cornetist can't play without teeth. In December, he wrote home from Raleigh, North Carolina, while on the way to Georgia:

Dear Niece:

I receive your card, you don't know how much I appreciate your thinking about the old man. . . . Thank God I only need one thing and that is clothes. I am not making enough money to buy clothes as I can't play any more. I get little money from an agent for the use of my name and after I pay room rent and eat I don't have much left. . . . I felt terrible when I met Allen, I didn't want him to see me, but his eyes fell right on me. . . . I've only got one suit and that's the one sent me while I was in Wichita,

Kansas. So you know the King must look hot. But I don't feel downhearted. I still feel like I will snap out of the rut some day.

Well, the old man hasn't got the price of Xmas cards so I will wish you all a Merry Xmas and Happy New Year. Now you must keep in touch with me. Love to the entire family including the bird dog and cat. Take good care of yourself and keep well.

Sincerely, Uncle

From Raleigh, Joe went down through Georgia and Mississippi, on a tour that left him stranded and penniless, with a landlord dunning for rent. The bus broke down completely in Mississippi; it was a long time before Joe could extricate himself from these troubles and return to Savannah, the base of his circuit. Here he received a letter from another booker in September, 1937:

Dear Sir:

Contrary to the usual way agents handle colored bands, my business is based on honest representation and fair dealing with both promoter and band. . . . My fee for nationwide exploitation and booking is twenty per cent. Ten per cent for each. There is no use to try and make any money on a band if they are not properly exploited and in the limelight all the time. . . .

I remember many years ago when I was playing vaudeville around Chicago with my own band, of hearing you play down on the South Side. . . .

It is my usual custom in the South to send a white manager along with the band so that nobody will be bothering the attraction at any time. We bond the man to keep him honest and I will pay half of his salary and you pay the other half. . . .

While Joe was negotiating with a new manager, he had to hire an attorney to write an order to the old agent, requesting him to "desist from the use of the name of King Oliver's Band and to cease accepting deposits for said band" when "you know as well as he does that he has no band just now: that the use of the name of his band is unfair to him, and the general public."

Then the new manager wrote:

I got a band lined up in Mississippi that I may be able to swing for you. . . . No use playing around this section as I hear that fellow killed it for you through this country . . .

If we are able to furnish transportation, etc. for a band, we will have no difficulty in getting a good band I am sure. But we must have a good looking bus in good shape as there is no use in going out on the road with an old rattle trap that is breaking down all the time putting your dates in jeopardy and killing the prestige of the band the minute it arrives in town. . . .

In November, 1937, Joe received his last letter from this man:

Your letter or card received today and I note what you say. I trust by this writing that you are well and able to be about. . . . You keep trying and I think before long we will be able to get lined up okay. I mentioned your name down through Mississippi and they are willing to book your band I believe that you could do well in Miss. La. Texas and up this way. . . .

Joe never went on the tour this agent proposed, because his health began to fail, and he was forced to stay in Savannah. During the next three months, he wrote to his sister and told her what had really happened:

Dear Sister:

I'm still out of work. Since the road house close I haven't hit a note. But I've got a lot to thank God for. Because I eat and sleep. . . . Look like every time one door close the Good Lord open another. . . . I've got to do my own cooking as my landlady and daughter both work out. I am doing pretty fair. But I much rather work and earn my own money. . . . Soon as the weather can fit my clothes I know I can do better in New York. . . .

Dear Sister:

I receive your letter which found me well and getting along pretty nice. I looked up another job. With little money. If hours was money I'd be drawing more money than Babe Ruth at his best. . . . We are still having nice weather here. The Lord is sure good to me here without an overcoat. . . . I have to see by lamp here. *Smile.*

Sincerely yours, Brother

Sunday evening

Dear Sister:

Well I hope you don't feel like I am lying down on you. I put in such long hours until I don't feel anything like looking at a bottle of ink or picking up my pen and you know I'm one who love to write. But I am going to see to you hearing from me often. I will get some cards when I go to town and will be able to drop you a card from the place. I am feeling pretty good, but just can't get rid of this cough. Don't like that sticking on me so long. I just can't get rid of it. I've tried most everything. My heart don't bother me just a little at times. But my breath is still short, and I'm not at all fat. . . .

I would like to live long as I can, but nothing like making all arrangements in time. . . . Don't think I will ever raise enough money to buy a ticket to New York.

I am not the one to give up quick. If I was I don't know where I would be today. I always feel like I've got a chance. I still feel I'm going to snap out of the rut I've been in for several years. What makes me feel optimistic at times. Look like every time one door close on me another door open. . . . Look how many teeth I had taken out and replaced. I got teeth waiting for me at the dentist now. . . . I've started a little dime bank saving. Got $1.60 in it and won't touch it. I am going to try and save myself a ticket to New York. . . .

Dear Sister:

I open the pool rooms at 9 A.M. and close at 12 midnite. If the money was only ¼ as much as the hours I'd be all set. But at that I can thank God for what I am getting. Which I do night after night. I know you will be glad when the winter say goodby.

Now Vick before I go further with my letter I'm going to tell you something but don't be alarmed. I've got high blood pressure. Was taking treatment but I had to discontinue. My blood was 85 above normal. Now my blood has started again and I am unable to take treatments because it cost $3.00 per treatment and I don't make enough money to continue my treatments. Now it begins to work on my heart. I am weak in my limbs at times and my breath but I can not asking you for any money or anything. A stitch in time save nine. Should anything happen to me will you want my body? Let me know because I won't last forever and the longer I go the worst I'll get unless I take treatments.

It's not like New York or Chicago here. You've got to go through a lot of red tape to get any kind of treatment from the city here. I may never see New York again in life. . . .

Don't think I'm afraid because I wrote what I did. I am trying to live near to the Lord than ever before. So I feel like the Good Lord will take care of me. Good night, dear. . . .

When Joe Oliver died on April 10, 1938, two months after he had written this last letter, his passing brought sadness and distress to the family. His sister could not realize that he was dead; the things he had accomplished in New Orleans and Chicago gave him such a strong claim to life, such a deep root in it, that it seemed impossible that he should be torn away so suddenly. When he did go, they were afraid; his sister was poor, it would cost too much to ship his body from Georgia and give him "a decent burial." But she knew Joe must not be neglected. She took her rent money to bring him North, and gave up her plot in Woodlawn for him. There was a funeral; a few friends helped here. But when it was over, there was no money left for a headstone; it is still missing from his grave.

His name is disappearing fast; music that derives from his Creole Jazz Band is played today by musicians who know nothing of King Oliver. Only his family, and his old friends from New Orleans and Chicago, remember him now; men like Bunk Johnson, to whom he once wrote: "I too, would like to see you, so we could sit down and talk about old times."

CHICAGO

"Every tub on its own bottom"

A BIG sprawling city jammed against the southwestern shore of Lake Michigan. The Chicago River cuts through it like a giant crank, the handle entering the lake. The river bends sharply around the Loop's encircling quadrangle of elevated lines, flowing down through the stockyards. South of the Loop, bounded on the west by the yards and on the east by the lake is Chicago's Negro district. This was where jazz was first heard when it came from the South:

> Have you heard Emanuel Perez's Creole Band? Have you heard that wonderful jazz music that the people of Chicago are wild about?

That's what the Defender said when it arrived. From here, it seeped into the white districts of Chicago, spreading eastward and westward over the country like a slowly opening fan.

Down State Street from the Loop the red-light district began, centering around 22nd Street. The two big places were Pony Moore's and the Everleigh Club. There was music by Negro piano players who traveled from city to city, getting their keep from the management and their pay from the clientele in tips and drinks. A good town on the circuit, they hit Chicago oftener and stayed longer. Tony Jackson, Benjamin Harney, and Jelly Roll Morton could be heard in "the district" regularly in the years around 1910. Tony Jackson had a band at the Elite in 1910 and one at Dago and Russell's in 1912.

But Chicago's South Side, where there had been no more than a bordello and a half-pint piano with a slot-kitty to nurture jazz, had its first taste of a whacky horn in 1911 when the Original Creole Orchestra came North for the first time. Fred Keppard, out of the Bolden school, was on cornet. And

95

the Grand Theatre at 31st and State, with its ornate pseudo-Roman façade, witnessed the début of New Orleans music in the North. For years after, "Creole" was a musical trademark for Negro bands from New Orleans. Surprisingly, the various Creole outfits channeled into one Chicago group in the early twenties: King Oliver's Creole Jazz Band.

No one knows even today how rich and varied was the un-written book of the New Orleans improvisers. Contributors to the book were not only the blues singers. There were Scott Joplin rags, marked: not to be played fast, and brass band tunes. Steamboat Blues. Roustabout Shuffle. Midnight Dream. Pepper Rag. Alligator Flop. Spencer and Clarence Williams, Alphonse J. Picou, Ferdinand Jelly Roll Morton, Joe Oliver, and others wrote them down. Played over and over, phrases from them, even whole choruses (written or unwritten) be-came part of the necessary nourishment of an anemic Tin Pan Alley and of an eastern jazz that had no melodic heritage of its own. Usually in this process the tune was lost, the rich-ness thinned out. But turn back to the early blues and jazz pieces and you'll find the vein, the way it was when King Oliver wrote to Buddie Petit:

> If you've got a real good blues, have someone to
> write it just as you play them and send them to me,
> we can make some jack on them. Now, have the
> blues wrote down just as you can play them, it's the
> originality that counts.

Some of the tunes were written down by Lil Hardin, pianist in Sugar Johnny's New Orleans Jazz Band, then with King Oliver's Creole Band. Lil came up from Memphis in 1917 to study music. One day she walked into a music store to try out a new tune on the piano. A clerk listened, asked if she'd like a job playing sheet music for the customers who came in. Another clerk countered with, "She's too little." But Lil got the job. They offered her only $3.00 a week, but it was a chance to learn the new tunes without having to buy the music. Then one day Sugar Johnny's New Orleans Jazz Band came to town and, like all those early groups from New Orleans, had no pianist. A hurry-call went out to the music stores, and when word came to Lil's store, the manager insisted she apply. But Lil hesitated, because her musical background had been so far away from New Orleans that she was reluctant to try out. When she came into the back room in the De Luxe Café where the boys were practicing, she found them hard at work. They stopped for a moment; Johnny motioned for her to take a seat at the piano.

"What piece is it?" Lil wanted to know.

"Hit it, gal."

Lil looked up from the piano stool. "But what key is it in?"

"Never you mind. Gwan and hit it, gal."

And that was the only thing left to do.

Not until Tom Brown's Band from Dixieland came North, did the white musicians begin to play the music. Before then, as Pip Villani told it:

> We used to go around Negroville, outside. We couldn't play it ourselves. It was too new. Before that it was strictly ragtime. There was no precision. The rhythm was slow and the notes fewer. One rhythm would predominate throughout. They would all play around that same rhythm, solo choruses and all.

And when La Rocca and the Original Dixieland Jazz Band came North it was possible for him to say with complete truthfulness: "The great musicians were at a loss to see how we could play and get so much music out of so few instruments."

There were Chicago musicians in the New Orleans Rhythm Kings when it went into the Friars' Inn, but the bulk of the personnel was from its name city. Chicago musicians hadn't arrived at anything like their music, though they were coming close, what with Muggsy and his crowd. In those acoustical days, string bass did not record, but when the band went out to the old Gennett studio in Richmond, Indiana, Steve Brown slapped the bass anyway, so that they would have a full rhythm section. Years later, on electrical re-recordings, the percussion emerged, plunking away like the ghost of the doghouse.

Legends have clung to Rappolo, as they have to Bix. Probably the best of them are true. How he leaned against a telephone pole, playing clarinet against the weird harmonies of the singing wires. How he couldn't stop when a number was through, but went on playing until the manager, pulling his hair, pleaded with him, anxious for the customers to sit down and spend.

And of Bix, George Wettling's succinct account is as good as any legend:

"The first thing Bix did was to go to the closet and pull out a pint of gin. Then we went to a Chinese restaurant."

The Wolverines were younger than the Rhythm Kings. They came to the Friars' Inn, as George Johnson put it, "to listen and learn, and to wait long hours until, late at night when the regular members in the band tired, we were permitted to sit in with the orchestra to give a member a few moments' relief. This was a privilege, of course, since the Kings were all Kings and we all less than that, excepting Bix."

From Pontchartrain to Schiller's Café, from the Friars' Inn to White City, jazz was what you made it. Chicago made it pretty good. Young kids could say straight out:

"We didn't give a damn about the customers."

"We played for the kicks between the guys in the band."

And the penalty that was as prompt as it was inevitable:

We got our notice the first night we worked there at James Lake. They expected a novelty band, wearing fancy hats, doing novelty tunes with talking vocals. They didn't know our music. We were playing like the Friars' Inn, and we played Tiger Rag. They fired us . . . so we all figured on getting back to Chicago.

A popular place with Chicago musicians was Kelly's Stable, across the river from the Loop. A real stable (that went big in Prohibition) with an old watchman who came out with a lantern to guide customers up rickety steps to a black-painted interior. Johnny Dodds played there, and Baby Dodds, who learned drums from Ma Rainey's drummer, a man called "Rabbit." Also popular was the Entertainers' Cabaret, where Earl Hines played a miniature piano. Both piano and stool were on casters. Earl wound up a chorus with an involved break, gave the piano a shove to the next table, picked up where he left off. And when morning came along, and there was nowhere else to go, musicians went to the buffet flats down in the old Ellis Building.

"They didn't have music in the buffet flats, just Victrolas, the orthophonic kind, but you could sure spend your money."

But 35th and Calumet was the center of the universe. The words aren't Latin but to a lot of jazzmen they mean alma mater. Louis Armstrong, doubling at the Sunset and the Vendome. Little Louis, big Louis. Little cornet, then shiny trumpet. Fate's words about Louis (he hired him for the Strekfus Line):

> I first heard Louis in the Cooperative Hall, with Kid Ory's band, playing Chris Smith's Honky Tonk Town.

Louis. Oliver. Keppard. And the long procession of New Orleans clarinets: Baquet, Bechet, Simeon, Dodds, Noone.

Diagonally across the street from the Sunset, Joe Oliver and his Dixie Syncopators played at the Plantation Café. Joe sends word over to Louis:

"Close those windows or I'll blow you off 35th Street!"

Louis loved the old man (who didn't? who wouldn't?) but he kept the windows open, swinging around and away from the beat.

Because of the music, 35th and Calumet became more a symbol than a street address. Probably at the time, the only person who could arrange this music was Jelly Roll Morton. Black Bottom Stomp, recorded with Omer Simeon on clarinet, tells the whole story. Break down its complex parts, put them on paper, and you see how jazz was played, you see that the harmonic conventions that were to become such a fetish in arranged jazz had nothing to do with it, and that when the boys got set at 35th and Calumet it was just a case of

every tub on its own bottom.

C. E. S.
S. W. S.

IV

BLUES

BY E. SIMMS CAMPBELL

1

When Ma Rainey
Comes to town,
Folks from anyplace
Miles aroun',
From Cape Girardeau,
Poplar Bluff,
Flocks in to hear
Ma do her stuff;
Comes flivverin' in,
Or ridin' mules,
Or packed in trains,
Picknickin' fools. . . .
That's what it's like,
Fo' miles on down,
To New Orleans delta
An' Mobile town,
When Ma hits
Anywheres aroun'.

2

Dey comes to hear Ma Rainey from de little river settlements,
From blackbottom cornrows and from lumber camps;
Dey stumble in de hall, jes' a-laughin' an' a-cacklin',
Cheerin' lak roarin' water, lak wind in river swamps.

An' some jokers keeps deir laughs a-goin' in de crowded aisles,
An' some folks sits dere waitin' wid deir aches an' miseries,
Till Ma comes out before dem, a-smilin' gold-toofed smiles
An' Long Boy ripples minors on de black an' yellow keys.

3

O Ma Rainey,
Sing yo' song;
Now you's back
Whah you belong,
Git way inside us,
Keep us strong. . . .
O Ma Rainey,
Li'l an' low;
Sing us 'bout de hard luck
Roun' our do';
Sing us 'bout de lonesome road
We mus' go. . . .

4

I talked to a fellow, an' the fellow say,
"She jes' catch hold of us, somekindaway.
She sang Backwater Blues one day:

'It rained fo' days an' de skies was dark as night,
Trouble taken place in de lowlands at night.

'Thundered an' lightened an' the storm begin to roll
Thousan's of people ain't got no place to go.

'Den I went an' stood upon some high ol' lonesome hill,
An' looked down on the place where I used to live.'

An' den de folks, dey natchally bowed dey heads an' cried,
Bowed dey heavy heads, shet dey moufs up tight an' cried,
An' Ma lef' de stage, an' followed some de folks outside."

Dere wasn't much more de fellow say:
She jes' gits hold of us dataway.[1]

FIRST LET me say that I am no music critic, neither do I
look upon myself as a fumbling layman—appreciating the
blues form in American music from the pew of an enthusias
tic but incoherent follower of Le Jazz Hot, that strange hybrid that has ripened in France under the aegis of Monsieur
Hugues Panassié, who has an ear to the ground as well as an
ear for Le Jazz Hot. Not that M. Panassié is insincere, neither
are "jitterbugs" insincere, but an intellectual· approach to
blues that borders on the ridiculous with the attendant erudite
mumbo-jumbo is doing one of the purest forms of American
music much more harm than good.

It is not necessary to form a cult, to read hidden meanings
and mystical expressions as well as pretentious symbolism into
something as elemental as blues.

Books, essays and reams of scholarly European treatises
have been written extolling jazz, the blues and all of the
music that American Negroes have written and played—and
it can only be forgiven because of the grossest ignorance on
the part of intellectuals who delight in faddism.

There was in this country a "Negro Renaissance," as they
called it—when every Negro who was literate was looked upon
as a "find." New York in 1925 and 1926 was the hotbed of
intellectual parties where Negroes who were in the theatre
were looked upon as social plums, and the dumbest and most

[1] Sterling Brown, "Ma Rainey," Southern Road, Harcourt, Brace, 1932,
pp. 62-64.

illiterate were fawned over by Park Avenue—Negro Art had arrived—African Art—Negro Music—with Carl Van Vechten, recently turned candid camera addict, as its Jehovah. I know what I am talking about because I attended many of these parties, and the intellectual stink could have been cut with a knife—a dull knife.

The blues are simple, elemental. They have the profound depths of feeling that is found in any race that has known slavery and the American Negro is no stranger to suffering. Out of the work songs and spirituals that they sang sprang this melancholic note, rising in a higher key because of its intensity, and enveloping the spirituals because of its very earthiness. One cannot continually ride in chariots to God when the impact of slavery is so ever present and real.

"Some day ah'm gonna lay down dis heavy load . . . gonna grab me a train, gonna clam aboh'd . . . gonna go up No'th, gonna ease mah pain—Yessuh Lord, gonna catch dat train"— this isn't mystical. It was the cry of a human being under the lash of slavery—of doubts—of fears—the tearing apart of families—the caprices of plantation owners—these hardships of slavery all fusing themselves together to burn into the Negro this blue flame of misery.

And yet it was never a wail, but a steady throbbing undertone of hope. "Times is bad but dey won't be bad always," is the lyric carried in a score of blues songs—times are tough but somehow, somewhere, they'll get better.

"Gotta git better 'cause dey caint git w'us"—stevedores sweating on the levee, chain gangs in Georgia, cotton pickers in Tennessee, sugar cane workers in Louisiana, field hands in Texas, all bending beneath the heel of southern white aristocracy, the beautiful "befo de wa'h" South of the crinoline days.

One might as well be realistic about slavery. The South was as cruel as any Caesar to its slaves, and many slaves were

as vindictive as any Richelieu to their masters, but both sides
have profited. Without pain and suffering there would have
been no blues, and without an understanding white America
there would have been no expression for them.

And now, what are the blues and into what category of
music do they fit? They are not spirituals and they are not
work songs nor do they fit into the pattern proscribed by
many music critics as folk music in a lighter vein.

To me, they are filled with the deepest emotions of a race.
They are songs of sorrow charged with satire, with that po-
tent quality of ironic verse clothed in the raiment of the buf-
foon. They were more than releases, temporary releases, from
servitude. The blues were the gateway to freedom for all
American Negroes. In song, the Negro expressed his true feel-
ings, his hopes, aspirations and ideals, and illiterate though
many of them were, there was always a spiritual and ennobling
quality to all of the music. True, many of the blues lyrics are
downright vulgar and the suggestive quality has crept in with
the passing years, understandable enough when you realize
that many audiences, both white and colored, wished to find
those meanings in them. As paid entertainers, Negroes were
only catering to popular taste—and the taste of the American
public in the mauve decade was decidedly that of a slumming
party toward any reception of blues.

They did not wish to hear lamentations in any form. They
wanted something "hot"—knowing nothing of blues, other
than that they were "dirty," they received what they expected.
As court jester, the Negro had long since learned that his very
existence depended upon his ability to please the white man.
One was either a "good nigger," one who acquiesced to the
wishes of the plantation owner or overseer and lived, or a
"bad nigger," one who had decided ideas about what he
would or wouldn't do, and who usually died.

This heritage and birthright of fear ground into the smallest Negro child a chameleon attitude toward life, and Negro musicians and entertainers were well schooled and versed in this pattern. As long as the field hands were singing on a plantation, the "boss man" would go into town; he had no fear of any uprising or discontent. A singing darky was a good darky. All Negroes knew this.

Picture the long fields of sugar cane in Louisiana, glinting in the sun, and rows of cane workers acres across all singing their work songs as they rhythmically cut cane; fields of cotton in Georgia—sweating stevedores in Memphis and St. Louis stripped to the waist while they swung two hundred pound bales of cotton—chain gang workers and railroad tampers, pile drivers on the southern tracks—a race of black people singing as they worked—and it was hard physical work. There is little creative ability in work that requires dextrous hands and strong backs; there is only rhythm and timing and these songs which they sang lightened that burden. "Ah'm gonna swing my pick, gonna throw dis hammer—uh yes, Lord—gonna throw dat hammer—uh yes, Lord." The punctuation of "Yes, Lord" that occurs throughout many blues was the sigh, the sigh of physical exertion, the brief fraction of a second of suspended effort before the task was accomplished. As the *combite* works today in Haiti carried over from the *combites* of Africa, in which large communal groups of Negroes work a field together, working to the rhythmic thumping of a drum and singing in time with it—just so did the American Negro work on the plantations.

They worked and sang together and many of these songs carried a meaning only to Negroes. To the white mind, it was perfect peace and contentment among the blacks, but to Negroes it was often a means of communication.

"Ya bettah breeze on down dat road—son—ya bettah breeze on down dat road. Mistuh Charlie from town ain't feelin' good—ya better lighten dat heavy load"—from one to another the song was taken up and passed along the field. It simply meant that there was a white man from a different town who had arrived on the plantation and the young Negro who was working among them, guarded zealously from the whites "at de big house" had better leave town. Negroes frequently hid one of their own who had sought refuge among them, and they were telling him in code that he had better leave the plantation that night.

Such lyrics interspersed among well-known songs carried a world of significance to black ears.

A race that has been continually on the defensive for so many years has developed a keen sense of impending danger and the blues grew out of this form of protection. Melancholy though they were, they could be interpreted a hundred ways, but the circumstances under which they were sung had everything to do with their proper interpretation.

Basically, the blues are similar to spirituals and it is important to note that the musical bars are of practically the same length. For those musically minded take the song *Minnie the Moocher* or *St. James Infirmary*. The spiritual—*Hold On—Keep Your Hands on the Plow*—is identical with them—and it was written more than forty years ago.

This background of the "why" of the blues is essential to understand them properly and to get a fuller understanding of their true meaning. None of them was ever written to music before the 1890's because the majority of Negroes had had no musical education and the flood of ragtime pieces that immediately followed, in the early nineteen hundreds, were merely melodies that have followed the blues pattern these many years. There is a definite pattern to the blues, just as there is for poetry and other forms of creative expression that have survived the centuries. It is no hit-or-miss musical form. For example take the key of C:

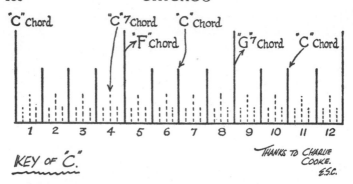

KEY OF "C."

THANKS TO CHARLIE COOKE.
E.S.C.

The above diagram is the harmony of the blues. In other keys the same relationship as far as harmonic changes are concerned would exist.

"C" chord is retained for 3½ measures or bars.

The next half bar is the "C" seventh chord.
The next two bars are the "F" chord.
The next two bars are the "C" chord.
The next two bars are the "G" seventh chord.
The next two bars are the "C" chord.

The dotted lines equal four quarters to each measure. The heavy lines represent a bar of music consisting of four quarters or beats.

The blues always consist of twelve bars—the "C" seventh after the first four bars—the "F" chord and the remainder of the piece is essentially the same. An original blues composition must be original in the first four bars, the next four bars are merely relief—then one returns to the major chords.

Often one hears pieces on the radio termed blues which are merely bastard products because some well-known orchestra insists on stepping up twelve bars to twenty-four or even thirty-two. This is "swing" as we know it today, but it has nothing in common with the blues and, as Clarence Williams told me: "The flavor and color are taken from the blues when one tries variations and liberties with their original form."

Clarence Williams is now a music publisher in New York who has written hundreds of blues and who I think, as do many of America's finest musicians, is the greatest living blues writer. If you know blues at all, I'll give you a few of his compositions, and then perhaps you'll know this man better. He wrote *Sister Kate*—remember the *Shim-me-sha-wobble?*— *Royal Garden Blues*—*Gulf Coast Blues*—*You Don't Know My Mind*—*West End Blues*—*Sugar Blues*—*Squeeze Me*—*I Ain't Gonna Give Nobody None of This Jelly Roll*—*I Can't Dance, I've Got Ants in My Pants*—and that greatest of all blues (unless of course you are a *St. Louis Blues* fanatic), *Baby Won't You Please Come Home*. The list is endless and he's still writing.

When he was fourteen he wrote the *Michigan Water Blues*:

Michigan water—taste like champagne wine
Michigan water—taste like champagne wine
Ah'm going back to Michigan
To see that gal of mine

Ah believe to my soul—mah baby's got a black cat born
Ah believe to my soul—mah baby's got a black cat born
'Cause every time ah leave
Ah got to crawl back home

This naturally led us into a discussion of the fact that blues, as we know them today, were always written about love, someone's baby leaving them, hard luck dogging one's trail, and the "misery 'roun yo door." "It's the mood," he exclaimed. "That's the carry-over from slavery—nothing but trouble in sight for everyone. There was no need to hitch your wagon to a star because there weren't any stars. You got only what you fought for. Spirituals were the natural release—'Times gonna git better in de promised lan' '—but many a stevedore knew only too well that his fate was definitely tied up in his own hands. If he was clever and strong, and didn't mind dying, he came through—the weak ones always died. A blue mood— since prayers often seemed futile, the words were made to fit present situations that were much more real and certainly more urgent."

"Ef ah kin jes grab me a handfulla freight train—ah'll be set—" Always the urge to leave, to go to a distant town, a far city, to leave the prejudices and cruelty of the South. Superstition played its part, too, a large part—black cats, black women, conjures, charms, sudden death, working in steel mills, cotton fields, loving women, fighting over women, all of the most intimate and earthly pursuits. As I talked with Clarence Williams, his eyes brightened: "Tell you what I'll do." He pressed a buzzer near his desk and whispered a hurried message into the phone.

"I'm canceling all appointments for today. We'll just talk about blues. You ask the questions and I'll try and answer them if I can," he said as he pushed a large sheaf of letters aside.

I only asked one question and that question started a discussion that ended when the neons began to blink over Broadway and Forty-fifth Street, and the taxi horns aroused us from a bygone period. I started: "Mr. Williams, if you were a white man, you'd probably be worth a million dollars today, wouldn't you? Because the radio and motion picture rights as well as all mechanical rights to all of your songs would be copyrighted. You'd have a staff of smart boys working for you ferreting out tunes and buying them for a song from colored fellows who had no musical education and you'd never have a material care in this world—think hard now—wouldn't you have rather been born a white man?"

He laughed out loud, uproariously, and replied, "Why, I'd never have written blues if I had been white. You don't study to writes blues, you *feel* them. It's the mood you're in—

sometimes it's a rainy day—cloud mist—just like the time I lay for hours and hours in a swamp in Louisiana. Spanish moss dripping everywhere, but that's another story—it's a mood though—white men were looking for me with guns—I wasn't scared, just sorry I didn't have a gun. I began to hum a tune—a little sighing kinda tune—you know like this—"

Clarence Williams was seated at the piano, and his large muscular fingers caressed the keys. Eerie chords rumbled along. He sang: "Jes as blue as a tree—an old willow tree—nobody 'roun here, jes nobody but me"—the melody trailed off. "Never wrote that down, never published it either. I don't know why I'm playing it now."

I didn't intrude on his thoughts. "You never knew Tony Jackson, did you? No, of course not. You were too young." Williams was not conscious of my presence in the room. He talked and played. I listened.

Tony Jackson was probably the greatest blues pianist that ever lived. He was great because he was original in all of his improvisations—a creator, a supreme stylist. This all happened thirty years ago when the wine rooms flourished.

These were nothing more or less than sedate saloons, with a family entrance for ladies and potted palms and the usual ornate bric-a-brac in every corner. There was the inevitable three- or four-piece orchestra with the diva belching out ballads, trailing her ostrich plumes as she coyly made her exit, and the mustached dons of the period keeping a sharp eye out for a well-turned ankle. Informality was the keynote, and any of the patrons who wished could render a song, vocal or otherwise, provided of course that they weren't too terrible. Booing was much too mild for a poor performance in those days. Negroes had their wine rooms, patterned as nearly as possible after the white ones, but they were necessarily less pretentious in every way. Often their wine rooms were combination billiard and pool parlors, saloon and clubroom for the tougher gentry. There were no paid entertainers, no orchestra, and the only music provided was that played and composed on the spot by these ragtime and blues piano players.

New Orleans was the focal point for Negro musicians, all of them coming down from the various river towns but particularly from Memphis and St. Louis on the many boat excursions that would wind up in the Delta. Blues was looked upon as "low music" forty years ago because its greatest exponents were hustlers and sports, itinerant musicians who played in river joints and dives because these were the only places sympathetic to their type of playing. Negroes have always loved the blues, but in attempting to imitate the white man, many of them were trying to stamp out of their consciousness this natural emotional tie because of its background of slavery.

Being ashamed of one's heritage is usually predominant in minority groups—and in imitation of the music of white America, many Negroes were contributing nothing worth while to American music. The blues musicians were the pioneers, those who refused to compromise with their music; and they were creating and forming the basis for present-day American music. Gershwin's *American in Paris* as well as his *Rhapsody in Blue* are outstanding examples of blues harmonies—you don't think he pulled them out of the air, do you?

Cities and towns figure in the names of so many blues because the writers of these pieces were definitely associated with the towns. In these early "jam sessions"—many of them held in these wine rooms in New Orleans—individual musicians would compete with one another. They came from the length and breadth of the Mississippi and their styles of playing were as different as the sections of the country from which they came. Boogie Woogie piano playing originated in the lumber and turpentine camps of Texas and in the sporting houses of that state. A fast, rolling bass—giving the piece an undercurrent of tremendous power—power piano playing.

Neither Pine Top Smith, Meade Lux Lewis nor Albert Ammons originated that style of playing—they are merely exponents of it.

In Houston, Dallas and Galveston—all Negro piano players played that way. This style was often referred to as a "fast western" or "fast blues" as differentiated from the "slow blues" of New Orleans and St. Louis. At these gatherings the ragtime and blues boys could easily tell from what section of the country a man came, even going so far as to name the town, by his interpretation of a piece.

Even today, the finest clarinet players in the world usually come from New Orleans, and this is because of the French influence. France has always led the world in the making of reed instruments, and the first musical instrument that many of these Negroes owned was the clarinet. It is simple to trace their influence in the formation of blues as we know them today. The West Indies, Martinique in particular, always used the clarinet and bass viol in the *béguine* and in all of their other folk dances.

Clarinets were handed down from one generation to the next in New Orleans, and almost any young boy who showed any musical aptitude at all could play a reed instrument.

I would say that through New Orleans, the Spanish and French rhythms were interjected into the blues. The late Chick Webb had it with his drumming, as does Zutty Singleton. Gene Krupa, the great white drummer, is another who acquired it.

St. Louis and Kansas City were noted for their piano players as well as their honky-tonk joints. To the Southerner, St. Louis and Kansas City were looked upon as northern cities and a great many Southerners, both black and white, settled there. The Negroes that came brought with them the blues of the cotton fields and plantations of the deep South not influenced in any fashion by the Spanish or French. That is why even today among musicians, the purest blues, and the real "low-down blues" as they frequently call them, were born in these cities. New Orleans gave a lilt to the blues. The other cities gave them their solidity. Having been born in St. Louis and intensely interested in blues, I was on many a boat excursion that carried these early Negro bands—and all of them never played any other type of music. Jelly Roll Morton from Kansas City had probably the greatest blues band—there was Fletcher Henderson, Charlie Creath, Fate Marable, and Bennie Moten. I could go on by the hour. All of these men, however, were preceded by Tom Turpin, Scott Joplin, and Louis Chauvin, a great natural piano player. In 1896 Tom Turpin of St. Louis (his full name was Thomas Million Turner) had published *The Harlem Rag, The Bowery Buck,* and *The Buffalo*—and Scott Joplin had just written *The Maple Leaf Rag.* This was white America's first introduction to ragtime, which was patterned after the blues. The blues were so essentially a part of Negro life that many musical pioneers rightly felt that America would not accept them, thus this offshoot, ragtime, which did happen to strike the public's fancy. It was gayer and was more in keeping with the mood of the American white man. Blues were always played among Negroes, seldom among white audiences, and when they were played, they were set apart as the *pièce de résistance* of the evening.

The first blues singer on a record was Mamie Smith, and the first band to play blues on a record was the white Dixieland Jazz Band, an aggregation of young white men who came up North from New Orleans in 1916. The boom years for the blues were from 1919 through the twenties. The five Smiths were among the greatest single artists to interpret the blues for the country. They were all Negro women, and were not related in any manner, neither by family nor by their varied vocal interpretations. Mamie, Bessie, Laura, Clara and Trixie were their names; today among musicians and lovers of the blues, the hottest type of argument may be started over the respective merits of the five. Bessie Smith is usually given credit for being the greatest, but to single any one out for that honor would not be fair. As I have mentioned before, style was important, and whereas Bessie Smith would sing certain numbers with all of the pathos and feeling that a certain blues number required, and would wring the song dry, as it were, Mamie Smith could do certain blues numbers much better in her own style. Bessie Smith was the depressed, mournful type; her blues were eloquent masterpieces of human misery bordering on the spirituals. She was blues personified.

She had a powerful voice, and she sent her music in great waves of misery over audiences. Her *Empty Bed Blues* and *Backwater Blues* will forever remain classics.

Mamie Smith, and this is purely a personal opinion, had much more music in her voice. In her rendition of certain numbers, she might be compared today with Ella Fitzgerald.

Another great blues star was Sara Martin, who had a great flair for the dramatic. In a darkened theatre, with only candles on the stage, she would begin to wail in a low moan: "Man done gone— Got nowhere to go—" She literally surged across the stage, clutched the curtains in the wings, rolled on the floor, and when she had finished, the audience was as wilted as she. There are too many names to give them all: Ida Cox, Virginia Liston, Eva Taylor. Most of the greatest vocalists were women with rich contralto voices. When blues were sung by a woman the voice, that is, the female voice, carried tragic implications—the rich overtones of the cello— the man always imparted background on a guitar or piano— she was the hub of the family—black America crying out to her sons and daughters.

The great Ethel Waters started her career as a blues singer, as did most of the Negro's greatest dramatic actresses.

It is interesting to note that many who are still living are finishing their careers in church work. Virginia Liston and Sara Martin at this writing are both singing spirituals in churches. There is no doubt that blues and spirituals are closely interwoven.

As I started this article, I wished to tell of the St. Louis, Kansas City, and Chicago periods of the blues.

When Earl Hines and Louis Armstrong were going strong, and Jimmy Noone, the great clarinetist who wrote *Four or Five Times*, was hitting those high notes at the old Nest and Apex Club. The night I was there when Nora Holt, a celebrated Negro entertainer, just returned from China, handed me an autographed copy of George Gershwin's latest piece— 'Swonderful—and she played it for us.

The night I had my overcoat, as well as hat, gloves and my first silk neck-scarf stolen, as did ten other fellows at the old Warwick Hall in Chicago, because we were gazing open-mouthed, watching beads of perspiration pour off the head of a trumpet player by the name of Louis Armstrong while he played a new piece called the *Heebie Jeebies*.

The night King Oliver started his famous talking on a trumpet, actually preaching a sermon with it. Johnny Dunn was later to do the same thing, and played it on a record, so that America was soon to hear amazing things with the instruments they thought were finished as to technical virtuosity. I wished to tell about the old Vendome Theatre in Chicago— with Weatherford at the piano, playing his eccentric solos— how a fellow by the name of Freddie Keppard could blow rings around Armstrong, and when Louis was given the featured spot, we youngsters booed.

The night there was that great fight on the steamer *St. Paul*, an old paddle-wheeler out of St. Louis with Fate Marable's Band playing. Five miles downstream a knife fight started and the boat wheeled around to put ashore.

The band continued to play; as I climbed up on the bandstand to get a better view of the proceedings, I soon found myself atop the old upright piano. The fight was overflowing to the bandstand. How those fellows continued to play, I'll never know until this day, but they played as if everything was serenely quiet on the old Mississippi.

The boat did not come into the wharf but hung out in midstream until the "Black Anny," as we called the patrol wagons, had lined up on the dock.

Then we landed, and three loads of celebrants were carted away—and not once do I remember Marable's Band stopping. He played blues after blues—and they sounded grand, too. All of the musicians who played on the boats and the river front were inured to fisticuffs of all sorts. As one musician told me:

"I don't care what they do as long as they don't break this snare. It set me back thirty bucks." Of such stuff are musicians made. They had come up in the toughest of all schools. They had played the levee front from one end to the other. Night life, sporting houses, gamblers, rounders, they knew them all.

"—And today," broke in Clarence Williams, "their music is played in Carnegie Hall before a selected group, one sees many a full dress, high hat, ermine wrap there, you know." We had been exchanging experiences, talking nothing but the blues for over five hours, and the lights of Broadway were beginning to flash. I made another false start to leave, although I really didn't want to leave, when the door was quietly opened and a straight, elderly, copper-colored man walked in.

"Didn't knock, Clarence. Knew you'd be here. Just dropped in for a chat," he said as he sat down in an overstuffed chair and deposited a briefcase on the desk.

I got up and was about to make my departure for good when the amiable Williams stayed me.

"I'd like you to know Reese D'Pree," he said. I shook hands with the man, and I could see a look of resignation in his face. He seemed very tired and worn. Williams went on, "Reese D'Pree wrote a number about forty-three years ago, wrote it in Georgia, Bibb County to be exact. Will you tell Campbell about that piece, Reese?" In simple language he told me of the number he had written and sung—made money on a ship in 1905 wearing a chef's cap and apron and singing his song. He used to sing it at pound parties in the South—pound parties were community affairs given by Negroes at that time where one would bring a pound of "vittles" of anything edible, a pound of chitterlings, of pig's feet, of hog maw, barbecue, butter—anything that contributed to the feast. It was a simple little piece, but everywhere he went they wanted him to sing it. At the present time he is having copyright trouble. D'Pree did not impress me as being a wealthy man, but the song must have earned over a million dollars for someone. Possibly you've heard it, too. It's called *Shortnin' Bread*. Reese D'Pree loves the blues as much as Clarence Williams. I will always remember what that man told me the blues meant to him, as I left the office.

"Son," he said, "the blues regenerates a man."

V

LOUIS ARMSTRONG

BY WILLIAM RUSSELL

Mah mule is white, mah face is black,
Ah sells mah coal two bits a sack!

THIS PLAINTIVE call of the rapidly vanishing coal peddler still echoes occasionally through the byways of the Vieux Carré. A quarter of a century ago, before the increasing popularity of gas heating drove the coal carts from New Orleans streets, one particular cart could often be heard rumbling over the uneven and scattered cobble-stones down the back alleys on the wrong side of town. Perched on top, fresh from the reform school, was "Little Louie," crying his wares in a hoarse, froggy voice.

Louis at the age of twelve had been sent to the Waifs' Home charged with "firing firearms within the city limits" during his 1913 New Year's celebration. At that time his musical ambition was to sing bass. He had been singing tenor in a quartet with some other kids from the Perdido Street gang including "Happy," "Shots" and "Kid" Rena, all of whom sooner or later landed in the Home. This strolling quartet haunted the streets of Storyville, singing for pennies in the honky-tonks and dives until they were chased out of "the district" late every night. Louis' only instrument had been a four-string guitar made of a cigar-box, copper wire, and a piece of flat wood for the neck. Years before, Louis had wanted to be a drummer. When a boy, Louis lived only two blocks from the Masonic Hall, and often heard Buddy Bolden's Band warm up on a few numbers outside the hall to draw the crowd down Rampart Street. Louis' eyes, like those of many a boy, were on the drummer man. But since he had no money to buy a drum, all he could do was to sing and whistle.

The usual story is that Louis first started playing cornet when he came under the influence of Captain Joseph Jones, the man in charge of the Waifs' Home whom all the boys called "Pops," but it is evident from the following statement by Bunk that Louis had already begun to play cornet when he was sent "back o' Jones":

When I would be playing with the Diamond Stone Brass Band or most any other brass band in the uptown section Louis would steal off from home and follow me. Now here is Louis' gang, Nicodemus, Black Benny, Henry Rena and his brother Joe, Johnny Keelin Jr, and so many other boys that used to be in that gang that followed prades.

During that time [1911] Louis started after me to show him how to blow my cornet. When the band would not be playing I would have to let him carry it to please him. Then he wanted me to learn him how to play the blues and *ball the jack*, and *animal ball*, *circus day*, *take it away*, and *salty dog*, and *didn't he ramble* and out of all of those pieces he liked the blues the best.

Now here is the time I began showing Louis I took a job playing in a tonk for Dago Tony on Perdido and Franklin St. and Louis used to slip in there and get on the music stand behind the piano. He would fool with my cornet every chance he could get until he could get a sound out of it. Then I showed him just how to hold it and place it to his mouth and he did so and it wasn't long before he began getting a good tone out of my horn. Then I began showing him just how to start the blues. Little by little he began to understand what I was showing him about the blues. Now that was every time he could get a chance to steal in Dago Tony Tonk.

I was hired to play in the tonk on the nights that the Eagle

Band had no jobs. On Saturday the Eagle Band used to play at
the Masonic Hall and the dances used to last until four o'clock
and then I would go over to that tonk. My crowd would be waiting for me. I had a piano player and a drummer. They would play
until I knock off at the Masonic Hall with the Eagle Band. Then
I would go there and play the blues and nothing but the blues
and one of Louis' favorite pieces, *Balling the Jack*. Louis would
be on the music stand behind the piano sleeping, waiting for
Bunk to come. When I would get there I wouldn't call him. I
would take my horn out of the case and tune up and crack down
on the blues and Louis would wake up and stay awake a long time.
He did that until he got the hang of cornet and that tonk later
was the first job Louis had with the same piano player and
drummer.

Now that is just how Louis started on cornet. As for Waif's
Home Louis did not start cornet in there because when Louis
began going there he could play on cornet real good. He could not
read at all. Now Jones had a little band trying to do his best with
them. He began taking them every Decoration Day which is the
30th of May, to Camp Shallmet. When they got so they could
play a few little marches they played for the Old Civil War
Veterans and other little jobs that Jones would get for his little
brass band.

Now here is the year Louis started in behind me to begin showing him how to play the blues. It was in the latter part of 1911
as close as I can think. If I am not mistaken Louis was about 11
years old. Now I have said a lot about my boy Louis and just how
he started to playing cornet. He started playing it by head, and
as for learning to read music he began that after he started playing with Jones' little band.

No one outside the Home knew Louis was playing cornet
until his mother and sister visited him one day. Beatrice, his
sister, felt badly when she thought of Louis having to stay
there in the Waifs' Home, and began to cry. Louis tried to
cheer her up:

"Hush up. Stop cryin'. See, I'm learnin' how to play cornet.
Don't you cry now." Then for good measure he played her a
few notes on the piano.

Louis had first been given a bugle to learn. Captain Jones

didn't want his home to sound like a jail so used bugle calls rather than a police whistle to call the boys. Louis soon mastered the bugle and was given a cornet. He immediately cut notches in the mouthpiece so it could be held firmly against his lips. Peter Davis, an amateur musician like Captain Jones, taught Louis to read. Joe Howard, of the Allen Brass Band, helped Davis and Jones with their instruction. The brass band formed at the Home was well known in New Orleans.

Although Louis had acquired exceptional skill by the time he was released from the Waifs' Home, he was still too young, at the age of fourteen, to get a job playing in a band, so he turned to odd jobs such as selling papers and working for a dairy. His earnings were occasionally augmented by a lucky "take" in a game of craps with the other boys. One of the easiest ways the boys of the tough Third Ward gang had of scraping together a few nickels and dimes was selling coal. They took a gunny sack at night down to one of the Basins and filled it with coke the stevedores had dropped when unloading barges. Then the next day they were ready to peddle from house to house. New Orleans is famous for its Creole cuisine, and eating ranks as a fine art. There was a ready market for charcoal, which was used in little tin furnaces for preparing many of the Creole delicacies such as bouillabaisse, grillades, and gumbo.

Louis could always use a little extra change to take out his girl Daisy. Daisy Parker was a pretty girl and as tough as they came. Louis says he "used to swing some mean dukes," but Daisy also knew how to use her fists, and was a match for Louis any day or night. If Louis tarried too long with his Storyville friends, and didn't get around on time, he might be greeted with a well-aimed brickbat when he opened Daisy's door.

When Louis took Daisy to dances on Saturday nights, he knew just where to go. He had hung around the best spots for years, peeping through the windows and listening from the outside. His favorite music was that played by the Eagle Band with his idol Bunk on cornet. Louis has never forgotten how this barrel-house bunch used to swing; recently, speaking of Willie Johnson, he said:

"Bunk is the man they ought to talk about. Man, just to hear him talk sends me!"

Many a day Louis followed Bunk on parades. If he didn't have his tin fife with him, he whistled along with Bunk's music anyway, for he was a great natural whistler. Armstrong says that Bunk made them cry on funeral marches with his beautiful, vibrant tone and the feeling he put into dirges.

Not long afterwards Louis began to pick up a few jobs playing in the gin mills around the Gravier Street tenderloin for a dollar a night with his pal Sidney Bechet. Sidney came from down in the Creole section but like Louis had a love for freedom. Both boys "always had the seats of their breeches out"; as fast as they got Bechet a new suit, it was torn again.

In 1917 Louis came under the influence of Joe Oliver, and with "Little Joe" Lindsay, organized a band patterned after Kid Ory's Brown Skinned Babies in which Oliver played. When Oliver went to Chicago the next season, Louis was chosen to replace him with Ory's band.

Louis, who meanwhile had married Daisy, wasn't getting along very well at home, and didn't like sleeping on the doorstep either; so he was glad of a chance to leave New Orleans the next year and travel up and down the Mississippi with Fate Marable's Jazz-E-Saz Band. He played on several of the big excursion steamers of the Strekfus Line with some of the best jazzmen from New Orleans, including Picou, Sam Dutrey, Pop Foster, Dave Jones, and Baby Dodds. After two seasons on the river Louis stayed in New Orleans and got a job at the Orchard Cabaret on Burgundy Street, where his friend Zutty Singleton had organized a small band. When Storyville closed and resorts were scattered, many moved back into the French Quarter, which again became the center of the city's night life.

Forty years before, the lowest of the cribs and cheap parlor-houses had been concentrated on Burgundy and neighboring streets. In those earlier days, the entire district was overrun with street-walkers who carried an old mat which they spread out on the sidewalk for the standard price of ten cents. If they got too near the steps of the brothels, they were showered with hot water by the inmates inside who were trying to keep their rates up to fifteen and twenty-five cents. The block on Burgundy between Conti and Bienville, known as Smoky Row, was the center of the lowest class of prostitution, and was notorious for its battling bawds, such as "One-Eyed" Sal, "Fightin' " Mary, "Kidney-Foot" Jenny and "Nutcracker-Clutch" Kate.

At the Orchard Cabaret Louis received twenty-one dollars a week, a considerable increase over his pay during the Gravier Street days. He soon got a better offer from Tom Anderson and moved over to The Real Thing, Anderson's cabaret on Rampart Street where Luis Russell, Albert Nicholas, and Barney Bigard were members of the orchestra. During that period Armstrong also composed a number of tunes, among them, *I Wish I Could Shimmy Like My Sister Kate.* He sold this to Piron for fifty dollars, the usual price for original numbers. Later Clarence Williams revised the song and it swept the country. One day in the summer of 1922, after a parade of the Tuxedo Brass Band, in which Louis also played, he received a telegram from Oliver offering him a job at the Lincoln Gardens.

Months before Louis left Rampart Street, he had become a legend in Chicago, according to Paul Mares, who used to go down to the Lincoln Gardens and "get his kicks" from the Creole Jazz Band led by "Bad Eye" Joe Oliver. (The scar from the broomstick-wound on Oliver's head had contracted his eyebrows into what resembled a puzzled scowl. Hence the nickname "Bad Eye," given by street urchins in New Orleans, had stuck.) Whenever Mares came to the South Side, he talked with Oliver of the kid he had heard back home, and threatened, "If he ever gets here, you're dead."

And Joe knew whom he meant, because he not only liked the boy, but had heard him play in New Orleans. After Louis joined them at the Lincoln Gardens, Oliver remarked to another member of the band, "I never could nor will play the cornet Louis does, but as long as he's with me, he can't hurt me." This same band member says Oliver wouldn't give Louis a chance, and seldom let him take a solo. Dutrey and the Dodds brothers practically went on strike because Joe wouldn't let Louis, with his better tone, play the lead. But after all, it was King Oliver's Band and one could hardly expect him to take a back seat and play second. Actually, Papa Joe helped Louis, made him feel at home in the big city, and encouraged him with his music, for in technique and musicianship the King was no ordinary man. He fully appreciated Louis' talent. It was only after Oliver's insistence that Louis was the greater cornetist that Lil Hardin, their pianist, began to notice the second cornet part. Lil soon saw that Oliver was right and began to take more interest in Louis' playing, although her main interest had always been in classical music.

They began practicing together, and Lil bought a book of standard cornet solos and proceeded to drill them into Louis. Already an excellent reader, due to the efforts of Dave Jones and Oliver, Louis was willing to learn wherever he could. A little later, to find out what all that talk of the non-pressure system was about, he took some lessons from a German teacher down at Kimbal Hall. He had long ago given up the notches cut in the mouthpiece of his first bugle, for he had no further need for them. He became such an excellent sight-reader that while other musicians hurriedly looked over their parts before a first playing, Armstrong never had to worry, knowing that when the time came he could "wipe those notes right off." But in those days, when Lil arranged public appearances for Louis at churches and other occasions, he was not so confident and would sweat even more than he does today under the Klieg lights of Hollywood. But Louis came through. At times, he picked up ideas from other pieces on the program, as for instance, the snatch of *Souvenir* he was to introduce in *Court House Blues*, when he recorded the next year with Clara Smith.

Once they practiced all week on *Dippermouth Blues*; that was discouraging. Louis had a tough time with the cornet choruses that Oliver always took. He just couldn't work his hand quite right to get all the wah-wahs. That peeved Lil, for she couldn't see why Louis had to adopt Joe's style anyway. It was all right to play along in the orchestra with him and work out intricate two-cornet breaks, but somehow it wasn't Louis' natural style. Ever since the warm days Louis spent loafing on the levees, he had never ceased his marvelous whistling. During the first years in Chicago, Louis still whistled the characteristic riffs we have come to identify with the Armstrong style. Lil knew it well, having heard it every time Louis came along the street within two blocks. And Louis had talked a lot about Bunk, his idol of earlier days, had tried to tell how beautiful Bunk's tone was, how intense his vibrato, and had sung phrases to Lil to show the facile, imaginative way Bunk had of embellishing them. Louis had not directly copied Bunk's style; a player as original and sincere as Armstrong wouldn't need to imitate. Somehow Louis had felt things the same way as Bunk, had the same inborn sense of beauty, the same melancholic and exuberant accents, and naturally adopted a similar mode of expression. A lesson of inestimable importance which Louis absorbed more than anyone else was the way Bunk had of hesitating, always a little behind the beat, a lazy yet most dynamic way of playing which is at the core of all hot jazz. All this Louis knew and had explained to Lil, only in those early Chicago times it came out more in his whistling than in his playing. Lil decided the time had come to encourage Louis to return to his own and Bunk's natural style and try to forget some of the Oliver influence, great as it was.

Lil, who was married to Louis early in 1924, cleverly engineered that he should leave Oliver and go to the Dreamland as first cornet, while she stayed on a few more weeks at the Lincoln Gardens. A short time later, in September of 1924, Louis was rushing around town, excitedly telling friends that next week they were going to New York. At last he had his big chance, and was off to join Fletcher Henderson's popular Roseland band.

In New York he was lost, not only on Broadway, but in Henderson's big band with its fancy arrangements. Louis could read them all right, and Fletcher gave him many chances to take solos which made quite a sensation among the musicians, but as Armstrong said, he couldn't "stretch out." It is amazing today to hear one of the old Henderson records of that period; thin, in spite of the size of the band, and somewhat threadbare of any interest or vitality, until suddenly out leaps a hot tone in a cornet solo as modern as anything played today. When, some time later, Henderson's Orchestra made its first visit to Chicago, this time without Armstrong, the Negro press was quick to hail it as "the greatest, not at all like the average Negro orchestra, but in a class with the good white orchestras, such as Paul Whiteman, Paul Ash, and Ted Lewis." To quote the Chicago *Defender*, their music was "soft, sweet, and perfect, not the sloppy New Orleans hokum, but peppy blue syncopation."

However, the year in New York was not wasted. Armstrong got a lot of experience and broadened out in many ways. If for no other reason, the stay was made worth while by the memorable series of recordings in which Armstrong accompanied many blues singers, including Bessie Smith.

The very first session, with Maggie Jones, showed a return to the purely melodic, hot style of Bunk. How Louis must have enjoyed those Clarence Williams Blue Five and Red

Onion Jazz Babies recording dates, which served as excuses for some real New Orleans jam sessions! At some of these sessions, there was a reunion with Sidney Bechet, boyhood chum of Louis', who since 1917 had been spreading New Orleans jazz around in Chicago and New York and had then been first to introduce it to western Europe. After the special arrangements of standard popular tunes Louis played at the Roseland every night, it was a relief to "swing out" on the good old numbers such as *Texas Moaners, Cake Walkin' Babies,* and *Coal Cart Blues.* The last title was in memory of the almost forgotten days in his early teens when Louis drove a coal cart "back o' town." Armstrong must have recalled those days again when he was on tour a few winters later, and passed out five hundred bags of coal to needy Negro families on a cold day in Baltimore.

Lil returned to Chicago after playing on the Red Onion records, and organized her own orchestra for the Dreamland Café on South State, then persuaded Bill Bottoms to make Louis the unusual offer of $75 a week to return from New York. Louis thought at first that they were kidding him, but on November 14, 1925, an ad appeared in the Chicago *Defender* announcing that Lil's Dreamland Syncopators would feature the "World's Greatest Jazz Cornetist," Louis Armstrong. ("Every Thursday night—Barn Dance.") A few weeks later a review in the same paper reported that:

Louis Armstrong, greatest jazz cornetist in the United States, is drawing many white musicians to Dreamland nightly to hear him blast out those weird jazz figures. This boy is in a class by himself.

At last Louis was in his element and was playing the kind of music he knew and loved. The public loved it too, for they wanted gut-bucket jazz. It had to be loud and hot for the hip-liquor-toter of the mid-twenties.

A month after Armstrong opened at the Dreamland, Erskine Tate also engaged him to play in his Vendome Theatre Or-

King Oliver's Creole Jazz Band

Johnny Dodds, Baby Dodds, Honoré Dutrey, Louis Armstrong, Joe Oliver,
W. M. Johnson, Lil Hardin at piano

photo from Victoria Johnson

This seven-piece band is named by most musicians as the first important
influence in the development of today's hot jazz.

Dave Peyton's Symphonic Syncopators (1924-25)

Joe Oliver kept his music book closed. *photo by Woodard Studios*

Joe Oliver brings the nucleus of the later Luis Russell band into the Plantation Café.
Left to right, Kid Ory, Joe Oliver, Paul Barbarin, "Little Tick," Junie Cobb, Luis Russell, Darnell Howard, Rudy Jackson, Bertrium Cobb, Barney Bigard *photo from Victoria Johnson*

Bix

The Wolverines when they first came to Chicago.

When Voynow proposed they use music someone said, "What would we do if the lights went out?"

Bix Beiderbecke

Frankie Half Pint Jaxon with chorus at the old Sunset Café

"Now Corinne Brown from Chicago Town
Was a snake-hip shakin' queen."

With Erskine Tate's "Little Symphony" were Louis Armstrong, trumpet, and Teddy Weatherford, piano. Louis had given up his short horn.

To Kid Muggsy
from
Louis Armstrong

Louis Armstrong's Hot Five

Louis Armstrong, Buddy St. Cyr, Johnny Dodds, Kid Ory, Lil Hardin

"Serve it up hot for my chillun."

Louis Armstrong

Louis Armstrong and his Stompers at the old Sunset

Earl Hines, Peter Briggs, Honoré Dutrey, Louis Armstrong, Bill Wilson, Tubby Hall, Boyd Atkins; *standing*, Rip Bassett, Joe Dixon, Al Washington

"I've got the Heebies—I mean the Jeebies"—Boyd Atkins.

Carroll Dickerson's Orchestra, with Louis Armstrong and Zutty Singleton

"There's the pig we passed around the band.
Anybody hit a bad note we put the pig in front of him."

photos from Zutty Singleton

Jimmy MacPartland and Husk O'Hare's Wolverines, Des Moines, 1925-26

Left to right, Teschmaker, Lannigan, Freeman, Jimmy MacPartland,
Tough, O'Brien, North, Dick MacPartland

    "This was right on the note. You pushed on the
    beat; that was what gave you that fine rhythm."

photo from Jimmy MacPartland

At the end of the White City engagement Tesch left Husk O'Hare's
Wolverines to join the Midway Garden Orchestra

Muggsy and Stacy standing together, Tesch extreme right

Although his mind was shattered, Rappolo (*third from left*) could still play out near Lake Pontchartrain with Abbie Brunies' Halfway House Orchestra after leaving the New Orleans Rhythm Kings. He wore white socks with evening clothes; the photographer blacked them out.

Muggsy Spanier   Frank Teschmaker

Cow Cow Davenport

BOOGIE WOOGIE PIANISTS

"At a house-rent party they start'd a-steppin' that's all."

Cripple Clarence Lofton

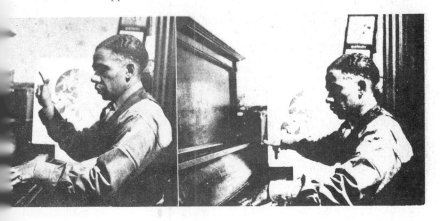

Bessie Smith

"See that long lonesome road,
Lord, you know it's got to en'."

Johnny Dodds   photo by William Russell

ORLEANS CLARINETISTS

Sidney Bechet (soprano sax here)   photo from John Reid and RCA-Victor

Fletcher Henderson's Roseland Orchestra, 1925
Left to right, Scott, Hawkins, Armstrong, Dixon, Henderson, Marshall, Bailey, Chambers, Green, Escudero, Redman *photo from Fletcher Henderson*

Luis Russell's Saratoga Club Orchestra
Back row, Otis Johnson, Foster, Henry Allen, Jr., W. Johnson, Higginbotham
Front row, Hill, Barbarin, Holmes, Armstrong, Russell, Nicholas
photo from Luis Russell

chestra. At the Vendome, Louis played solos before a large and appreciative audience. Here also began Louis' stage career as an actor-singer *extraordinaire*. This phase of his talent soon won equal recognition with his instrumental ability, leading finally to Hollywood. The stage show attracted so much attention that the movie was secondary; many in the audience came to hear the orchestra and left immediately afterwards. At a typical Vendome show, one first heard a standard overture interpreted with musical freshness by Erskine Tate's Little Symphony Orchestra. Then Louis, all smiles, climbed out of the pit and hopped on the stage, toting his cornet in one hand and his indispensable handkerchief in the other. Instantly the house was in an uproar, feet stamping on the floor, cheers and whistles rending the air.

A few preliminary flourishes of the handkerchief and Louis was off on his feature number, *Heebie Jeebies*. Before he hit the second note they were swaying back and forth in their seats all the way to the last row. He kept that up for a while and as suddenly picked up a little megaphone and in a husky voice poured forth the words of the song with all the warmth of the Southland. He took another vocal chorus, not with words but with a guttural mouthing of incoherent nonsense, supplemented with unearthly grimaces. This hair-raising hokum had about it a chilling fascination, all the more because the steady beat helped to create a background for Armstrong's rhythm which itself added to the suspense.

After a moment's rest he was back again with a new stunt. He donned a frock coat and identified himself as the Reverend Satchelmouth. He proceeded with throaty stuttering to announce his text. If anyone asked Louis about the voice he said, "I got a cold." While he exhorted his flock, he thrust his chin out, looking for some response from the brothers and sisters. He always got it. Then his voice really went low—he'd fulfilled his ambition to sing bass by then—and when the congregation was ready for the light he whipped out the little cornet, and gave it to them.

Louis is a born actor and magnificent showman, has a talent for comedy and loves a spotlight. As early as 1917, he had worked out "a little jive routine with dancing and fooling around between numbers to get laughs" with Ory's band at Pete Lala's. So many critics and too-serious purists among the hot fans who object to the showmanship, facial contortions, and bodily antics of the New Orleans musicians forget that in the public eye they were only entertainers, along with the "dancing girls," and that their livelihood depended on their comic as well as musical ability. The customers expected "jive"—kidding, clowning, nonsense—and went away disappointed if they didn't get it. We should be under no illusions about the artistic aspirations of those who worked in Storyville; the musicians were trained to entertain the customers of brothels and barrel-houses. In this amusement business the gift of gab in kidding the patrons had a telling effect when the players came down from their balcony to pass the hat. People are prone to forget the environment that gave jazz its birth and nurtured it along in its formative years, where, according to the *Blue Book* ads, "good time" and "to give satisfaction" were mottos, where "everything goes, and pleasure is the watchword" set the tone of an evening.

Soon after his return to Chicago, Armstrong organized the Hot Five for the Okeh recording sessions. When we consider their size, make-up, and repertory, we see that the Hot Five was the inevitable reaction to a year of Harlem sophistication and Broadway artificiality. For Louis just had to "stretch out," and that meant with a five-piece, New Orleans barrel-house bunch.

The first title to come out, *The Gut Bucket Blues,* was typical of the series. To make sure that the trombone would be played in the crude, sliding, tail gate fashion, Armstrong sent for his old friend Kid Ory. The other members were all from "the swingingest band of all time," Oliver's Creole Jazz Band. The choice of clarinetist Johnny Dodds was most fortunate. His round tone was just what this gang needed. Johnny's playing has always been so consistently inspired that one takes it for granted, and tends to underestimate his contributions to the Hot Five and to Oliver's Creole Jazz Band. Even today Dodds is little appreciated. Who else could have followed Armstrong's solo in *Wildman Blues*, for instance, without a most disastrous letdown? And how many clarinets could have wailed and sobbed out the blues as Johnny did in *Lonesome Blues*, or pounded out stomps with the fire and drive Dodds had on *Potato Head Blues?* His tone could at times be sensitive or, to suit other moods, its quality became coarse and arduous, with a big vibrato.

Ory, who played occasionally with subtle and sorrowful accents, as in *Savoy Blues*, more often played as he did in his own classic, *Muskrat Ramble*, which must have startled the Okeh people into thinking someone was demolishing the El structure out on Wells Street.

Lil, the only member of the Hot Five not from New Orleans, nevertheless had enough of the "down-river" touch to give a true honky-tonk atmosphere to her solos, as in *Drop That Sack* and *Put 'Em Down Blues*. Her "chording," in the New Orleans tradition, always gave excellent support to the improvised ensembles.

When Armstrong enlarged the Hot Five to Seven, to help Buddy St. Cyr give more punch to the rhythm section, we find Baby Dodds playing drums on a notable group of records beginning with *Gully Low Blues* and *Alligator Crawl*. For subtlety of nuances, Baby has never been surpassed, and for obtaining the greatest variety of color and effects from the smallest drum set, he has no equal. In the Hot Seven days recording engineers put a damper on dynamic drumming; hence we do not get the entire picture of Baby's enormous vitality.

Their recording sessions were the height of informality. Sometimes they met in Armstrong's front room, over on 44th Street, to try over a new tune Lil had thought up, or Louis might demonstrate on his cornet a few ideas he had for some of the other parts. Then, with the help of a bottle of Miss Urzey's gin, they were "ready, so help me." These recording dates were never very serious affairs, not after the first afternoon when Johnny Dodds broke down the session. Louis had wanted Johnny to introduce his cornet chorus near the end of *Gut-Bucket Blues*. Johnny had memorized his line, "Blow that thing, Papa Dip, ho-ld it," by heart, and rushed forward to the horn when he heard his cue and opened his mouth wide, but no sound came out. That finished, for that afternoon and for all time, Johnny's vocal efforts on wax. The others ruined several more "takes" with outbursts of laughter before Ory finally got them over that spot. Louis had to have his fun, too; he must have re-discovered the old slide whistle he had used with Oliver's band, for it turned up at the *Who's It* session. The acoustical recording used in the Lincoln Gardens days had been supplanted by electrical recording; the sobbing is better recorded, but just as sentimental. But Louis' most important contribution to these records was the fire and fury which he put into his work; his enthusiasm had a catching quality which compelled the others to do their best, from the opening bars till the end, where he drew them into breath-taking "all-in" choruses.

The *King of the Zulus* was Louis' burlesque of a scene which has been graphically portrayed in the *New Orleans City Guide* of the Federal Writers' Project:

At ten o'clock Mardi Gras morning, with the coming of Zulu, . . . one enjoys the heartiest laugh of the day. King Zulu arrives . . . on a decorated yacht steaming through the New Basin Canal. In early days the King wore a grass skirt, with tufts of dried grass at his throat, wrists, and ankles. His body was incased in black tights, on which were painted stripes of red and green. His face was further blackened, and was decorated with green and red circles and lines. His throne was a Morris chair, his headdress a tin crown, and his scepter was a broomstick with a stuffed white rooster atop. The throne was shaded by a sacking canopy, and the float was decorated with bedraggled palm and palmetto leaves, paper flowers, and red and purple flags. Painted warriors stood in attendance . . .

The float second in the parade was occupied by a cook, a basket of fish, and a cooking stove. The fish-fry float was for the feeding of subjects along the route . . .

King Zulu . . . has a Queen . . . who awaits her monarch on the balcony of a sumptuous undertaking parlor on Jackson Avenue near Dryades Street. The King drinks to his Queen in champagne, and beer and sandwiches are served. The parade is routed down South Rampart Street to Tulane Avenue. . . . The climax of the day is a large ball at which the city's best Negro bands play "as long as anybody has rhythm."

Louis had *his* King of the Zulus at a picnic like the ones "up the river near Baton Rouge" for which he used to play. The fish-fry was supplanted by "chittlin's." Just as the band gets under way with a solo by Ory, a stranger appears:

"Wayit mahn, wayit, stop, stop, wayit!"

"Why, looky here, what do you mean by interrupting my solo?"

"Mahn, I come from Jamaica and I don't mean to interrupt the partee but one of me countrymahn tell me there's a chittlin' rag going on heah!—Madoum, fix me an order of those things you call 'chittlin' ' but I call 'em 'in-a-daube' and I play juanami-'niaca jazz, too."

"Madoum" Lil Armstrong answered with: "Serve it up hot for my chillun!" as King Armstrong swung into his solo, and the "partee" carried on. No wonder the Okeh Company advertised that for this record there would be "no advance in prices, both sides for six bits!"

There was, so far as we know, only one public appearance of the Hot Five, all their work having been done in the Washington Street studio. It was on a Saturday night, June 12,

1926, and the occasion was the gigantic benefit at Chicago's Coliseum, which was arranged by Richard M. Jones, of the Okeh "Race Record" Department. Every Negro jazz musician of importance in Chicago participated, including King Oliver and the Plantation Review, Erskine Tate's Orchestra, Cook's Orchestra with Keppard, Butterbeans and Susie, Bertha Hill, Sara Martin, and the "king of them all, Louis Armstrong, world's hottest jazz cornetist." That week the *Defender* carried an extra eight-page music supplement and announced that Louis Armstrong, the "iron lip cornet wonder," would be featured with the Hot Five in a demonstration recording session making *Heebie Jeebies.* Louis added his own personal message: "The old cornet is just itchin' to make blue music, mister, so I just can't stay away." The audience of ten thousand hailed Louis, who blew "the meanest cornet ever heard," as the sensation of the big ball. Fortunately, the promised performance of *Cornet Chop Suey* and *Come Back Sweet Papa* by all twenty-one orchestras at once failed to materialize.

In the spring of 1926, Louis left the Dreamland to join Carrol Dickerson's Orchestra at the Sunset Café. The *Defender* described the newly enlivened scene:

The boys are red hot. Just across the street at the Plantation Café is King Joe Oliver and Band, another hot one. The fire department is thinking of lining 35th Street with asbestos to keep those bands from scorching passersby with their red hot jazz music. Atta boy!

With Earl Hines "spanking the ivories," the Dickerson band took the cake as the best in Chicago. Dancers at the Sunset stayed in the middle of the floor, refused to leave, and yelled for more: "It's too bad Jim, when Lou-ie blows that wicked trumpet."

It was at the Sunset that Louis first saw his name go up in electric lights, for when Dickerson left, early in 1927, he took over the band and reorganized it. Every night there was a battle of music at 35th and Calumet. In addition to Oliver's

Plantation Syncopators on the opposite corner, there was Jimmy Noone's small band straight across the street, at The Nest. Louis, still doubling at the Vendome earlier in the evenings, could tell if he were late at the Sunset by the volume and hotness of the music emanating from the windows as he came down 35th Street. Armstrong's new band was not quite as large as Dickerson's had been, but lacked nothing in enthusiasm.

Buck Washington, who played one of the two pianos in Armstrong's band, tells how, as the spring season came on and they opened up the windows (the Sunset was not so fancy then as its re-modeled, air-conditioned successor today), the battle of music was no mere fabrication of the imagination.

In spite of more and better music per square foot than had ever been heard, even in the almost fabulous New Orleans pre-war days, Chicago did not lack its critics, who were ready to pounce then, as now, without very much understanding of the music itself. One of them commented:

You have to put your ear muffs on to hear yourself talk in the place. Louis will learn in time to come that noise isn't music. He should have a capable violinist-director with experience who knows expression and orchestral conduct. . . .

Who, besides a critic, would want to go to the Sunset in those days just to hear himself talk? Fortunately, the "roughneck from Rampart Street" continued to blast out his New Orleans music to an appreciative mob of Chicagoans, only a few of whom had not yet gotten over the Creole invasion.

These were the nights that found the white musicians packing the Sunset, too. Joe Glaser considerately waived the $2.50 cover so these kids could come as often as they liked. In the early morning, Muggsy Spanier, Frank Teschmaker, Jess Stacy, and George Wettling would rush in, through with their night's work over on Cottage Grove, all ready to take over for Louis during the intermission. Nor did they always wait for the intermission. If Earl Hines wanted a rest, the boys told him to go out in the kitchen, and Jess sat in. Muggsy got a kick from playing second with Louis and, incidentally, learning his new tunes so that when Louis made his occasional guest appearance on a big night at the Midway, Muggsy's bunch could cut loose with Armstrong's best numbers as soon as they saw him come in. All Louis could do was to shake his head and say, "I b'lieve Muggsy's out to cut me tonight."

Some of the more established and commercially successful white musicians, who had little understanding of what it was all about and no inclination to get at the core of things, also crowded the Sunset and "offered fabulous sums to learn Armstrong's tricks." Others had the idea that by buying and learning the *Fifty Hot Choruses of Armstrong* which Melrose published during the Sunset days, they could assimilate Armstrong's style.

Meanwhile, Louis was playing day and night, at the Vendome in the afternoons and evenings, then rushing over to the Sunset and playing until dawn, with only one intermission. Strangely enough, he kept getting stronger and better as the night wore on; his lip and wind were still in perfect shape as he played the long tones of *The World Is Waiting for the Sunrise*. Frequently the sunrise found Louis stopping in at the after-hour joint where Zutty Singleton, who had just come up from New Orleans, was showing how the drums were meant to be played. Here the jazz was still jumping at nine or ten in the morning, and Louis invariably had to play *Big Butter and Egg Man* before he could get away.

After resigning from the Vendome, Louis, "running wild," regularly tied the show at the Metropolitan Theatre in a knot. When Armstrong's band closed at the Sunset, he decided to enter the amusement game himself and buck the Savoy, which had just opened on Thanksgiving night, 1927. So in December he rented the Warwick Hall on 47th Street, called his new "dancing school" the Usonia, and with the Hot Six began once more to "serve it up hot for his chillun." The Hot Six was all right. Hines and Zutty were among those present. But the expected thriving business was not, and Armstrong's thousands of friends must have stayed at home. So despite his eminent reputation, it was a cold, hard winter for Armstrong and the "Hungry Six." The Warwick venture soon folded, with Louis taking a loss on the year's lease.

But the first week in April found Louis back with Dickerson's band for an opening at Chicago's Savoy Ballroom. Here he was a riot, "the only musician who, with his cyclonic jazz figures, really stops the ball, just as an actor stops the show." Today the Savoy has several clusters of horns to amplify the music of its fourteen-piece bands, for the acoustics are not the best and the crowds inclined to be noisy, but in those days a public address system was unnecessary to make Louis heard; in fact, his powerful tone could be heard out on the street in front of the Savoy.

Armstrong's fame was rapidly growing. At a special afternoon dance, he "knocked all the tin off the roof" of Chicago's ritzy Congress Hotel. He left the Savoy for two nights to go to St. Louis at a hundred dollars per night plus expenses, a new high. And when Henderson, during his Chicago engagement, attempted to lure Armstrong back to his orchestra, the Savoy had to raise Louis to two hundred dollars a week. Although the Savoy had a two-band policy, Dickerson's band, with Louis as the propelling power, had things their way and were the dancers' favorites.

White and colored musicians again flocked to hear Louis. Out-of-town bands on tour to Chicago, such as McKinney's Cotton Pickers whom Don Redman had organized, were seen listening to Louis nightly, and whenever Bix came to town he could be counted on for a trip to the South Side to jam with him.

When the Savoy engagement came to an end in the spring of 1929, most of the boys decided to stick together, put the band in Armstrong's name, and try their luck in New York. Armstrong still had the old yellow roadster in which he, Zutty, and Hines used to ride around the South Side before the Savoy days. Three others had broken-down rattle-traps too; so with the twenty dollars apiece which Lil had helped to dig up for them they started out for New York.

They finally pulled in, broke. Zutty's vibraphone, which had been strapped to the outside of one of the cars, was rusty and ruined. Louis found his friend, Wellman Braud, who helped tide them over until the day they substituted for Ellington's band at the Auburn Theatre in the Bronx. But before they could take the work at the theatre, they had to round up the boys, who had dispersed by this time. Each had gone his own way in the attempt to find work. The trombonist was in Atlantic City so they got Jimmy Harrison. When the band's turn came, they played the *St. Louis Blues.* Before they were through the first chorus the house orchestra was standing up in the pit looking at Louis.

The week after that, they opened at the Savoy Ballroom in Harlem, and their success gave them a big chance at Connie's Inn. While he was playing here, Louis doubled in the Broadway review, "Hot Chocolates." The renown which this double employment gave him started Louis on the most successful part of his career, which carries us into the present. After the termination of the Connie's Inn engagement, Louis went to California; from there, he worked his way back across the country, and made a trip to Europe which earned him wide acclaim.

Many separate factors have combined to make Armstrong an outstanding jazz musician. He possesses most of the qualities which arouse superlatives from critics who approach the field of jazz. Each one of these qualities is alone enough to make an interesting musician. Louis is lucky in having almost all of them. One of the most remarkable is his endurance,

which was developed in a harder training school than that
which most jazz musicians of today have to go through. His
physique, lung power, lip control, and throat relaxation, which
enable him to obtain such fullness of tone throughout his
entire range, were developed by many a long march under the
semi-tropical New Orleans sun, and by long nights of playing
in Storyville's cabarets. The technique which this rigorous
early life helped him to perfect has been the marvel of "legitimate" musicians, who couldn't believe that the glissandi and
brilliant solos which they heard played, coupled with such
amazing virtuosity in the highest register, were actually performed on a trumpet. Louis paid no attention to them, because he was always working, trying something new, and was
never content to remain merely "the best." Even today, when
the band stops during the intermission of a rehearsal, Louis
goes right on practicing, experimenting by himself. If he's at
a dance, he doesn't want to stop at all, even when the dancers
themselves are exhausted.

The beauty of Armstrong's tone has brought forth many
elaborate treatises. There is about it a bigness and warmth
of spirit which melts everything he touches. Undoubtedly,
there is some of Bunk's unusual tone and vibrato here, for
Louis can neither play, sing, talk, nor whistle without letting
the grandeur and glow of this warmth come forth. This quality
is controlled by his vibrato. A musician's vibrato is as individual as his fingerprint and has little to do with his consciousness, but is produced under stress of emotion. Thus it
is not surprising that no one has been able to simulate Armstrong's broad, smooth, yet unusually fast vibrato.

Armstrong evidently has always felt that open horn tone is
more capable of hot intonation. Thus, he did not fall into
the habit of using the dozens of mutes which many have
found necessary to give variety to their playing. For years, like
others from New Orleans, Armstrong used a cornet, with its
more mellow, lusty tone. When he did finally switch over to

a trumpet, it was not because he liked the more brilliant tone, but because his little sawed-off horn looked ludicrous beside the other trumpets in the Vendome Theatre.

In addition to hot intonation, jazz depends on the swing which is generated by rhythmic accents and intervals. Most important is that small interval of delay in which a musician holds back the expected attack. Through this, the listener is not only disturbed but stimulated when the impact is finally felt. This is a matter much more subtle and dynamic than the syncopation that Tin Pan Alley supposed to be the basis of jazz. Just as one swings away from the straight melody in improvisation, the rhythmic patterns must also be broken up and vitalized. Armstrong has the right rhythmic instinct and sense of timing in "swinging around and away from the regular beat," as he expresses it. And so all this talk of rhythmic interval, of making an instant more intense, is not just theory. Nor is this phenomenon of delay produced by instinct alone. The retardation is done consciously, at least to some extent; for instance, in the early twenties Louis described to Lil Bunk's way of hesitating, always just a fraction behind the melody, and then of catching up. Veterans from the bayou country, when asked about Bunk's style, invariably reply: "He seemed to be kind of behind all the time and then catching up at the end of the phrase"; or, "He played like he was missin' all the time and holding back a little." With Louis, we can feel this swing, even when he plays or sings alone, without any accompaniment to mark off the regular pulse, as well as when he carries the entire band along. .

Equally remarkable is Louis' melodic variation. Although characterized by unity of feeling and sureness of direction, Armstrong's solos take shape in an amazing variety of styles. There are solos which are full of fast little runs and descending arpeggios, and the florid breaks he frequently uses in the blues. On the other hand, there are those of extremely simple structure, which use sometimes only a single note throughout a chorus, but with a seemingly endless rhythmic and dynamic modification of African genesis.

Armstrong at times uses only one pitch throughout and varies the dynamics with crescendos, or he may use a series of glissandi centered around one note. The glissando, ruled out of European music as "bad taste," is an essential part of all other musical systems, including the African and Oriental, which recognize curves as well as straight lines of pitch. Actually, the glissando may be considered a simplification of a very complex scale of the most minute intervals, infinitely finer than even quarter tones. Thus in melodic as well as rhythmic sources, the hot jazz of the Negro proves its independence from the Western music of the white man.

The glissando is an essential part of all vocal blues where the small curves and subtle inflections are particularly expressive. We find in the accompaniments to blues singers some of Armstrong's most stirring and characteristic playing. Louis, who never adhered to the conventionalities of European music, is continually getting away from the diatonic scale and altering with chromatics the modal material often found in the blues. The blues frequently give him opportunity to use his style of embellishment by inserting fast runs and figurations lightly between the main phrases, as though they were comments in parentheses, or added footnotes. This technique, derived to some extent from Bunk's style, is often carried over to Armstrong's instrumental improvisation with an orchestra.

Louis has an individual way of not only taking his time to attack each separate note, but also of applying this technique to an entire phrase as a unit. After the orchestra starts a phrase, it sometimes seems as if Louis, who daubs away with his handkerchief and silently fingers the valves while "getting his chops set," would never come in; that he has decided to rest for a bar or two; but before you realize it, there he is, rocking away, fitting in his obbligato, each note in just the right place to make its maximum effect. Part of Armstrong's spell and charm is in the notes he doesn't play. No one ever made more startling and effective use of the "rest" and the "pause."

Armstrong's vocal style has changed very little through the years, since it is dependent upon the natural limitations of the human voice, which is not capable of taking the flights that are possible with instrumental virtuosity. This is not to say that Louis' vocalizing is not varied, for he has sung tenor and bass, smoothly and roughly, with humor and melancholy, and at times with the most frightening, insane incoherency. He has murdered everything from Cuban and Hawaiian folk songs to blues, stomps and spirituals. Louis' voice has a huskiness which accentuates its hot quality. In his innovation of the "scat" chorus he created an abstract form well suited to hot expression. Whatever the original inspiration for this was, whether a desire to approximate musical timbre, a subconscious straining away from the words he disliked, or merely that he could not remember words, Armstrong's scat singing proved to be a unique contribution to vocal art. Like his contributions to the trumpet style of jazz, it had a far-reaching influence.

Richard M. Jones said that better than anyone else when he remarked, "As long as those pearly teeth hold out, Louis'll still be playing something new, and all the others will be running after him trying to catch up."

VI

BIX BEIDERBECKE

BY EDWARD J. NICHOLS

BEFORE BIX becomes all legend, it's better to set down some facts. He died young. That gives the legend a head start. Of the other top men of jazz only Teschmaker shares this luck of an early death, and Tesch stayed in one spot, where the tale-tellers could keep the record straight.

So Beiderbecke was gone before the jazz revival, with its researchers asking, "And did he really play with Charlie Straight?" You see, Armstrong is still alive where they can get at him, but the quiet years following Bix thinned out the little facts in the memories of those who were with him. Not the sound of his horn, mind you, but only the little facts. His friends don't even care much about the places and the dates. Sometimes they get impatient with your questions and they say, "Listen, how do I remember where it was? Maybe it wasn't *Dinah* and maybe it was only ten choruses, but you hadda hear that horn. If you heard the horn that's all there is. That's Bix and you don't need any more."

They all remember the horn all right, and most of the boys remember a particular session. They're like Paul Morris out in Hammond, Indiana, who followed the Wolverines from campus to city to the joints on the Indiana lakes: "I got to show you the house. Right off that porch there, by the side window. Six of them came off the job at Gary and we threw a little dance in there. Bix was sitting against the wall right by that window. You heard him out at the Beach, but you were only hearing the best cornet in your life. What I'm saying is the greatest music out of a horn or anything else blew right through that window. It was open and Bix would lean by it for air, only he wasn't breathing anything but through the cornet. If I was all the way sober I wouldn't tell you, but I'll admit Buck and I still park here some nights and try to recall the choruses all over again."

They never know exactly when it was or who else played with him (and usually they're surprised that you care), but they get that across-the-campfire look and you can see a legend in the making.

Sure, did you know that the young Bix would take a rowboat out on the Mississippi and wait for the riverboats up from New Orleans? He would listen to the great Negro bands, mostly to the trumpets. Then back at his house Bix could copy them phrase for phrase, beat for beat.

Did you know how Beiderbecke and Hoagy Carmichael, on the way up Indiana for a recording date at the Gennett Company in Richmond, stopped their car, climbed out, and blasted two horns (Carmichael did occasionally play the trumpet) for half an hour across a Hoosier cornfield?

And how about the night at the Plantation Café on the South Side of Chicago? Bix and Louis were having a battle of horns. When Armstrong heard Bix he broke down and cried, then admitted he could never play as well as that.

Perhaps you've heard how the Whiteman band kept an empty chair in the brass section when Bix was sick near the end. And how some of the boys went out to Davenport one August seventh, on the anniversary of Beiderbecke's death, and played jazz over his grave.

These are some of the stories. There are many others: drinking stories, tales of his eccentricities, and always that melodramatic account of Bix and gangsters whose tortures "really caused his death."

That should be enough to show a legend in the building. Some of the stories have a core of truth; others probably have none. But they all add up to making a musician's hero. In the eyes of the tellers is the insistence that you feel this man above and beyond the facts. The stories, liquor as well as music, are all to the good.

But hell, you should have heard that horn!

And the truth is closer to this. Leon Bismarck Beiderbecke was born on March 10, 1903, in Davenport, Iowa. The "Bix" was picked up from his older brother, who was called that before him. His family are well-to-do lumber people, and Bix's background was cultured and musical. This is a bad break for the legend, which would be more romantic had his heritage conformed more closely to the recent novel inspired by Beiderbecke. You can make a pretty good hero out of a musician if you can make his power and genius seem mysterious.

But actually his mother was a student of both piano and pipe organ, who at the age of ten had won a medal for her playing. On his father's side there was also musical talent. His grandfather led a chorus of German Americans in Davenport and his grandmother's father played an organ in Europe. His sister is an able pianist. Bix himself took at least a few lessons on the piano from Professor Grade of Davenport, who said that the boy responded well for one who played so entirely by ear.

That matter about the ear must have been right, for Mrs. Beiderbecke testifies that Bix began picking out tunes when he was just tall enough to reach the keyboard. At the age of three he was playing the air of the *Second Hungarian Rhapsody*. No wonder Bud Freeman thinks Bix had the greatest ear he has ever known.

Bix never took a lesson on the cornet. He picked it up himself and that is why his playing was unconventional. For instance, Bix never thought of the cornet as a B Flat instrument. He thought of it as being a whole tone higher—that is, in the same key as the piano, with which he was somewhat familiar. Since violin parts were scored in concert key, like piano, Bix could read them better than cornet parts. So he relied on them from the time he quit the Wolverine Orchestra until he played with Jean Goldkette.

Another difference in Bix's playing was his heavy reliance on the third valve of the horn. The usual fingering employs the first two valves more than the third. In fact, Joe Gustat, nationally known symphony trumpeter and teacher, said Bix would have to forget all he ever learned by himself and begin all over by taking lessons if he ever wanted to be a cornetist. But this "wrong" technique may account for the easy tumbling flow of some of his most celebrated rapid passages.

People often ask why Bix chose the cornet instead of the trumpet. The timbre, or tone, of the cornet is mellow and full bodied—closer to the human voice than the longer and smaller-bored trumpet. Dance musicians have favored the trumpet because of its brilliance or "sting," and also because it is better adapted to tonguing and to mute playing. In the early twenties any trumpeter who didn't carry at least a satchelful of mutes on the job wasn't modern. But the growl, the wah-wah, and other muted effects irritated Bix. He himself had only one straight mute and rarely used it. He preferred a legato style and the round singing tone of the cornet rather than the virtuoso potentialities of the trumpet.

As to the musicians who first influenced Beiderbecke, the controversy which should properly surround a legendary figure is hotly present. The argument is still going on.

"Oliver and Armstrong were the influences on Beiderbecke."

"The hell they were. La Rocca got Bix started; he says so himself."

"Oh, so I guess you never heard Bix give most of the credit to Emmett Hardy."

To these you could add Fate Marable, Paul Mares, and a guy named Johnny Dunn, if you want. In fact, practically every trumpet man who played before Bix except Louis Panico has been advanced by someone as *The Influence*.

Bix's mother tells it this way: when he was in his early teens he used to wait to see if the family were going out, and if they were he would come downstairs in his pajamas, sit by the Victrola, and play his cornet along with the music. She remembers hearing him accompany a recording of *Tiger Rag*. Given Bix's age, the horn would have had to be La Rocca's and, as Charles Edward Smith pointed out in *Tempo* (July, 1936), you can't listen to La Rocca and Bix playing the same Dixieland tunes, a decade apart, without finding a fair case to support the Italian's influence.

Yet as Smith adds, if Bix fell into the Dixieland tradition, he was brought much closer in freedom of expression to Negro jazz than to La Rocca. Since Bix never played in a band until he left Davenport, his only outlet was to accompany the phonograph. In addition to the Dixieland records, he later played to those of King Oliver. Either these records or the earlier presence of Oliver and Louis on the riverboats at Davenport would have given Bix the chance to hear that off-scale tonality which is so strong in his music. He admired them both, though he considered Louis a great improvement over Oliver in style.

Emmett Hardy, a white trumpet player on the riverboats, may also have influenced Bix. Red McKenzie says Bix himself named Hardy. But this whole business of the riverboat musicians is confused. One friend of Beiderbecke's, who grew up in St. Louis, insists that no good New Orleans bands ever got up as far as Davenport. Then at the other extreme is a detailed account of how King Oliver and Louis Armstrong came there on a Strekfus Line boat, the *Capitol*, and of how Bix went on board and was even allowed to whack the ship's calliope.

However it is, no doubt is left concerning the influence of Negro jazz on Bix—particularly Oliver and Armstrong. Bill Challis, who knew Bix intimately during the great days with Goldkette and Whiteman, remembers that Bix named La Rocca, Armstrong, and Ethel Waters. While it is common to hear of the effect Bessie Smith had on Bix, the mention of Waters is strange. Yet another friend of Bix's said Ethel Waters "impressed Beiderbecke by her fine dramatic style and her excellent phrasing." But she didn't move him as Bessie did. Neither of these men recalls any admission on the part of Bix that Hardy influenced him.

Whatever the controversy, the point is that Bix had found his medium—the cornet—and that's what counts.

Beiderbecke spent two and a half years in Davenport High School and in the fall of 1921 entered Lake Forest Academy on the North Side of Chicago. Starting in a school dance band as pianist, he was soon the featured cornetist. When his father visited him there he found that Bix belonged to every musical organization in the vicinity. His mother still has a locket with a lyre on it, given him by the Academy for his outstanding musical ability. But meanwhile his scholarship was winning no prizes; in fact it was low grades that caused his exit before the school year was out, his mother being surprised he had hung on so long.

Bix was no student, but the music was in him and even the campus couldn't supply enough. An instructor at Lake Forest says Bix used to sneak off campus after hours to play in a band downtown. And already there was plenty of gin. He may have been a faculty problem but the headmaster still remembers his popularity among the students and emphasizes the amiable nature and the unselfishness in Bix that friends are constantly pointing out. The band he ditched school to play with included several members who later helped form the Wolverine Orchestra that started Bix on the climb to the

top. Meanwhile he jobbed around Chicago after his year at
Lake Forest until the Wolverine period began.

The Wolverines got under way when Dick Voynow booked
them at the Stockton Club, a roadhouse near Hamilton, Ohio,
late in 1923. Drummer Vic Moore says the band's first job was
in Doyle's Pavilion in Cincinnati, but there is more evidence
to support the Ohio opening, which took place before Moore
joined the group. Besides Bix and pianist Voynow, the personnel included George Johnson, tenor sax; Jimmy Hartwell,
clarinet; Bobby Gillette, banjo; Al Gande, trombone; and Bob
Conzelman, drums. After a couple of months Vic Moore replaced Conzelman, and when later Vic Berton took over the
band, the two alternated at the drums and in directing. Gande
did not accompany the band when it left Ohio.

The Wolverines were the third great white band of jazz.
But unlike their precursors, the Original Dixieland Jazz Band
and the New Orleans Rhythm Kings, here was a style well on
the road to that of the Chicagoans, whom they influenced.
If they hadn't any other justification than helping to provide
the direction to musicians like Teschmaker, Russell, Tough,
Freeman, etc., it would be enough. But of course the Wolverines did more. They gave Bix the first important surroundings
in which he worked, and if the general impression of the
group, apart from Bix, is a little vo-do-de-o-do today, in the
years 1924-1925 it satisfied some pretty discerning ears.

Hoagy Carmichael heard of the band and got them on the
Indiana University campus for a fraternity dance in the spring
of 1924. This meant a great deal to the Wolverines, for in
those days when Carmichael liked a musician or an orchestra
the publicity pretty well covered the state of Indiana. Hoagy's
own campus band at the time was the best known in the
region. Hoagy himself, Wad Allen on sax, and violinist Bridge
Abrams were far enough along the right road to have discovered the Wolverines. So the band drove up to the Kappa Sig
House and a fraternity member writes about the date:

The Wolverines came—drove up in a battered car, everybody and all the instruments spilling over the sides. And such banged up, dented horns. We were all worried at this introduction, because not even Hoagy had ever heard them play. So the boys decided they ought to hear the band before the dance. But when they played, their dubious entrance was forgotten, and the entire campus tried to jam into one fraternity house to catch the music. Bix was in the band, blowing down into his lap on an old second-hand brass cornet he had picked up for eight dollars. Hoagy went nuts. He and Moenkhause [a swell classical musician and a good jazzman, since dead] began the Bix cult that had the band back on the campus ten weekends in a row.

The I.U. dates were followed by an engagement at the Casino Gardens in Indianapolis. Meanwhile the famous series of Gennett recordings was beginning to come out of the studios of the Starr Piano Company in Richmond, Indiana. Drummer Vic Berton heard *Jazz Me Blues* in Chicago and became an immediate convert. He came down to the Indiana campus and booked the band for a summer theatre tour which included Indianapolis, Louisville, Terre Haute, and other cities in the circuit. Later in the summer the Wolverines opened the Gary Municipal Beach Pavilion for a two months' stay. Every night here was like college night, with Hoagy usually leading the worshipers. Pushed up into a small corner of an immense brick structure with open sides, the band would look completely licked at the start. But midnight always found the players tucked in warmly by what must have been one of the first rings of jitterbugs.

Sure Bix had his little "jug." He always had it, but most of the musicians disclaim the stories about "those bang-up, out-of-the-world choruses that a knocked-out genius blasted at the ceiling when friends had to support him in his chair." Too far along and the lips get stiff; the tongue is fuzzy; the fingering slows up. The great choruses out of brass aren't likely to come then.

But late at night Bix could turn to the piano. At Gary

Beach he did this often, and the characteristic figures that had carved from the horn out over the artificial lagoon beside the pavilion merely piled into and out of the piano chords.

It was a great two months for everybody, certainly for Bix and the band. Music—lots of it—on the job and after. Also gin and girls. The girls liked Bix. His mildness and good manners were untypical of the usual jobbing musician, and it got the women who wandered in and out of the dance halls. One girl followed Bix all over the Middle West during these days, and two women in St. Louis are still said to be in love with him. But these wouldn't be the girls to hold Bix, whose great regard for his mother set for him a very high standard. Later, when he hoped to make a trip to Europe with the Whiteman band, it was his mother he planned to take with him, and her influence on Bix was always greater than that of any other woman. Not that there weren't any girls who counted. At least there is evidence of a girl in these early Chicago years, also of one near the end. Neither of these women has any resemblance to Bix's legendary gangster's moll any more than to the intellectual stiff neck in the fictional story based upon his life.

It was still a great two months, with Bix in demand everywhere in the region, including one session with Milt Mezzrow at a joint called the Martinique in Indiana Harbor.

For a while the story of Bix is easy to follow. The jazz world knows how Red Nichols came to listen and to imitate; how Sam Lanin with a band full of stars, at once hired Bix to make recordings; how Local 802 knew a musicians' band when it heard one, and how Beiderbecke became the idol of every man who carried a card. That was the trouble, of course—it was a musicians' band. The people who danced had to feed the band and these people wanted to hear the same tunes Don Bestor or Emil Coleman put on the air each night. With two exceptions the Wolverines, Bix included, couldn't read music, or at least very little, and their repertoire was standard and limited. Ten choruses on *Riverboat Shuffle* might knock out a listening musician, but there weren't enough musicians to pay the way. So other engagements in the city were not available, and rather than go on the road Bix preferred returning to Chicago and a spot in Charlie Straight's Orchestra. For Bix the first leg of the stretch to the top was over; the Wolverine period was closed for him.

When Bix was playing at the Rendezvous with Straight he kept a wildwest novel propped up on the rack and played from his knowledge of the tunes and the ability of his ear. But Straight would often leave the band on its own after midnight; then down came the novel and arrangements both, while the band jammed it out until time to quit. His work with Straight was brief, not more than a few months. He quit when he learned that the members of the band were chipping in for half his salary because his presence was a drawing power.

While Bix was with Straight's band, he and the other Chicagoans spent a great deal of time in the colored night spots, especially on the South Side. In 1925 Oliver and Louis had separate bands, Jimmy Noone was a local favorite, and Bessie Smith had just come to town. The first night Bix heard Bessie he threw his whole week's pay out on the floor just to keep her singing. He especially liked to hear her sing *I'll See You in My Dreams* and became very fond of the tune. A story goes that Bix featured the song for a week in which he and a trumpet player, Frank Quartel, from Fio Rito's Orchestra, did an act at the Riviera Theatre. They were billed as "The Pepper Boys," and Bix would sit on the steps leading up from the orchestra pit, playing up at Quartel, who was on the stage with a concertina. One night Bix got up to take a bow and fell down the steps—and knocked both troupers out of the act.

These must have been some of the best days for Bix. It was a kid's life, and Bix was just a kid. You had your music; you played it right; and around you were friends who knew you were playing it right and who could play it that way along with you. There was drinking, sure. It was the middle of Prohibition, and who that sang or played or lived wasn't drinking? So all the tush-tush of certain friends of Bix's today seems far aside from the point. Many of those who drank hardest with him love him best today; that ought to be enough to take this alleged stigma off the facts about the liquor.

The times may have been good, but not so good in money for the musician who wanted to play hot jazz. The big commercial bands who played it sweet usually didn't want you, and if they did you probably didn't want any of them, or couldn't have fitted in if you did. Beiderbecke, almost a year away from his first large orchestra, found, like most of the hot musicians, that the going was tough for him. At this time he went up to Detroit where he played on a lake boat and jobbed around the city. While there he became acquainted with members of Jean Goldkette's orchestra in time to make a return to Indiana University for a prom date under the Goldkette name, though he was not a member of the band. Bix was still remembered on the Indiana campus and he liked to play there. His appearance was also a homecoming for those alumni who had heard him the year before.

In September, 1925, an offer came for a steady job in a band of Frank Trumbauer's and Bix left to play for a year at the Arcadia Ballroom in St. Louis.

Here was good money. He was making $100 a week. But so strong were the hand-to-mouth habits of the Chicago barnstormers that Bix lived in a third-rate hotel and even then left bills around the bars in excess of two or three hundred dollars. When he left town in the spring he was wearing the pants of one friend and the coat of another. Toward the end of the season at the Arcadia his tuxedo trousers had become so worn in the seat that Bix would have to mount the bandstand with his cornet held carefully behind him.

Only this wasn't all of the St. Louis year. Bix was fond of

symphonies and especially modern concert music: Stravinsky, Ravel, Debussy, as well as the American MacDowell (*Woodland Sketches*). Bud Hassler, a friend of Bix's who played in the Arcadia Band, tells about their regular attendance at these concerts. Hassler thinks that Bix's love for the modern whole-tone scale and the whole-tone chord was noticeable all through his playing. Bix wore out a recording of Stravinsky's *Firebird Suite* while he was in St. Louis.

At this time, too, his piano improvisations were gaining in melodic context and beauty. The classical models at hand, along with the hours Bix spent on pianos in the joints around the city, were developing a talent that his friend Hassler calls the greatest index of Bix's genius.

During the year at St. Louis there came another prom date at Indiana University, in April, 1926. Bix was billed as assistant director and in the college paper was pronounced "the most efficient exponent of 'dirty' trumpet playing in jazz circles." So Bix played dirty! Today's critics can talk about his almost classic line, the restraint, and the echoes of his favorite Debussy; but the college kids in 1926 called him dirty and that's the way they liked it. It was a great reunion for Bix, back again on the campus where Hoagy and the boys had started the fame of the Wolverines.

It was only a short time later that Trumbauer broke up his band and moved with Bix into Jean Goldkette's Orchestra. This was a marked step upwards for Bix. Goldkette was first of all a business man, to whom a band must be an impersonal commodity that never lagged behind the best commercial market. He had sensed the growing popular interest in hot jazz to the extent that his big band was a mixture of two styles. The band could play it sweet or play it hot. The musicians themselves, of course, were supposed to play both. This meant for Bix more reading of music than he had ever attempted before. But here was a band working out from a large booking office, and already famous in the Middle West; a band with its own special arranger and yet one in which the boys were often allowed to blow it out for themselves. In all a good spot.

In the summer of 1926 the band was playing in two sections, a hot and a sweet band. Bix joined the hot group, which included, among others, Trumbauer, Pee Wee Russell, "Sonny" Lee, "Itzy" Riskin, and Ray Ludwig. There were eleven pieces in all, and they worked a dime-a-dance system in the Blue Lantern Inn at Hudson Lake in northeastern Indiana. Sometimes the band would alternate in five- and six-piece combinations, at which times Bix invariably played cornet in one unit and piano in the other. Freeman says he even played drums several times. Bix loved to play so much that when the going was right neither rest nor paycheck mattered.

One night Milt Mezzrow came out to Hudson Lake and took Bix back to Chicago to hear a band at White City which included Frank Teschmaker, Floyd O'Brien, Bud Freeman, Jim Lannigan, Dave North, Jimmy MacPartland, and his brother. Bix went up to the stand and said, "How do you fellows do it? You're the best white band I ever listened to." That was the band that had got its first inspiration from the early Wolverine recordings, and here was the star of the Wolverines paying the tribute right back into their horns.

By now Bix was close to the top. He was in the best group he'd ever play with regularly, and on the stand he was the one pointed out among a group of stars. And an arranger like Challis knew at once what to do about Bix. How did he want the brass trio to go? he would ask Bix. And what kind of harmonic background did he want for his solos? It would be the way Beiderbecke liked it, and there were two smart readers like Ludwig and Farrar in the brass to help him make it go. Too bad this is seldom the Goldkette you hear on the recordings. *Pretty Girl*, *Clementine*, and one or two others maybe; but the studios wanted most of it sweet and that's the way it came out.

In the Greystone Ballroom in Detroit, at Castle Farms in

Cincinnati, at the Roseland Ballroom in New York they played more often the way Bix liked. If it wasn't a great band, at least it came closest to offering the surroundings Bix required.

But Goldkette's was a high-priced band and stars are temperamental. It couldn't last. No booking for the band was in sight beyond the Greystone early in the fall of 1927, and the boys were restless. Adrian Rollini had been up to hire some of them to open a spot in New York. Paul Whiteman was also showing interest, though he hesitated to break up another's band. Since the band was on the way out anyhow, Rollini picked off Bix, Farrar, Bill Rank, Venuti, Lang, Signorelli, Moorehouse, and one or two others to open a club called the New Yorker. In two weeks the place was closed, but for Bix and several others it meant moving into the Whiteman Orchestra.

A story goes around that Bix had refused a previous offer to join Whiteman because he doubted his own ability to read music well enough. It's a story that doesn't trace down. On the contrary, Challis, who already had talked with Whiteman several times about changing over from Goldkette, says that Whiteman seemed indifferent to Bix, thinking he might not fit into the organization. Nevertheless, when the New Yorker folded, Bix went into the Whiteman band.

Commercially this should have been the highest reach for Beiderbecke. At the time no doubt he thought it was. The musical scores provided by Ferde Grofé were intelligent and complicated—whether they rode or not. Since Bix was a follower of modern concert music, there was something in the glitter of all this flash that at first impressed the young man from Davenport who had never had a lesson on the cornet. In fact he worried and was self-conscious. Letters to his mother express fear that maybe the big league would prove too tough, too advanced for him.

Still, you can't shake the boys who know. Pretty soon the same wise fingers who pointed to the Goldkette stand and said, "Get a load of that!" were stabbing at the bulge-eyed young man (who was getting a little stout by now) in Whiteman's brass section. There was a Beiderbecke following that began to have its way. When the band was in Los Angeles in 1928, two of Bix's cousins in the audience heard a large crowd of collegians stamping and shouting, "We want Bix!" Finally Whiteman had to promise to let them have him as soon as the printed program was completed. In the stage shows it was customary for Whiteman to use Bix only in a hot group from the band, which gave a brief concert of its own. So there was early precedent for the Goodman quartet.

The fine arranger from the Goldkette days was still on hand to feed the material around his horn whenever he got the chance; so for a while, even though the band was heavier and the demands more commercial, much of the music was good for Bix in the old way. His confidence came back. The band loved him, and his own section—Goldfield, Margulies, and Busse—were always glad to help with the tough spots in the scores.

There still was Chicago too. Every time back meant reunions and jamming all over the town. Like the afternoon "Slick" Condon got Bix to come over to Sam Beers' place at 222 North State Street, just to play for Teschmaker, Bud Freeman, and Joe Sullivan. That was between shows at the Chicago Theatre, and it was only a beginning. The next morning at two one of the dream sessions of all time got under way. Bix, Sullivan, the two Dorseys, Freeman, Benny Pollack, and others played it out until dawn. And that was just one time, one place. There were other nights and other spots; there was still White City and the colored clubs on the South Side. With Crosby, Malneck, and others of the band, Bix was the white-haired boy wherever he went. He knew he was good all right, and why not? But he never let it spoil him. And the money was good too—$300 a week to start, not counting the records.

In 1929 the downward curve began. The demands on the Whiteman band were heavier than ever. The direction was more and more commercial. Columbia signed the orchestra for a series of recordings. Commercial! Radio signed them to compete with the terrific pace set by B. A. Rolfe's Lucky Strike program. Commercial! These assignments were tough for Bix, especially the radio hour. Twenty numbers in sixty minutes, and often five or six of them new. Never a good reader, buried in the complicated scores demanded of the band, Bix began to lose his grip.

So what do you do when you can't play it right? You are sitting for an hour and they give you maybe eight bars to think out yourself. Well, and you love the music played right and you can't get it. So what do you do? You drink more.

That's what Bix did. Pretty soon they couldn't depend on him the way they used to, for he was a sick man. His absences from the stand became more frequent. Finally Whiteman sent him to a cure and from there he went home for a time. Then in the spring of 1931 he came back to New York hoping to rejoin the band, but he must have known he couldn't. So he picked up what he could get. Somebody got him a job on the Camel Hour. He played one night, then had to give it up. Friends worked hard to interest him in trying to join the Casa Loma Orchestra. Once they even got him halfway through Central Park on the way up to Connecticut for a tryout. But when he found out where they were taking him he refused to go. Finally he did go up, and the Casa Lomas were glad to have him. Yet four nights steaming through the Gifford arrangements with their exacting ensemble mechanistics told him off.

He made several recordings for Victor, one of them among

such good company as Tommy Dorsey, Joe Venuti, Eddie Lang, Hoagy Carmichael, Bud Freeman, Gene Krupa, and "Bubber" Miley. Freeman says Bix was very happy that afternoon and to hear his cornet on *Barnacle Bill* is to know that for at least one day Bix had it again the way he liked it. Thirty-two bars of his music stemming back to the greatest days and no doubt about it.

The curve was still down. Bix was broke most of the time and his way of living grew more careless, but there was still one job to be done. He and Challis worked out together some of the piano improvisations he had been playing for a number of years. *In a Mist* had already been scored while Bix was still with Whiteman. That job had taken him and Challis three months or more, for Bix seldom played anything exactly the same way twice. Finally, when the Robbins edition of *In a Mist* did come out, it still differed slightly from the record Bix had made for Okeh in 1927. These last pieces were put on paper more easily, and although Bix never recorded them they have since been given effective interpretations by Jess Stacy of Goodman's Orchestra.

That was pretty close to the end. While there was still fun to be had and plenty of friends, the music was just about done. His apartment in the Forty-fourth Street hotel had lots of company. Bix was playing the piano almost exclusively now, improvising on Debussy themes, or maybe just improvising. He was cheating the cure now, telling himself he wasn't getting the drinks he never ceased to take. Babe Ruth used to come around frequently those days, because Bix was a great ball fan, a great drinker, and a great guy. Babe could never get through the rooms of the little apartment, so he would unscrew the doors from the hinges and set them aside. Fun yet —but not much music.

One of the last desires Bix had was to take an all-star white band to tour Europe. He had heard that they knew what good jazz was over there and you wouldn't have to play commercial. He actually succeeded in getting some good men together for an audition, among them Krupa, Sullivan, Tom Dorsey, Freeman, and either Jimmy Dorsey or Pee Wee Russell. But without backing it never came off.

For Bix the end was quick. With a bad cold he got out of bed one night to play a Princeton club date. It was either Bix or no job, the boys said—so Bix went. Pneumonia set in and Beiderbecke died a few days later, August 7, 1931.

Then the legend began.

VII

THE AUSTIN HIGH SCHOOL GANG

BY CHARLES EDWARD SMITH

IN 1922 five kids from Austin High School out at Chicago's west end, got up a little band. The buff brick high school they attended was so much like others it was hard to describe, and the boys themselves were the sort who might have gone on to college but for their interest in music. All played violin except Bud Freeman, the greenhorn of the bunch. Their interest in music, brought to a head when they first played together, was so keen that they played and practiced in school, in their homes, and even in the vacant apartment of a house owned by the father of one of them. "The poor people downstairs," Jim Lannigan commented, "they finally had to move out."

Jim Lannigan played piano in the little band. Jimmy Mac-Partland played cornet and his older brother Dick played banjo and guitar. Bud Freeman played C-melody sax, at that time a popular instrument for home study, and changed to tenor sax a few years later after the band had got under way professionally. Frank Teschmaker was also a member of the original group. At this time he was learning alto sax, but still played violin. The ages of the group ranged from Jimmy Mac-Partland, the baby, who was a mere fourteen, to Jim Lannigan, seventeen. Dick was seventeen before the first season was over, Teschmaker sixteen, and Bud Freeman slightly younger.

Drawn together by a common ambition, they went as a group to theatres, parties, and restaurants. Coming from comfortable middle-class homes they could, in the beginning, pursue their musical ambitions as a hobby, a circumstance that gave them much more freedom of choice than would have been the case with a different background. At that time the Al Johnson Orchestra, heard in a local theatre, was their inspiration, though it was not to last long. It did, however, give them the incentive they needed and they improved rapidly. Soon they were good enough to play at the afternoon high school dances that were then becoming popular in Chicago. These dances, held usually from three until about five-thirty, had the endorsement of the Parent-Teacher Association, no doubt on the theory that they were a healthy social outlet for youthful energies. Over at Hull House was a band made up of neighborhood kids, most of them from the tenements. There, membership in the band was a double inducement. Some, like Benny Goodman, joined it to get a chance to play on a real instrument; others were chiefly interested in the fact that the band got a free trip to summer camp.

In the Austin Gang the oldest boys, Jim Lannigan and Dick MacPartland, were best grounded in theory. Although Jim was jazz crazy with the rest of them he wasn't sure that he always wanted to play in jazz bands. He'd watched and listened to the foundation work of a contra bass in a symphony orchestra, and this had become the measure of his ambition. Jimmy MacPartland, on the other hand, wouldn't trade his jazz cornet for the best symphony job. Handsome and athletic, there was a sturdy quality in his ambition that showed in his personality.

And Tesch? Well, you couldn't, to this day, get an accurate word picture of him. He was of medium height, blond, and outwardly quiet. He had a full mouth, long upper lip, slightly snub nose, high rounded forehead, and brooding eyes that were often hidden by glasses. He was patient and impatient by turn. Some said that this was because of his extreme sensitivity; others insisted there were those two sides to his nature. Whatever it was, Tesch remained to the end the white-haired boy of the Austin High School Gang, the one they listened to and the one they followed.

The little band played at high school fraternity dances, at the homes of fellow students, for supper or for nothing at all. Practicing day and night and never quite satisfied, their studies had been forgotten. Tesch wasn't always convinced that Bud would learn to be a musician. On one occasion he said that he wished Bud was out of the band. But this was a passing mood. As the band shaped up, Bud's musicianship was not merely to be vindicated but was to become, for many, the source of an instrumental style. In the give and take of criticism the boys built upon what knowledge they already had. Dick, whose father had taught him musical theory, got Bud to learn arpeggios. "He pounded harmony in his head," Jimmy explained.

Across the street from Austin was an ice cream parlor known as "The Spoon and the Straw." The boys dropped in there often, as did other students from their high school, and usually someone had a nickel to feed the automatic phonograph. One day they made a tremendous discovery. It was a record by the New Orleans Rhythm Kings, made under the name of the Friars' Inn Society Orchestra. They played the record over and over, none of them knowing who the clarinet was on Tin Roof, but all of them getting a kick out of hearing that kind of music for the first time. They turned to each other and said, "That's the stuff!" "That's it!"—so voluble in their amazement that even the soda-jerker looked over at them in surprise.

The Rhythm Kings, to whom the young Chicagoans were listening for the first time, had grown up when jazz was at its height, when in a few compact blocks in New Orleans you could hear jazz that was authentic because no one had yet learned to be cornfed. And so, patterning their style after the veterans of New Orleans, the Rhythm Kings had had the satisfaction that they were getting their music from its source.

The Austin High School Gang had no such opportune environment. By the time the toddle was dying out in Chicago, the word jazz had no more meaning than had the word ragtime before it. What you heard when you listened to jazz might be a four-piece honky-tonk combination playing as though there were nothing to go by, not even instinct, or it might be a fourteen-piece band emasculating the already dreary strains of Tin Pan Alley's most commercial output. Somewhere in between were the small bands that could or couldn't read, traditional but going places. In an atmosphere of such confusion the significance of the records on the nickelodeon at "The Spoon and the Straw" may be appreciated. Listening to the Rhythm Kings, the Austin High School Gang heard real jazz for the first time.

The Austin Gang came definitely and immediately under the influence of the Rhythm Kings. They tried to get the same steady, compelling rhythm, contrapuntal improvisations, a comparable quality in tone color, a similar economy of notes and ease of melodic interpretation. When a bit later on they heard Gennett records made by Bix and the Wolverines, their pre-professional training was almost complete. In this way the impact of New Orleans music, strained first through the Rhythm Kings and next through the Wolverines, stamped itself on the musical style of the Chicagoans at the very beginning. What was more natural than that they should name themselves after the Friars' Inn Society Orchestra—Husk O'Hare's nom de plume for the Rhythm Kings—and call themselves the Blue Friars? Having heard records, they went out to hear the bands themselves. It was about this time they discovered King Oliver's Creole Jazz Band. From then on, their identity with New Orleans jazz was complete.

One of the first dances given by the Blue Friars was at the

Columbus Park Refectory. They paid eight dollars' rent to get the hall from three until six in the afternoon, and they charged fifty cents admission. Jimmy "borrowed" type from the school print shop to make up tickets and handbills on a home press. On that day, each of the boys felt a responsibility that was less to Austin than to Rappolo and Bix. "The kids came from Austin and other high schools," Jimmy said. "They went crazy."

Sometimes the band played at Lewis Institute, which Dave Tough attended, and he added his drums to the little band. (It was Dave who found Floyd O'Brien playing trombone at a University of Chicago jam session. The latter was a musician whose restraint of mood gave emphasis to a gifted imagination and a constantly surprising technical equipment.) The dances at Lewis were "tea dances," on the model of those endorsed by the P.T.A. Each of them got fifty cents for the afternoon's work. Benny Goodman occasionally played with them, though Tesch felt that he was not close to their musical ideas. Joe Sullivan also played at Lewis. They played *Jazz Me Blues*, the Dixieland pieces, and numbers from the repertoire of the New Orleans Rhythm Kings.

Jim Lannigan got hold of a bass viol, watched how Chink Martin slapped it, and was soon able to play it in the band. Then, with Dave North on piano, they could call themselves an orchestra. They didn't have a business manager and hardly needed the inducement of cold cash to make them work. "Let's get together and play," was the first law of their land. Once when they (unsuccessfully) auditioned for a job, the manager commented, "All right, boys, we'll let you know." Jimmy said, "But you don't understand, mister, we just got to have this job."

Probably the manager was scared by the absence of written music. There was no system to their playing. The Blue Friars, often with Tesch leading informally, decided upon a number, then played chorus after chorus. At the end of 32 bars Tesch would nod and whoever was in the direction of the nod took off by himself. Musicians went for this kind of music and among them the Blue Friars were beginning to have a name. But in the fall of 1924 the Wolverines lost Bix. They were in New York at the time, playing the huge Cinderella Ballroom on Broadway. They tried out Sharkey Bonnano of New Orleans but he hadn't ripened; so they wired to Chicago for Jimmy MacPartland. While in New York the Wolverines recorded for Brunswick and many listeners, hearing MacPartland's cornet, mistook it for Bix. Actually his tone was bland compared to that of Bix and his style hadn't the rolling quality of the original Wolverines' cornet.

The Wolverines spent the winter in Florida, coming back to Indiana, their old stamping ground, for the spring college dances. Hartwell and Moore had left the band. Vic Berton, who had made the trip East with the Wolverines, was on drums, Jimmy Lord on clarinet. Voynow, the pianist, was finally the only member of the original outfit. Though there were temporary changes in personnel, every member of the Wolverines was eventually replaced by a member of the Austin Gang.

During the lean months the boys who'd been left behind had temporary jobs of varying duration. One was as the pit band in a movie house before the days of sound. Their job, of course, was to play music appropriate to the film. On one occasion the band, interested in the piece it was playing, was unaware that the newsreel was on. Marshal Foch solemnly laid a wreath on the tomb of the unknown soldier while the Austin Gang had an informal jam session, beating it out. Suddenly one of them noticed the discrepancy. "Holy smoke!" he exclaimed, "we're playing the wrong tune!" The manager of the theatre had made the same discovery and was on his way down the aisle, to give them their notice. It was funny, in a way. But they needed work and were relieved when Jimmy came back and with chubby Husk O'Hare, the most unmusical Chicagoan of them all, they formed Husk O'Hare's Wolverines. Over WHT the band was labeled O'Hare's Red Dragons.

With Floyd O'Brien, Dave North, and Dave Tough added to the Austin Gang, Husk O'Hare's Wolverines got a job at White City, a large dance hall of Chicago's south side amusement park. On Saturdays Mezz Mezzrow or Fud Livingston played third sax. A Goldkette unit consisting of Bix, Pee Wee Russell, and Trumbauer, was playing at Hudson Lake, Indiana, and sometimes came in to hear the band. Ben Pollack, who was at the Southmore, and Louis Armstrong, who was at the Sunset, both came out. Louis stood near the bandstand, said, "Hit it. Yeh, boy!"

While the band was still playing tea dances at Lewis, Tesch was practicing clarinet, blowing on Bud's before he got one of his own. Oftentimes he'd practice in the locker room of the Y.M.C.A., his style showing traces of the glissandi from violin playing.

At the Sunset and at Kelly's Stable Tesch heard Johnny Dodds, learning from him, as well as from Bix, a method of playing that was somewhat like trumpet phrasing. He also went to The Nest (later the Apex) where he sat in with Jimmy Noone, a clarinet player whose style was typical New Orleans,—fast runs of notes that seemed evenly spaced in tempo made up flowing passages, interspersed with long, sustained notes and sudden excursions into the upper register. Tesch learned the one without losing the other. Bud, meanwhile, had become interested in the tenor sax. When he heard Coleman Hawkins later on, in a Detroit ballroom, it was exactly the lesson he needed in order to develop a style of his own. Hawkins, who has since become known as a virtuoso of the tenor sax, then had a simple direct style, characterized by clear and precise attack.

The style of Husk O'Hare's Wolverines, at its best, was one stripped of the superfluous. It was strictly musical interpretation in which feeling had to be so welded to the music that you were not aware of it as a quality apart from the music. Naturally, they didn't formulate this. It remained for the critics to name it. But it should be possible to distinguish Chicago style on the basis of instrumentation alone. The Rhythm Kings had come nearer than any other white band in New Orleans to the Negro style while retaining much in the way of tradition that belonged to white Dixieland. Similarly, white Chicago style approached the style of Negro jazz in Chicago but held on to the white traditions kept alive by the Rhythm Kings and the Wolverines.

The music of the O'Hare Wolverines hadn't the flow of New Orleans (Negro) style, yet there was the same tendency to define each note. There was also, as no white band had developed it, the ability to cradle the note in the swing of the rhythm. Ensemble passages were marked by a closely knit polyphony and a sour tonality that became more pronounced as Tesch learned clarinet, Bud tenor sax. With Tesch it was not merely a dissonant tone quality, it was an unconscious hankering for the quarter-tone scale. Well-meaning friends told him what a bad tone he had. At times he professed to be worried about it but his playing was not affected.

Chicago style was closer to the beat than most styles having a comparable "swing." Describing it, Bud Freeman said, "This was right on the note. In order to keep time you have to think of pushing on the beat, all the time. There are fellows who play ahead of the beat or behind the beat. But on the beat gives you that fine rhythm. We worked it out from playing together. We studied and listened a lot." He said that you could compare it with the way Negro bands played; though it was not the same thing, it was similarly motivated: "It came from playing together. We used to listen to and love the same things."

At White City O'Hare's Wolverines stayed in the shell a great part of the night and when feeling good, begrudged themselves time off. They had some stocks, but usually played without arrangements. Sometimes Jimmy stood up to lead. In the band were Teschmaker, Jim Lannigan, Bud Freeman, Jimmy MacPartland, Dave Tough, Floyd O'Brien, Dave North, and Dick MacPartland. Later George Wettling played traps. Late at night when they played New Orleans tunes you could hear the high strong tone of Tesch's clarinet cutting through the dance hall din. A big hall and a big tone. Tesch showed the way in collective improvisation, slashing the tones of the upper register, the band getting hotter and the dancers so excited that the floor shook and the manager begged the musicians to take it easy.

On week ends at White City Sig Myers' Orchestra with Muggsy Spanier played opposite them. This band had tremendous sock, and was even closer to the spirit of the Negro bands than Husk O'Hare's Wolverines. The two bands undoubtedly affected each other. Muggsy was an old-timer. Back in the early twenties he'd had a cornet team with Bix. Keeping to the middle range of the cornet, Muggsy played in the rhythmic style of Oliver and Armstrong, and from the former may have gained his dexterity with mutes. A warm tone riding easy—that was Muggsy. And he kept to this style, even when playing in name bands. Years later, when a baton wielder told him to play high notes, Muggsy retorted, "Aw, get a piccolo!"

At the Columbia Hall "dancing school" where Myers' band played opposite a band with Louis Armstrong, there were real battles of music. It was tough, rough, and so noisy that the bands had to play loud to be heard! One band was on the floor and the other on a balcony. For a time the Rhythm Kings played there, and apparently felt a trifle condescending toward the younger musicians. One reaction was "We killed those guys!" But the Myers' band were not lacking in confidence, either, and boasted of how they "blasted" the Rhythm Kings.

For the White City job Myers had Volly De Faut on clarinet; Myers, violin; Floyd Town, sax; Shorty Williamson, piano; George Petrone, drums; Marvin Saxbe, banjo and guitar; Arnold Loyocano, bass; Muggsy and one other cornet; Bob Picilli, trombone. At the end of the White City engagement the band was re-formed to go into the Midway Garden at 60th and Cottage Grove. Tesch joined Muggsy for this job and the Wolverines broke up at last, Freeman, Lannigan, and Jimmy MacPartland going with Art Kassel.

The Midway Garden band shaped up around Tesch and Muggsy. A musician with whom he played on this job described Tesch, indicating how little his personality had changed: "He was a very odd guy. Not a whoop-it-up guy. He had lots of character and he was a fine musician, tough with every sax. He could really make them play. He learned from Jimmy Noone and from Dodds and Pee Wee. But Bix was his idol."

And Tesch was the same in other ways. Once, while playing a fashionable job on the North Side, Tesch needed a haircut. The customers kidded him about it so much that he finally had it clipped short. Seeing him come in that night the men in the band stood up and applauded. Tesch glared at them, embarrassed, sore. He walked out and didn't come back for three days.

For more than a month after he began playing at Midway Garden he came in each night, said hello, then sat down and got to work. Not a word out of him. Later, when he and Muggsy became friendly, they went to jam sessions together and often at night they'd have a few drinks, then go down to a French restaurant in the Loop.

Muggsy was from the South Side, where he'd gone to parochial school. So was George Wettling, who became the drummer in the Midway Garden band. Another recruit to this band from Husk O'Hare's Wolverines was Floyd O'Brien.

Jess Stacy came into the Midway Garden one night, wearing a tuxedo but no overcoat, shivering. None of the men in the band knew Jess very well, though some remembered him from the tea dance days. Stacy came directly to the point and said that he was looking for a job. He had been playing piano at a little place in the Loop that had closed down. Muggsy said, "Go on upstairs; we got all the gin upstairs." Stacy headed for the stairs, Muggsy watching him as he blew softly into his cornet. While Jess was getting warm the band played *Poor Little Rich Girl*, a number they really swung out on. Jess came down, feeling warmer inside. Muggsy asked him if he was ready to play and Jess nodded. "What would you like to play?" Muggsy asked. Jess said, "That *Poor Little Rich Girl* suits me fine." He sat down at the piano, chording skillfully with an easy rhythm. When the musicians came in with him they played softly so that they could listen to the piano.

Although Chicago's local of the American Federation of Musicians was Jim Crow (almost all locals except New York City are, even today) the musicians themselves got around this policy. They played together in the Negro district, at speakeasies patronized by musicians, and in the homes of such musicians as Johnny Dodds. "It was jam session all the time," Wettling remarked. Joe Marsala at that time did more listening than playing. But he liked Noone and Tesch and Dodds, and was learning clarinet himself. He drove a truck for a living, and bought records on pay day.

They jammed at The Cellar with Wingy Mannone, and at the 3 Deuces Bix often led the sessions. Eddie Condon played there a lot and after a night of it would buy a bottle of milk (from the wagon) to drink on the way home. The idea that the Chicagoans were at this time (1926-1928) amateurs was of course without foundation. Condon, for instance, had his first union job at the age of seventeen.

There was among them one bona fide amateur. This was Charles Pierce, a south side butcher who played jazz for the love of it. He used what profits he derived from the meat market to pay high salaries and thus attract the best men to his band. It was not a regular band but a pick-up outfit playing week-end engagements and making phonograph records. Pierce always supplied a bottle for these jobs. The first recorded example of Chicago music was made in 1926 when Charlie Pierce, with Muggsy and Tesch in the band, made some records for Paramount, a company that specialized in "race" records. Because no one knew the tune, Muggsy had to sing the verse of *Darktown Strutters*, then they waxed it. Tesch was nervous and kept pushing up too close to the mike.

Pierce played alto sax, and though his style lacked brilliance it was clean-cut and in the mood. Once Pierce heard a clarinet player he didn't like, hired him and put him in the band so that he could hear Teschmaker. He'd have the newcomer play a chorus and then have Tesch play six to show him.

Although the Chicagoans had jobs, the big hotels still went for the name bands. Often the Chicagoans, who were far better musicians, generally speaking, eked out a living in the joints that flourished during the Prohibition era. Most of these places were really low down, like a café on North Clark Street, described by Wettling, where the cab drivers came in with guns sticking in their leggings.

They'd get drunk and have battles. Then they'd begin to shoot. We'd duck into the back room, behind the safe. We would see those rods come up and duck.

The little clubs were settings for many fights. Young gangsters, coming in from outside, tried to break up the dance. If the law got around it was usually when the fighting was over. When it was too close, the drummer had to hold the bass drum in the air so it wouldn't get smashed. "But we got good money then," a musician confided. "One job on South State Street paid $118 a week."

The Midway Garden Orchestra got a job at the Triangle

Club at the end of its Midway Garden engagement. Although he paid the regular men well, the boss of the Triangle Club hired substitutes and extra men without paying them. They'd take out what they could in meals and drinks. When the union threatened to get tough the boss said he'd bomb the union. He meant it, too. But the regular men liked the job. As one of them put it: "We had the best band and conditions were good. It was cabaret class. Strictly west side crowd. Plenty of takers. The boss was shot in the stomach one night but we kept working. After that he walked sort of bent over."

North and south side gangs had their own leaders but Capone was boss. He would come into a place with seven or eight men. As soon as he got in, the door was closed. Nobody got in or out. He had a couple of hundred dollar bills changed into fives and tens and his bodyguards passed these around to the waiters and entertainers. The musicians always got five or ten dollars each for playing his favorite numbers, all of them sentimental things.

During these years George Wettling often worked on jobs with Joe Sullivan, with whom he went up to James Lake. Joe studied piano at the Conservatory of Music. When he first came around to play jobs—such as at Lewis Institute—he didn't know standards like *Tiger Rag*. He was influenced somewhat in this formative period by the trumpet-piano style of Earl Hines, but Sullivan's own style was characteristically gin-mill, reminding the listener of places he played in—smoky, raucous, dimly lit. Sometimes on the slow blues he would use a heavy left hand roll that he had learned from the obscure Negro "party-piano" players.

A music relatively free from the inhibitions and constraints of arranged popular music was bound to attract younger men. Some of these entered the picture early and stayed on. Some, like Joe Marsala and his brother Marty, were not to become known until the thirties. Others were lost sight of in later years. Nor were all of the Chicagoans from Chicago. Wettling was from Topeka, Zurke, a younger pianist than Sullivan who came under the influence of the latter, was from Detroit, and Jess Stacy was from Cape Girardeau, Missouri. Bud Jacobsen, the clarinet player, and John Mendel, trumpet, are usually called Chicagoans because they played on the Okeh record of *Crazeology*. In other words, it was the style that made the man. Rod Kless, the clarinetist, decided to come to Chicago after hearing the Austin Gang when the latter, né Husk O'Hare's Wolverines, were playing one of their first jobs, a summer place at Riverview Park near Des Moines in May, 1926. (He's also a Chicagoan by marriage. His wife is Bud Freeman's sister.)

Jack Teagarden wasn't very much in the Chicago picture though he recorded with Chicago musicians. Many of the Chicagoans met him for the first time in New York, when Pee Wee Russell said, "Come on, I've got a trombone I want you to hear."

Like Teagarden, Russell played with the Chicagoans more often on records and at jam sessions than in bands. He was born Charles Ellsworth Russell, Jr., March 27, 1906, in St. Louis, Missouri. Tall, thin, and apparently vague, Pee Wee's whole personality seems to change when he blows on a clarinet. Off the stand he looks like the sort of person about whom anecdotes are told, an attitude he inspires whether he wills it or not. One story told about him concerns the Chicago El, on which tokens were three for a quarter. Passing through the gate, Pee Wee paid a quarter each time, pocketing the two tokens change. Gradually they accumulated and he talked it over with an acquaintance. He explained how he'd got the tokens, and said, "Now what do I do with them?"

When Pee Wee was still much too young to venture across the river to East St. Louis or even go down to the wharves and listen to riverboat music, the family moved to Oklahoma. There, at the age of seven, he took violin lessons from a "lady teacher." After a few months he gave up the violin. In rapid succession he took up piano, drums, and clarinet. He was still playing the latter at the age of twelve, when he was a student at Western Military School, Alton, Illinois. In the school band he was fourth clarinet and that, in his own words, "meant there were four clarinet players in school, and I was the fourth worst."

When he entered the University of Missouri, Pee Wee took his clarinet with him. This time he did get down to the wharves. Negro bands, such as Fate Marable's, played on the riverboats. In St. Louis itself he heard Charlie Creath, a local cornet player who created his own blues style, playing with a deep, rough tone. There were also piano players and small bands in East St. Louis. Pee Wee got Saturday night jobs; "Sometimes," he explained, "I'd go away on a Saturday and turn up in college on Tuesday afternoon in time for a Monday class at eight o'clock."

Although in and out of Chicago, Pee Wee had an influence on its music. Goodman, on his early records, seemed to vacillate between Tesch's phrasing and Pee Wee's growl. Tesch, by his own admission, was an admirer of Pee Wee's style. Besides the growl, that sounded as though he were trying to play two tones at once, Pee Wee played with a sustained rhythmic flow in a tone that was very blue. Pee Wee was surprised that Tesch's opinion of him had survived. He said, "I learned plenty from Tesch. If he was alive today he would play more clarinet than anyone in the world."

As in the familiar blues line, he's "traveled all over," and on one job near Houston, Texas, played in a band with such a curiously mixed personnel that it's worth mentioning. Peck Kelly was on piano, Joe Loyocano, who got his apprenticeship with Papa Laine, played bass, and Leon Prima was on trumpet. The band also had in it Leon Rappolo, mentally ill but playing sensitive clarinet characterized by fugitive tone and delicate vibrato. And Pee Wee, who could double on saxes, probably did.

In the early twenties Red McKenzie was back in his home town, St. Louis, the Mound City from which the Blue Blowers got their name. "I was a bellhop in the Claridge," Red said, "and across the street was a place called Butler Brothers. Slevins worked there and there was a little colored shoe shine boy who used to beat it out on the shoes. Had a phonograph going. I passed with my comb, and played along. Slevin would have liked to play a comb but he had a ticklish mouth, so he used a kazoo. He got fired across the street and got a job in a big soda store. He ran into Jack Bland, who owned a banjo, and one night after work they went to his room. He and Slevin started playing. They got me. Gene Rodemich's was a famous band at that time. His musicians used to drop in at the restaurant where we hung out. They were impressed and told their boss.

"He took us to Chicago to record with his band, as a novelty. When we got to Chicago we went down to the Friars' Inn. About 1924 it was. Volly De Faut and Schoebel were there. Isham Jones was at the place and he asked us what instruments we were playing. He had us come to his office next day, and set the date for Brunswick. That was the time we made *Arkansas Blues* and *Blue Blues*. They say it sold over a million copies. Brunswick put us in a café in Atlantic City called the Beaux Arts. I met Eddie Lang in Atlantic City. In New York the Blue Blowers played the Palace in August, 1924."

After a trip abroad, where the band played at the Stork Club in London, McKenzie returned to America, and has been busy in the music business ever since. It was Red who fixed the first Okeh date for Bix, Eddie Lang, and Trumbauer, on which the band made *Singin' the Blues*. In 1927 he arranged a Paramount recording session at which a small band of Chicagoans made *Friars' Point Shuffle*. The following year four sides were made for Okeh under the band name McKenzie and Condon's Chicagoans. At this time Condon was with Morris Sherman at College Inn. Bud was with Herb Carlin at the Hollywood Bard. In between jobs with Art Kassel, Jimmy MacPartland and Jim Lannigan had had a run at the Friars' Inn. But it was already a cheap, dingy cabaret. The crowd had moved on.

On the McKenzie and Condon recording date were Jimmy MacPartland, Bud Freeman, Frank Teschmaker, Joe Sullivan, Jim Lannigan, Eddie Condon, and Gene Krupa. They made the discs in the old Okeh studio on Washington Street, standing on soap boxes. Jimmy said, "It was so wonderful to be together again that we really played." Bix (who wasn't allowed to record with musicians other than those in the Whiteman band) heard the records soon after they were made. "They were fine," he said, "the greatest I ever heard." "It was all right," Tesch admitted after playing *Nobody's Sweetheart* over and over, "but Bud played too much Armstrong."

Improvisational in spirit, *Nobody's Sweetheart* has an ensemble passage in the middle of the record, written by Teschmaker. It is proof enough that such passages may be written if the proper instrumentation is followed—one of a kind and a balance of almost equal melodic and rhythm sections. There has been much original writing done for the twelve- and fourteen-piece band, by such arrangers and composers as Fletcher Henderson, Jimmy Mundy, Bob Haggart, Mary Lou Williams, and Duke Ellington, yet it is usually only in fragments of even the good orchestrations that one finds a utilization of the discoveries made by the ensemble of small bands. Indeed, most arrangements adapt themselves to the conventional orchestra set-up and are in turn swallowed up by it. They resort to juxtaposed brass and reed choirs, harmony abounding in tone color and technical tricks useful in themselves but no more than a means,—the end must still rest on the arranger's skill, or lack of it. A further point is that *Nobody's Sweetheart* grew out of playing together. "The money didn't matter; we just had to play," may have been a slight exaggeration but there was some truth in it.

Just as the four Okeh sides represent adequately the type of Chicago music played by O'Hare's Wolverines, two sides recorded by Brunswick show to some extent what the Midway Garden band sounded like. Though the personnel differs from that band, Muggsy and Tesch dominate the records in the same way they dominated the playing of the band at Midway Garden. The titles are *There'll Be Some Changes Made* and *Darktown Strutters' Ball*. On the date were Muggsy, Tesch, Mezzrow (tenor sax), Sullivan, Krupa, and Condon, with McKenzie doing the vocal on *There'll Be Some Changes*. After playing until six in the morning, the musicians reported for the Brunwick date at nine, played around to start the tune, then put it on wax.

Benny Goodman is sometimes identified with Chicago-style music, a point that proves confusing to those who listen to his recordings. Few of them would be considered appropriate to the *direct melodic* approach of Chicago music. One of the Chicagoans explained this difference by saying, "Benny and his bunch liked Red Nichols; we couldn't go for that at all." Yet they saw quite a lot of Benny and there were certainly times when he played in a style that fitted well with theirs. An excellent example is from a Nichols' recording made in New York after Nichols had begun to use the Chicago men on his records. This was the Brunswick record of *Lazy Daddy*, on which Krupa and Sullivan also play. Benny's chorus is creative and along definitely melodic lines; the decorative phrases that often mark his playing are absent. Hot musicians in New York jumped when they heard the record, for the rhythm was exciting and the solo work of Sullivan and Goodman excellent. Benny's clarinet on this record has a thin reedy tone, not at all unpleasant but utterly unlike the round limpid tone with which he was to play a few years later.

Among the Negroes who have made records with one or more of the Chicagoans are "Happy" Cauldwell, tenor sax; Jimmy Noone, clarinet; Coleman Hawkins, tenor sax; Henry Allen, Jr., trumpet; and Zutty Singleton, drums. Not all of these men played Chicago style, or anything like it, nor can there be any attempt here to list the innumerable Chicago-style records and their personnel. However, it does seem essential to give the reader a starting point. For the rest, he can pursue the exhaustive research by Delaunay, Panassié and others, as to the merits of this and that record. Though the total number of Chicago-style records is somewhat limited, the fact that they were recorded under various pseudonyms made their discovery a sort of collector's nightmare. The two most recent masters to turn up were *Windy City Stomp* and another *Jazz Me Blues*. The former record is actually a metamorphosis of a popular song.

The Chicagoans were not always sure they were on the right track. Sometimes they wondered if they ought to go commercial. But most of the time, they didn't think about it. If you were a musician depending on the gangster joints and the taxi-dancehalls for a livelihood, you didn't think too much of today, much less tomorrow. Most of the Chicago musicians went in for bathtub gin and a few smoked marijuana. The continued use of marijuana resulted sometimes in a nervous "jive" playing against background harmonies, in contrast to straight melodic improvisation. From being ripe, the jive would soon get over-ripe. A musician would lose his talent for improvising on the melody and eventually his instrumental technique might also be affected. The ones who suffered most were not the famous ones, who had some patch of ground to stand on, but the obscure musicians who, as one jazz player expressed it, "climbed the bush to get out of this world." Then he said, "It's not a very pretty picture, is it?"

Another curious side to the Chicago story is that while the music was obviously a fusion of Negro and white influences, depending for its most significant qualities on the former, the musicians themselves were not always free of prejudice. Among Chicagoans, one who was imbued with the most naïve race prejudice, was himself famous for having come close to the Negro style of playing, and has acknowledged the indebtedness! But the anomalous stand taken by a few of the Chicago musicians was due most of all to the attitude of the society in which they lived.

When the 1928 recordings were made, most of the Chicagoans got offers of jobs with name bands. Jim Lannigan, however, soon fulfilled his boyhood ambition to play bass viol in a symphony orchestra. Jimmy MacPartland went with Pollack, and Tesch finally got a job with Jan Garber. Except for one trip East, Tesch did not leave Chicago. However, Tesch made several records while in New York, among them the Ted Lewis discs on which both he and Muggsy play. Garber's Orchestra was much better than the average name band but even so Tesch was not happy. He said, "I wonder if we'll ever be able to play hot jazz for a living."

Tesch is often pictured as having been a musical hermit at this period in his life. Of course, that was not so. He played jam sessions with such friends as Noone and Johnny Dodds. He was married, too, and happily so. But music was always an important part of his life. He saw a lot of Rod Kless, with whom he had become friendly in Des Moines, and he jammed with younger musicians such as Joe Marsala. At home he played Holst's *The Planets*, much as Bix played Debussy. His own records he played repeatedly, always listening closely. Here both his tenacity and his humility were apparent. A chorus might sound a little off, or the tone not quite right. As the conviction grew that something was wrong, Tesch would lay the record aside, take it up again, play it through once or twice more, then smash it deliberately.

Because Tesch had natural talent some of his friends were inclined to overestimate it and assume that he came by the style as you and I breathe or walk or talk. Seeing him with the clarinet held carelessly to his lips, notes tumbling out, spreading in broad crescendos that cut through the noise of a crowded hall,—it did look spontaneous. But he practiced continually and listened critically to his own playing.

That was Tesch and that was the spirit of Chicago style. That it was a melodic and rhythmic style having its own measurable qualities may be determined by listening to records. That it had a perceptible influence on subsequent hot music will hardly be questioned. Yet Chicago style as such began to decline in the late twenties, when its best exponents were absorbed in name bands. The musical spirit of the Chicagoans was swallowed up in the maw of something bigger and considerably less great than itself, the popular music business. This business, to exist, must predicate its methods on what it thinks the public will take, not on what it thinks the musicians themselves have to give. Thus, the music they had to play depended no longer on their creative ability but on how they could adapt themselves and their talents to the name band business.

With some fortunate exceptions, this transition was noticeable even on records. Many of them had less and less the "feel" of Chicago music. The Mezzrow sessions of the early thirties were largely jive music. *Mutiny in the Parlor* was worth listening to because, like Armstrong's *Tight Like This*, it was jive to the bone. One listened to the spurious *Sendin' the Vipers* because on it Floyd O'Brien none the less played beautiful trombone. The record that was good all the way through, with everyone playing "like crazy" was a very dim memory. For the panic was on, as one of the Mezzrow titles inferred, and it was to continue until the coming of a jitterbug era that, however ridiculous its excesses would seem to a sober public, was to give hot music a re-birth.

Chicago style went out with Tesch, who was given to strange quirks and unexpected moods. He was afraid of riding in automobiles. He didn't know how to drive and he got nervous when anyone drove a little too fast. He'd say, "Slow down or I'll get out." One night in January, 1932, Tesch and Wild Bill Davidson, who led the orchestra in which he played, were on their way to work. They were a little late but they weren't driving fast. A truck rammed into them. Tesch was thrown clear of the car and killed instantly. Davidson was hauled off to jail to answer questions. They told him Tesch had been killed. Davidson is said to have turned dazedly to his informant and asked, "Now what the hell am I going to do for a sax man?"

VIII

BOOGIE WOOGIE

EVEN BEFORE Prohibition the house-rent party flourished in Chicago's South Side. When rent day drew near often the only way to pay the landlord was to throw a party, which was called "pitchin' boogie." That meant open house for the entire neighborhood. The only entrance fee was fifty cents and a sack of sandwiches, or a jug of gin. One person who never had to bring any half-dollar, nor even his own gin, was Jimmy Yancey. He was always welcome. Jimmy, a born comedian and an old vaudeville trouper, was the life of the party. Around five o'clock in the morning when almost everyone was knocked out and things were getting pretty dull and awfully quiet, someone over in a corner came to life and yelled out, "Let's have some blues." Then Jimmy obliged with his *Five O'Clock Blues*, known as the *Fives* for short. No one called it *Boogie Woogie* then, but it had all the peculiarities of the piano style known today as Boogie Woogie.

Aside from its immense vitality, the most striking characteristic of the Boogie Woogie blues style is the rapid, incessant rhythm of the recurring bass figures, usually of a jerky or rolling nature. In making full use of the resources of the instrument, the Boogie Woogie is the most pianistic of all jazz styles.

183

As jazz came up from New Orleans each instrument of the orchestra developed its own characteristic style, so suited to its total possibilities and limitations of sonority, timbre, and technique as to make even the most modern instrumentation of a Stravinsky or Varèse sound incomplete. For the first time the instruments were allowed to speak in a language of their own.

However, the piano, which had never found more than a temporary place in New Orleans orchestras, had developed no appropriate jazz style. Later, when it found a place in the orchestra, its players remained more or less under the influence of European classicists. Even Hines, great as he is, shows the influence of the music of Chopin, not to speak of Nevin, or Rube Bloom.

On the other hand, Jimmy Yancey developed a style so pianistic that it could not be imagined on any other instrument; yet it shows not the slightest resemblance to the piano music of the nineteenth century Europeans. In creating his style Yancey had, apparently, never listened to conventional piano classics. He tried to get out of a piano just what was in it, and not to give an imitation of an orchestra, a trumpet, a voice, or a hurdy-gurdy. He succeeded most admirably. The piano is, after all, a percussion instrument and one capable of producing more than one rhythm at a time, although it takes considerable ingenuity to accomplish this. Not an instrument for intoning legato melodies of long-sustained sonorities, the piano was well suited to Yancey's style.

Rhythmically the Boogie Woogie is rather more primitive than most African music, but it is still more complex and polyrhythmic than the conventional piano style of Teddy Wilson or Fats Waller. The rapid patterns of the left hand which produce a hypnotic effect are often set against the ever-changing rhythms of the right hand, causing exciting cross-rhythms.

Melodically built of short scale-like figures, with many repeated notes and phrases emphasizing its economy of material, the Boogie Woogie style is nevertheless more chromatic than the ordinary blues. The most common motive seems to be a three-note descending scale passage. Sometimes, however, the melody for an entire chorus will consist of one note played with a great variety of rhythms and accents. The usual rhythm employed in this form of variation consists of a full chord in the right hand struck on the first beat and again a little before the fourth beat of each measure. The tremolo is a frequently used device. In heightening intensity, the tremolo has a percussive and rhythmic function rather than being used simply to sustain a tone.

The Boogie Woogie takes almost without exception the form of the twelve-bar blues, repeated with endless variation, but always in the same key. The harmony is principally tonic and dominant. However, there is no attempt at four-part harmony and the emphasis is often on the contrapuntal, with frequently only two parts used. In such cases the melody may be widely separated from the bass and progress in contrary motion. Throughout there is an ignorance of conventional harmony which amounts to a most refreshing disrespect for all rules. This is a music constructed out of the piano keyboard rather than a harmony book.

Jimmy Yancey has never played piano on the stage. Born in Chicago, he joined the Bert Earl Company as a boy of six and traveled across America singing and doing his "buck and wing" dances. He even made one trip to Europe and appeared before King George and the Royal Family in London. But his piano playing he saved for himself and for a few friends who liked the blues. On the piano, Jimmy just worked things out for himself. His brother Alonzo also played, specializing in rags and stomps, but Jimmy preferred the blues; that was all he ever tried to learn. When he left vaudeville in 1913 and went back to Chicago to settle down, he found more time to practice his blues. Playing in south side barrel-houses, or wherever he found a piano, Yancey soon became popular, especially with the ladies, and was in demand for house parties. All Jimmy had to do was to go in anywhere and sit down at the piano; the women flocked around and took care of him. He didn't have to worry about a job in those days.

In the years that followed, Yancey composed many blues. Today he has a bigger repertory, as well as more technique, than most of the Boogie Woogie pianists. His first piece, the *Fives*, is probably the germ from which most of the piano blues of the Boogie Woogie type grew, and after a quarter of a century, it can still hold its own in dynamic interest and vitality when compared with later versions.

Although Yancey has worked for the last twelve years as a ground-keeper at the Chicago White Sox ball park, down on 35th Street, where he keeps the infield in trim and rolls down the basepaths, he can still roll out bass rhythms on the piano. In his home at 3525 South Dearborn he has no piano, but once a week he goes over to his sister's place and practices. If you should happen to be in a gin mill or in one of Chicago's many small clubs along South State Street when Jimmy wandered in, you would have a night of unforgettable music. One such time occurred on a cold windy night during Christmas week of 1938, at the 29 Club. Those were the nights when Johnny Dodds was leading his small band, which included Nat Dominique and "Tubby" Hall. Not more than a dozen customers were in the place, for everyone had spent all his money for Christmas, and night life was at low ebb. Dodds' old clarinet was on the bum and he couldn't play much, which didn't add to the hilarity. The joints of his instrument wouldn't hold together and he kept lighting matches to try to swell the cork.

Then Dodds got Jimmy Yancey up on the stand, and things began to happen. Waitresses who had stood like wall-flowers all evening began an irrepressible swaying. The small dance floor had been deserted, but now everybody felt the urge to get up and "shake that thing." Even the cook came in from the kitchen, to see what had occasioned this unaccustomed life and strange noise. One by one, the men in the band joined in, and soon Dodds forgot all about his clarinet not working and wailed the blues as he must have done back in the low-life days of Storyville. Such an exciting racket hadn't descended upon the 29 Club in years.

Although Jimmy Yancey has not yet received the credit and fame so long overdue to him, several of his "boys" have taken Boogie Woogie out of its hiding places in the dives of Chicago. The most famous of Jimmy's boys are Meade "Lux" Lewis and Albert Ammons. "Pine Top" Smith was another. Poor Pine Top never lived to see Boogie Woogie make its Carnegie Hall début. Several years ago, he was shot down in a brawl over "some ol' gal in a cheap West Side dance hall," according to Mayo Williams. And Pine Top died as he had lived. Probably the most erratic and flighty character of Chicago's jazzmen, he kept everyone guessing what he would do next. He slept all day, wandered from one club to another all night, and was apt to drive up to a friend's house at 5:00 A.M. in a taxi, and get the friend out of bed to pay his fare. Like Yancey, Pine Top had traveled the Theatrical Owners' Booking Agency circuit as a tap dancer in vaudeville. He was one of Maddy Dorsey's pickaninnies. When he outgrew the part, he settled in Chicago in the early twenties. Even then he didn't stay put and, at certain periods, was a well-known figure around the red-light districts of Omaha and St. Louis. About 1928, a short time before he was killed, Pine Top lived in a Chicago rooming-house at 4435 Prairie, where, by some fortunate coincidence, Albert Ammons and Meade Lux Lewis also lived. Albert was the only one of the trio who had a piano, and there were frequent cutting sessions in Albert's room when the three got together.

Luckily, Pine Top recorded several numbers and his music has exerted an ineradicable influence on many other pianists. His composition, *Pine Top's Boogie Woogie*, is not only the most widely copied of all piano blues, but gave its title to the style. The title, incidentally, has no special meaning; it was just something he got together at a house party in St. Louis, he told Ammons. A piano solo with talking, the *Boogie Woogie's* words explain what sort of dance accompanies the music.

From the first somber tremolo of *Pine Top's Boogie Woogie*, his first record, to the end of *Now I Ain't Got Nothin' at All*, his last in the Vocalion series, there is not a superfluous note. We can only admire Pine Top's sincerity and zestful spirit in these records. One cannot describe the effect Pine Top produces with the most direct simplicity. In the sixth chorus of the original version of his *Boogie Woogie*, he builds his entire solo by repeating a simple four-note scale motif. In the corresponding eighth chorus of the re-issued version, with even greater effect, he constructs his solo by repeating a single tone throughout over the primitive rumbling of the bass. The fourth variation of both arrangements further illustrates Pine Top's genius in making thrilling music without any melodic movement. As a blues singer, Pine Top was a folk artist of rare distinction, in spite of a peculiar high-pitched voice.

Pine Top didn't quite make his last recording date. Mayo Williams had him signed for another session with Vocalion. The morning of the date, his wife rushed in an hour late, and as Williams began to bawl her out for not getting Pine Top up in time, she calmly said, "Pine Top's dead. He was killed last night." Pine Top, it seems, had been "rambling 'round the town" once too often. When "the butcher finally cut him down," America lost an artist of the first rank.

By some strange premonition, a few days before he died Pine Top called Albert Ammons aside and said, "Albert, I want you to learn my *Boogie Woogie*." With what success Pine Top taught and Albert learned the piece everyone may witness today. For no one can approach Ammons in his performance of *Pine Top's Boogie Woogie*. Pine Top's naïve and simple performance was splendid, but Ammons' greater power

and imagination make his own version an astounding masterpiece. Chorus after chorus flows from his agile and tireless
fingers; even the most intricate passages are played with clarity. As he piles up climax after climax, one thinks surely that
in the next second the piano must fly to pieces. But there is
always another chorus. The secret is, of course, in the joyful
flame which burns within Ammons, for no one, not even
Fats Waller, whom he admires, ever enjoyed playing the
piano half as much as he. Only this indomitable joy has kept
his creative spark alive and made him go on playing through
many lean seasons in Chicago. This shows in his music. Without trying, he can arouse more enthusiasm than a dozen ordinary pianists.

Albert Ammons is younger than most of the Chicago blues
pianists, but he was old enough to be a member of the Eighth
Illinois Home Guards during the World War. In his early
teens he joined the bugle and drum corps. They had fourteen
buglers and fourteen drummers; Albert was one of the drummers. Both his parents played piano. Not long after the war,
he started to learn the blues and soon knew two or three good
pieces. He listened to the Yancey brothers and to other Chicago pianists, including Hersal Thomas, another remarkable
musician who never gained more than local fame. Hersal
played all the favorite blues and was known especially for his
own *Suitcase Blues*. In those days if a pianist didn't know the
Fives and the *Rocks* he'd better not sit down at the piano
at all. Whenever Hersal Thomas, who made a deep impression on young Ammons, came to a party, the other pianists
were afraid to play; so he became unusually popular and got
all the girls.

It was about this time, around 1924, that Ammons, working for the Silver Taxicab Company, met another driver, Meade
Lux Lewis. Lux was also learning the blues, as were a few of
the other drivers, and occasionally they went over to someone's house and had a Boogie session. Once when the Silver

manager couldn't find a single company cab on the streets, he decided to fit up a clubroom with a piano for the boys, so he'd know where to find them when they got a call.

Albert and Lux began to make money playing for club parties and house "kados." Those were the big Prohibition days, and with several jugs on hand, everyone, including the pianists, got stewed. When a house party was raided, Albert and Lux hid outside on the window sill; after the Law had cleared out the mob they climbed back inside and finished the unemptied jugs.

Ammons, although strictly an "ear" man, has always been an excellent orchestra pianist, as well as a blues soloist, and has organized some of Chicago's best small orchestras. One of his first jobs with one of these combinations was on the Illinois Central Railroad excursions to the South. A baggage car was fitted up as a dance hall and the orchestra played for the passengers during the trip. Albert went as far as New Orleans, where his Boogie Woogie astonished local musicians. Although some of the same bass figures were used in the blues as played by early New Orleans pianists, their use was not so continuous throughout a composition as it was later in Chicago and the Middle West, and therefore not Boogie Woogie in the stricter sense.

Back in Chicago, after a few seasons with the Louis Banks Orchestra, Ammons got his own band into the Club De Lisa late in 1934. For two years he played there with a picked five-piece band, including Guy Kelly, Dalbert Bright, Jimmy Hoskins, and Israel Crosby, which packed more power than a fifteen-piece outfit. By 1936 he had lost his men to larger commercial orchestras, and the next season found him playing alone for "cakes and coffee" at the It Club. By the fall of 1938, Ammons had again assembled a band for the Claremont Club, when he got his chance to go to New York for the Carnegie Hall concert and a long engagement at the Café Society. In New York he was at last given ample opportunity to make solo discs. His *Shout for Joy* (Vocalion), *Boogie Woogie Stomp* (12-inch Blue Note), *Bass Goin' Crazy* and *Monday Struggle* (Solo Art), are outstanding.

It was Meade Lux Lewis who first made Jimmy Yancey's name known with his *Yancey Special*. Meade Lux was born in Chicago in 1905. Although his father was musical and had played guitar and composed a bit, Lux did not start to learn music until he was about sixteen. Then his father began to teach him violin. One night, about a year later, Meade happened to hear Jimmy Yancey play. He knew that was "the real thing." Lux resolved then and there to give up the violin and learn to play blues on the piano. Although he heard plenty of good music around Chicago, by "Cripple Clarence," Jimmy Blythe, Lem Fowler, and the Yancey brothers, Lux was self-taught on the piano. For four or five years he played nothing but blues.

After a few odd jobs, including taxi-driving and a little traveling to Michigan and Kentucky, Lux made his first phonograph record in 1927. It was the *Honky Tonk Train Blues*, one of the earliest and most famous of all Boogie Woogie records. Meade's father had been a Pullman porter, and for a while they had lived over on South La Salle, near the New York Central tracks. A hundred times a day the big expresses roared by, whistling shrilly, making the entire house quake. So it was natural for Meade Lux to work out a train piece. The result proved to be the most phenomenal Boogie Woogie solo ever composed. For a while it had no special name; then one night Lux tried it out at a house party. When he tore into it, some fellow who had just dropped to hear the new music exclaimed:

"What kind o' man is that! What do ya call that thing?"

Lux said, "That's a train blues."

The other guy said, "Well, we're all together here. You ought to call it the *Honky Tonk Train Blues*."

"Well, all right! Let's call it the *Honky Tonk Train Blues*."

The original record was made for Paramount, a small company in Wisconsin. It was recorded even before *Pine Top's Boogie Woogie*, but not released for two years. A short time later, the Paramount Company went out of business when the depression struck, and Lux's record was unobtainable. Lewis dropped back into complete obscurity; even his friends almost forgot that he played piano.

The story of his re-discovery has often been told. John Hammond, an ardent collector, who had a "beat-up" copy of the Paramount record, couldn't find a clean one or have more copies made; so he began to search for Meade Lux. For almost two years he had no success, although he asked everyone he knew, and advertised in the papers. Finally in the fall of 1936, he met Albert Ammons in Chicago's Club De Lisa. Ammons was the first person who had ever heard of Lux. In a few days Meade Lux was located in a south side garage washing cars. He thought he could still remember the *Honky Tonk*, and after a few days' practice was ready to record it again for release on Parlophone in England. The next spring he got a job with his three-piece band, known as Lux and His Chips, at Doc Higgins' Tavern. A few weeks later he was working by himself at Bratton's Rendezvous. During these days Lux had his Decca and Victor recording dates, and made a third version of the *Honky Tonk*.

The descriptive qualities of the *Honky Tonk Train Blues*, with the suggestion of latent power in the introduction, the signal to the engineer, the wheels clicking over the rail joints, and the furious journey as the train rushes through the various stations, are remarkable in themselves, but not as unusual as are the purely musical qualities of the piece.

The skill with which Meade Lux can improvise for twenty or thirty minutes on a theme such as the *Honky Tonk* is astounding. His ideas seem unlimited; in developing them, he always gives an unexpected twist to the melody. A new technical idea is used for each chorus; one composed of high tremolos and repeated chords is followed by a variation based on light glissandi, and that in turn by one strongly rhythmic, with heavy bass figures for contrast. Dynamic variety and cross-rhythms have been employed to a much greater extent by Meade Lux than by any other pianist. From the drive and complexity of rhythm one might imagine that the *Honky Tonk Train Blues* was played by two pianists; when one sees it performed, one wonders how such simplicity of technique can produce torrents of tone from a very small range of notes. Many passages which sound like three or four hands are played in the old pre-Bach hand position without even using the thumbs, thus aiding relaxation. The recurring bass figure does not suggest monotony or lack of invention, but holds the listener. In common with other self-taught pianists of this school, Meade Lux does not use the damper or any other pedal, except to strike with his foot for the percussive effect.

Whether all honky-tonk music should be played and recorded only on broken-down, out-of-tune pianos is a debatable issue, but even the most dilapidated pianos found in Chicago's barrel-houses failed to dampen Lux's inspired improvisations. Boogie Woogie men usually prefer an upright to a grand piano, the action of which is too stiff for their gymnastics. They need "a real limber piano," and when they find one, it's "just too bad."

So fabulous a reputation did Meade Lux gain from the *Honky Tonk* that many think of him as a "one tune" pianist. The falsity of this view is shown by the variety of Meade Lux Lewis' recordings, which appear on nine different labels. Further, his repertory is constantly growing. More remarkable is the large variety of styles he has at his command.

Yancey Special has been the vehicle for some of Lux's most inspired improvisations. After the spectacular *Honky Tonk* this blues seems rather sedate, but is equally great in its own quiet way.

One receives a new surprise on hearing the celeste played

by Meade Lux for the first time; for a more apt and natural style cannot be imagined for a celeste. Such a variety of beautiful and delicate shadings of tone as we find in the *Celeste Blues* is entirely unknown in Western music, and has been produced before only by the Balinese gamelan. To those who have heard Balinese music, this analogy is no fabrication of the imagination. Balinese and Boogie Woogie music are both intensely dynamic and full of joyous vitality. Both make effective and idiomatic use of percussion instruments in producing a variety of nuances and maximum sonority. In Bali, where music is also an integral part of the life of the people, it is used for dance accompaniment, and to precipitate a state of trance. Both Balinese music and the Boogie Woogie derive their strength and sureness of form from the fixed solidarity of the 4—4 meter which somehow is no hindrance to variety of rhythm. In Bali, too, music is strongly syncopated, with the rhythm often seeming ready to lose its balance in the rapid patterns of shifting accents.

A common observation of novices, even intelligent ones, is that the Boogie Woogie has no melody. Aaron Copland, in *Modern Music*, writes of the "lack of any shred of melodic invention." Granted that there is no tune in the Irving Berlin manner and that no one goes down the street whistling the *Honky Tonk*, there is nevertheless unusual melodic charm.

As in Balinese music, the melodic development consists of simple and logical yet satisfying patterns of notes in a limited range, usually proceeding conjunctly. Often in the more elaborate melodic texture there is incessant arabesque and figuration based on the essential notes of the melody.

Lux had never seen a celeste until the day in February, 1936, when he walked into the Decca Studio in Chicago. He was intrigued by the small box that looked like a toy piano, sat down to try it, and was soon absorbed in its strange sounds. So were the astonished engineers, who finally told Lux to let it cool off a moment and then try making a record. The result was the *Celeste Blues.*

For years Meade Lux has shown remarkable talent for whistling which resembles somewhat the early cornet style of Armstrong. Evidently he did not sit in vain at the feet of King Oliver's Creole Band at the Sunday matinées held at the Lincoln Gardens. In the *Whistling Blues,* we have the arhythmic phenomenon of swing exemplified in its anticipatory aspect rather than the more common one of retardation. Boogie Woogie pianists, more than most jazz musicians, tend to use anticipation. Repetition of this device produces an inner reaction of cumulative energy which strives to break its bonds. As with Bessie Smith's tiger, one has the feeling that Lewis is "ready to jump." The *Whistling Blues* is unusual in that the regular pulses, the heavy chords which mark the tempo, are all played just a little before the beat, which is indicated only by Lux's stomping.

The first appearance of Meade Lux Lewis in New York was at the "first swing concert" at the Imperial Theatre in May, 1936. Amid all the confusion, he had to play on a new grand and was not at his best. Hardly anyone knew who he was or paid any attention to him. A year later, Lux was engaged at Nick's old basement tavern in the Village, but the Boogie Woogie was still too far ahead of the times. Bad management and the usual summer slump may have contributed to forcing him out; anyway, after six weeks, Meade returned to Chicago and went on relief. In December, 1938, Meade Lux made his third try in New York; this time, he clicked. With Albert Ammons and Pete Johnson, the Kansas City Boogie Woogie artist, Lux was the sensation of the Carnegie Hall concert of American Negro music, which was held in December. Coast-to-coast radio network appearances, night-club jobs, and recording dates followed for the trio. National magazines and newspapers carried their story, and at Café Society, the three became the latest rage in swing. New York had finally caught up with the Boogie Woogie.

In "Cripple Clarence" Lofton, Chicago still has a character as picturesque and eccentric as Pine Top. An almost savage crudeness and intensity more than compensates for what he lacks of Pine Top's subtlety and refinement. Down on South State Street, a little above 47th, is a saloon, lately known as the Big Apple, which might well be called "Cripple Clarence's Boogie School." Here many young aspiring blues players meet to hear and learn from Lofton and one another. Sometimes a fellow who is only a beginner comes in and Lofton shows him a few things, and before long he can play a piece or two. As Cripple Clarence says, "I gotta help these boys along, so when us old fellows are gone there'll be some more comin' up."

Such a situation is hard to imagine in one of America's modern cities, when we consider how radio, the common leveler, has killed the blues throughout the country, and most youngsters, if they play at all, are seeking to copy Teddy Wilson or Eddie Duchin. Some nights there may be seven or eight piano players in the joint at one time, and occasionally other old-timers drop in. There was one evening when Jimmy Yancey, Meade Lux, and Clarence engaged in a cutting session and Clarence came out a poor third; but on other nights he has reversed the decision over the same men.

No one can complain of Clarence's lack of variety or versatility. When he really gets going he's a three-ring circus. During one number, he plays, sings, whistles a chorus, and snaps his fingers with the technique of a Spanish dancer to give further percussive accompaniment to his blues. At times he turns sideways, almost with his back to the piano as he keeps pounding away at the keyboard and stomping his feet, meanwhile continuing to sing and shout at his audience or his drummer. Suddenly in the middle of a number he jumps up, his hands clasped in front of him, and walks around the piano stool, and then, unexpectedly, out booms a vocal break in a bass voice from somewhere. One second later, he has turned and is back at the keyboard, both hands flying at lightning-like pace. His actions and facial expressions are as intensely dramatic and exciting as his music. Clarence likes to work with a drummer. Last winter, one night, he had two of them and was trying his best to keep at least one sober.

Clarence's joint is no high class place; beer and sandwiches are five cents, other drinks ten. There's no checkroom; you park your coat and hat on top of the piano, or leave them on, and pull up a chair beside the piano and get your ear full of the crudest and most honest-to-goodness piano playing you ever heard.

They close up early, about 1:00 A.M., and then Cripple Clarence is off to make his nightly round of South Side spots. Almost as soon as he walks in a place, he takes over the show and is sitting at the piano strutting his stuff. Or else he has found a girl, and is tearing up the dance floor. In spite of being lame, he could probably win a "shag" contest. Soon he leaves, and wanders down Chicago's dark streets until he comes to the next tavern or club that has a piano. Finally the dawn catches up with Clarence and he hurries home to bed to be ready for another big night.

One always has the feeling when Clarence sings the blues that he is really moaning his own troubles. For he not only sings the blues, but lives the blues. Sometimes, if you happen to meet him on a street corner, he'll stop you, and with out-stretched arms, sing his latest blues.

Years ago his prize piece was *Strut That Thing*. Now, remodeled a little and even better, it's called *I Don't Know*. One night recently he had a brilliant new number called *Streamline Train*. The next night, when a "pupil" wanted to hear it again and even tipped him a dime, Cripple Clarence couldn't recall ever having played it. A week later he again announced the *Streamline Train*, and out came the *Cow Cow Blues*, note for note.

Cow Cow Davenport, another pioneer of early Chicago days, came originally from Alabama. After playing in honky-tonks and houses of prostitution in the coal-mining districts, the T.O.B.A. circuit booked his vaudeville act in Negro theatres throughout the South. The act consisted of comedy numbers, as well as singing and playing blues. Cow Cow was a prolific song-writer. The lyrics were written by his wife, a snake-charmer. They still have the snakes, which they keep in their bathroom. The most popular of Cow Cow's songs is *You Rascal You*, which, however, was published under the name of his friend, Sam Theard, a member of the troup.

About 1920, Cow Cow went to Chicago, where he greatly influenced many younger musicians, and later made a large number of phonograph records. In recent years he has lived in Cleveland, appearing rarely as a musician, since he and his wife have opened a small restaurant on Central Avenue. In the front room is an old upright on which Cow Cow occasionally plays. Although he complains that his fingers are stiff, he can still knock off the *Cow Cow Blues* and a few of his other old tunes, including the widely copied *Chimes Blues*. His best known piano solo, *Cow Cow Blues*, is notable for its melodic treatment of repeated notes. Another outstanding characteristic of Cow Cow's style is his development of the "walking bass," an effect much used today by string bass players, consisting of a rapid movement of single bass notes up and down the chords. Before it became a purely instrumental piece, the *Cow Cow Blues* started out to be a train number, and even Cow Cow's name came from the words, which were about a cow-catcher.

Many other great early Boogie Woogie pianists have dropped out of sight altogether. Romeo Nelson is one of the ones who have disappeared. Apparently no one in Chicago has ever heard of him. Yet, about 1929, he made a record of a piano solo, *Head Rag Hop*, a masterpiece which alone places him in the front rank. With the spirit of "Man, I'm gonna *ruin* this piano," he plunges into his solo. His playing has brilliance and his crude but prodigious technique is used with startling and dramatic effect. The backing of his record, a vocal number, *Gettin' Dirty Just Shakin' That Thing*, contains piano passages which in their unrestrained enthusiasm equal the work in *Head Rag Hop*. It is certainly pitiful that a musician who could make so wonderful a record remains unknown, unappreciated, and entirely forgotten. But the Boogie Woogie is the most non-commercial music in the world, in the best and worst sense of the word. Since those who play it make no concessions to popular tastes and trends, the pianists have seldom been able to earn a living from their art, nor have they been able to fit into the conventional dance orchestra.

Head Rag Hop has fortunately been reissued recently (Hot Record Society, release #8) but what we need is the opportunity to enjoy Romeo in person. When he made his record Romeo lived down in the district between 37th and 39th Street, near Cottage Grove. This section was leveled to the ground about 1936 in a slum-clearance P W A project, and Romeo might as well have been buried beneath one of the enormous piles of brick, for all the chance there is of finding him today. Some time ago, after a long search, Meade Lux Lewis thought he had located Nelson; he heard of a Romeo who hung around a saloon at 43rd and South Parkway. We went to see him, but he turned out to be Romeo Briggs. He was a pianist too; evidently there's a Boogie Woogie pianist in almost every house on Chicago's South Side; Briggs's *Detroit Special* was very good.

Another Boogie Woogie artist who has disappeared is Montana Taylor. No one can tell what happened to him. His early record of *Detroit Rocks* employs the well-known "rocks" variety of bass, similar to that used in *Honky Tonk Train Blues*. His *Indiana Avenue Stomp* also shows that Montana was a pianist gifted with great rhythmic solidity and fertile melodic invention. Taylor, who lived in Chicago for a while, has also spent some time in Indianapolis and Detroit.

Another pianist lost somewhere between Chicago and Detroit is Charlie Spand, who was known principally as a fine blues singer. About 1929 he made an old Paramount record with guitarist Blind Blake titled *Hastings Street*, in which there is a rhythmic background played by xylophones, rattles, and a whole battery of tom-toms. Throughout is a dark and ominous quality not found in so great a degree in the works of others.

Spand plays his *Soon This Morning* on another unusual Paramount record called *Hometown Skiffle*, an all-star affair which gives realistically a scene at a house party. A similar Vocalion record entitled *Jim Jackson's Jamboree* presents the exciting "Speckled Red" doing his best to "hit that Boogie Woogie." He attempts to play Pine Top's solo, but it's his own old favorite, variously known as *Wilkins Street Stomp, The Dirty Dozen*, or *St. Louis Stomp*.

Speckled Red belongs to the group of pianists, including Cripple Clarence and Romeo Nelson, notable for abundance of power. Notwithstanding his apparent crudeness, he has amazing virtuosity. In Speckled Red's playing we find the simplicity of Pine Top, plus the sparkling brilliance and contagious enthusiasm found in Romeo's *Head Rag Hop*. He is one of the rare artists who seems to get better as he goes along, such is his abundance of ideas. Despite his zestful, almost frenzied style, he always gives a great impression of ease.

Will Ezell, one of the best and most popular of Chicago's pianists during the early twenties, fell into obscurity with the coming of the depression and the repeal of Prohibition. Before he faded into oblivion, Ezell made a great record for Paramount, *Pitchin' Boogie*, in which he had the help of a rhythm section and a somewhat wheezy cornet. This sensational record, labeled a piano solo with instrumental accompaniment, shows just what can happen when a small band gets "in a Boogie groove." For low-down, gut-bucket music with barrel-house atmosphere, this disc could hardly be excelled.

Chicago was not alone in its cultivation of blues pianists. One day during the World War, Doug Suggs blew in from St. Louis with his *Mr. Freddie Blues*, and after his legendary stop at a 31st Street saloon, the Chicago Boogie men had another classic on their "must list." The Mound City had been developing its own Boogie Woogie and Suggs left behind him a number of young pianists who carried on. After the disgraceful "race riots" of 1919 the blues continued to be played and sung in dives along the Mississippi, especially over on the other bank, in East St. Louis. The Paramount Company, intent upon recording the best blues, sent for several pianists to come up from St. Louis, and thus we have preserved a few examples of the best of the St. Louis school of Boogie Woogie.

Wesley Wallace's *No. 29*, which depicts a free ride on the railroad running from Cairo up to East St. Louis, is another train piece, entirely different in type but in its own way almost as great a *tour de force* as *Honky Tonk Train Blues*. Musically and descriptively, both these unaffected solo compositions are more stimulating and successful than Honegger's pretentious *Pacific 231*. Rather than featuring polytonality, *No. 29* stresses polyrhythm, using a juxtaposition of 3—4 and 4—4. With his left hand playing throughout in 3—4 meter, Wallace demonstrates convincingly that it is possible to swing in other than duple time. The reverse of this exciting record is *Fanny Lee Blues*, similar to the sparse style of Ezell's early work but with all the sobriety and drive of Pine Top.

Henry Brown, another talented member of the St. Louis group, has several good compositions to his credit, the most interesting being *Deep Morgan Blues*, *Stomp 'Em Down*, and *Henry Brown Blues*, which resembles the style of Cow Cow.

Jabo Williams also made the trip up from St. Louis. He is

a pianist of great imagination. Uninhibited by the restrictions of classical form, his enormous vitality leads him to the most unconventional modes of expression. His *Jabo Blues*, played at an incredible speed, sounds at times like a player-piano roll gone on a rampage.

Some two hundred miles up the Missouri River there early developed in Kansas City another center of American music. Pete Johnson, the ace Kansas City Boogie Woogie artist, remembers 'way back when the best blues were played by Slamfoot and Booty. In those days, the *Four O'Clock Blues* was popular at house parties. They must have passed out an hour earlier in Kansas City than they did in Chicago during Yancey's time.

Pete Johnson, whose uncle Charles was one of the old-time pianists, was born in 1904 in Kansas City. He started out as a drummer in a school band and didn't take up piano until he was eighteen. Even then he had no lessons, but in three years he could really play. Before long he was working in the small three- and four-piece bands which spring up like mushrooms in Kansas City.

There has often been a close correlation between political corruption and the development of hot jazz. The jazz band has always been an urban institution and flourished only in shady places of amusement which could support it, such as dance halls, houses of prostitution, gin mills, gambling joints, and other underworld spots. It was no mere accident that jazz first sprang up in the South's largest city, New Orleans, which was then the most wide-open, vice-ridden and corrupt city in the history of the New World. Kansas City has also provided abundant proof of the long-recognized fact that the quality of American government reaches its lowest ebb in the cities. The notorious Pendergast machine had been well greased for over a score of years, and by the time Prohibition was introduced it was really humming. With the attending graft and laxity in enforcing closing hours and other regulations, Kansas City's night life grew by leaps and bounds. Dozens of small clubs, all employing musicians, were opened.

Pete Johnson got a job playing in the Hawaiian Gardens. That was before it was finally raided and closed. There he met Joe Turner, and a partnership was started which has lasted over ten years. Joe was a bartender and occasionally did a little blues shouting on the side. He was a large, tall young man with a powerful voice; when he sang, he didn't need a microphone. For that matter Pete's piano playing didn't sound any weaker than Joe's voice. So when they teamed up they had dynamite. Pete Johnson can hold his own as a soloist with any pianist, and as an accompanist is almost unrivaled. The Boogie Woogie has often been found in conjunction with vocal blues and is ideally suited as a style to the accompaniment of the blues.

This pair worked in many a tavern along 18th Street and finally landed with their small orchestra in the Sunset, on 12th Street, one of the town's famous spots. When the Sunset closed in 1937, they moved across the street to the Lone Star, one of the gayest of Kansas City's Negro night clubs. When one of these Kansas City clubs gets roaring full blast there's nothing comparable to be found in New York's Harlem or even on Chicago's South Side.

The garden of the Lone Star was out-of-doors under a tent, back of a big doublestore building which housed a barroom on one side and a poolroom on the other. In one back corner of the crowded barroom was a barbecue stand and up a few steps was the garden cabaret. Gaily decorated, the place was full of rickety wooden tables and benches crowded with carefree people. Almost everyone drank beer, ten cents a bottle, and paid the waitress when they got it, or else they didn't get it.

Over at one end, on the other side of the small dance floor, was the orchestra shell with barely room for an old upright, the drum set, a bass, a few chairs and the omnipresent slot-kitty. Most small Kansas City orchestras depend on customers' feeding the kitty with tips to make up their night's pay. No one seemed to know just who was in the orchestra; its size and personnel were constantly changing. It started out each night about ten o'clock with Pete and his drummer Merle playing together; one by one others came in and dropped out. By one or two o'clock there might be six or seven in the band, and before closing time it had simmered down again to Pete and the drummer. There was a 1:00 A.M. closing law but no one paid any attention to that. Although practically outdoors, they kept up the racket until about four.

At midnight the first floor show went on, which was the signal for everyone from the poolroom and even persons out on the street to rush in and jam the place. They stood all over the seats and on top of the tables to get a view of the show. If the orchestra wasn't too crowded and you wanted to sit down you could sit on the stand while others stood on the seats. It sounds like a topsy-turvy mad-house and that's just what it was. After the show there was no lessening of tension, for almost before it was over a concerted yell went up, "Roll 'em, Pete," and Pete let go with a torrent of notes as everyone made a scramble for the dance floor. The fellows put on their caps to dance; there was no place to check them. With Joe shouting and whipping the crowd to a wild frenzy, the place literally "jumped for joy." There was hardly room on the floor for the dancers to do more than stand in one spot and "roll 'em." Once Pete and the band got started "rolling 'em," they were good for half an hour or longer without stopping.

Today the cabaret back of the Lone Star is closed as Kansas City attempts a house cleaning. A 12 o'clock closing law was clamped on and it looks as if Kansas City jazzmen will have a hard time for a while. Anyway, the Lone Star had seen its most glorious nights. Pete Johnson and Joe Turner have at last gone on to success in New York, where with Meade Lux and Ammons, they took the big city by storm.

Since the Boogie Woogie has finally arrived, the future looks bright for piano blues. There is no need to look backward for the golden age, as in the case of orchestral jazz; not when Jimmy Yancey, the Buddy Bolden of the Boogie Woogie, is still in his prime, and a dozen others are active throughout the country.

The Boogie Woogie has made its influence felt in present-day orchestration, and many leading orchestras have their version of the *Boogie Woogie*. But it is fundamentally a piano style and is most effective when played on this solo instrument. Although the Boogie Woogie was originally dance music, it transcends any secondary function as mere accompaniment to words or movement and today has come to be recognized in its own right.

NEW YORK

"I'd rather drink muddy water, Lord"

JAZZ SPREAD up and out, and New York, that was first in many things, trailed along. The river cities had it before New York. Chicago was putting every tub on its bottom while New York was learning how to spell the word. Chicago had the big money and it wanted its jazz that way:

> Hot!
> Get hot!
> Throw the jazz around!

But Tin Pan Alley was in New York, in a cheap walk-up off Broadway. You might get a song published. What usually happened was that somebody heard the song in Chicago and stole it in New York. So the boys came to New York, where songs were published and bands booked. They came to New York in broken-down cars and in buses. Some of the spenders came in Pullman cars. The Creole Band came first, breaking up the show at the Winter Garden and leaving behind it a wake of followers in Harlem. Then the Original Dixieland Jazz Band came, hitting the town hard. New York boys who'd been taught that notes came before music learned all the notes by heart. They wrote down what they heard but each time a little was lost. Somehow the notes were not the same as those the jazzmen played. There might have been a chance if the musicians had said, "Look, it's in B flat, we'll put it down that way, like the king played it." But always behind the shoulder were the smart boys:

> "You gotta give it refinement."

> "The public wants sentiment. Catch on? Home and mother and for crissake harmonize it!"

Chicago produced and was a big spender. New York didn't spend. It bought and sold. Like all traders, it knew what the public was buying that year and it wasn't eager to take on a new line. Not until it saw how it would go. To the men in the walk-ups off Broadway, jazz was a long chance. The thing to do was to mold the new spirit to the shaky framework of Tin Pan Alley. But it was something like selling glands to a scarecrow. Jazz in New York was jazz in the cornfield, and it stayed there until King Oliver came East from Chicago, until Fletcher Henderson graduated from college and Duke Ellington came up from Washington. Until then it was cowbells and cacophony.

Those who wanted jazz went to Harlem. They got a taste of it downtown, when "Yellow" Nunez was there (with Alfred Laine, the son of Papa Laine, and the Louisiana Five), or when some of the men came in from Chicago, but most of the time jazz was confined to a few blocks in Harlem, from Seventh Avenue eastward to what was called "The Jungle." New York musicians took their lessons there or on phonograph records. And because it wasn't close, there weren't many who got it. (Miff Mole had it, and when the Georgians played a dance hall late at night there would be a swing in what they did.) New York bought and sold, and not many bands could go through that kind of wringer and come out with the spirit. Count them off, and you'd find most of the bands in or from Harlem. Fletcher Henderson. Duke Ellington. Luis Russell. And the small bands in the small clubs. The Nest. Small's Paradise. Connie's Inn. The Sugar Cane Club. The Saratoga Club.

The boy whose watchword had been "get off my note," tried to become a sight reader in three months, took a job in Chinatown, a burlesque show, a speakeasy, or a clip joint. It was noisy and bad. Everyone blew so loud that no one knew quite how bad it was. So the boy from Chicago learned five-brass, four-reed, and pretty soon someone told him he was improving (as distinguished from improvising) but where did he get that foul tone? So he cried in his beer, laid off the vibrato, sweetened up the tone and got a job in a name band where he took a six-bar break on the master record they threw away because it wasn't what the public wanted. On an off night he played a twelve-bar blues, just like that, and the smart boys told him we'll clean that up and give it melody, you gotta think of a lyric, though, something about a girl and a moon:

> "And watch tomorrow's papers, buddy, they'll tell
> you who invented jazz!"

New York set orchestral style for jazz but in the twenties there was not one white band that could compare with Fletcher's, not because there were no white musicians playing jazz but because no agents and no leaders were ready to back it up. "That stuff is all right for the jigs," they'd say, putting the white boys off another ten years. Meanwhile, Negro bands were not making much money but no one questioned that they were having fun. Left alone, with their own audience, they built big bands on a standardized pattern but that was where standardization stopped. They made their own arrangements, keeping the tone because no one told them what the public didn't want. And if they sometimes lost the spirit in arrangement it was sure to come back late at night. It was sure to come back because they had an audience and no one in between to say what it wanted. They even had a press. In 1927, the year transition was published in Paris, the Oliver band was announced for an evening in Dexter Park, Brooklyn:

> The King gets the butter. Some Day Sweetheart—
> play that thing—KING OLIVER—you got it.
> Dance, dance, dance—Funny I'm not tired Aint he
> hot—Some Day Sweetheart—Get off that dime—
> What a Crowd—The King reigns—Long live the
> King of syncopation—KING OLIVER we love you,
> I can't resist your charms when you play—Some Day
> Sweetheart.

Hey—hey—hey—I want to holler—but there he
goes again—he just won't—won't hear that cornet
moan—the sax cry, I can't resist it—it gets into my
blood, won't he stop playing that music—hard
hearted KING OLIVER—I feel faint—Yes I'll dance
—Oh won't he stop—Your hand belongs on my
shoulder, buddie—Wow, wow, wow, hear that applause—Applesauce—applesauce—what that boy is
blowing through his drum. Best drummer in town—
KING OLIVER make New York your home, we
love you—Play that thing—play me your favorite
number—Some Day Sweetheart.

And all this time white boys from Chicago were out of work
or reading notes in a name band. Jack Teagarden sat around
the Louisiana, an apartment hotel on 47th Street, one of a
number of good white musicians who were at liberty because
something stood between them and an audience. Jack would
sometimes go uptown to hear Bessie Smith, to jam with Louis
Armstrong. The rest of the time he'd sit around with musicians he knew and they'd talk about Chicago, or New Orleans,
or some other place they weren't at. Maybe that's when he
sang those words for the first time. It was a twelve-bar blues
and he called it Makin' Friends. On the record he made for
the Perfect label, he sang the vocal, then did the rest with the
slide of his trombone and a drinking glass.

I'd rather drink muddy water, Lord, sleep in a hollow log,
I'd rather drink muddy water, Lord, sleep in a hollow log,
Than to be up here in New York, treated like a dirty dog.

C. E. S.

IX

NEW YORK TURNS ON THE HEAT

BY WILDER HOBSON

THERE WAS probably as much fine jazz playing in New York during the twenties as in Chicago. Matching the names already identified with the Windy City, the musicians more frequently in New York included Joe Smith, Tommy Ladnier, Albert "Cootie" Williams, Charlie "Big" Green, Jimmy Harrison, Milfred Miff Mole, Jay C. Higginbotham, Joe "Tricky Sam" Nanton, Coleman Hawkins, Benny Carter, Buster Bailey, Johnny Hodges, Harry Carney, Barney Bigard, and Thomas "Fats" Waller—and it was in New York that Fletcher Henderson, Duke Ellington and Luis Russell developed their excellent big bands, including most of the players mentioned above.

New York's genuine jazz was, of course, like that of Chicago, very obscure as compared with the popular commercial dance music. When the Original Dixieland Jazz Band quit the city in 1919, it left very few musical imitators. Most of the "jazz" bands which sought a popularity like that of the Dixieland copied merely the latter's gags and novelty effects, made a syncopated din which had little or nothing to do with the jazz language as the Dixieland had learned it in New Orleans; these Northern combinations were for the most part old-style ragtime "nut" bands with added comedy features, an extra set of pots and pans for the drummer, and the habit of playing their instruments on one knee or in other acrobatic positions. They were exactly as raucous as a good many ministers of the Gospel insisted they were.

The jazz center of Gotham through the twenties was, naturally enough, the Negro section—Harlem—which was to New York what the South Side was to Chicago. To this vast, drably architectured district the Coolidge-Hoover boom brought more money than it had ever seen before or has ever seen since, although, by downtown standards, it would have been necessary to call it very small money. A good fraction of it was paid out by sightseers, led off by the downtown esthetes who "discovered" Negro art, music, dancing, and vice in the early twenties. And of that fraction a sizeable sub-fraction was siphoned off by entertainment bosses who were not Negroes. Colored Harlem has long been exploited in its own precinct by opportunists not of the race. The well-known Savoy Ballroom, where practically every fine Negro band has played in its time, was not and is not owned by Negroes, and the old, uptown Cotton Club of Prohibition days, where Duke Ellington made his name, was operated by a white beer-running syndicate. During the boom, however, enough steady money seeped into Harlem's musical circles to encourage the organization of some of the best bands in the jazz annals. And Harlem gave them the kind of attention which stimulates good playing—from visitors who expected genuine jazz and, more especially, from strenuous, inventive Negro dancers who, as André Gide says of the African natives, were "learned" rhythmically.

The first fine Negro band in New York, however, spent a good part of its time downtown. While Paul Whiteman was filling the expensive Palais Royal, Fletcher Henderson was leading his colored combination at the public dance hall, Roseland, a few blocks up Broadway. Henderson has always had various distractions from his music, and has never been much of a self-promoter. He has perhaps joined in more fine jazz performances than any man alive, both with his bands and as accompanist to Bessie Smith and other blues singers, but he has never sustained the discipline and routine, either personal or orchestral, which seem necessary for the really big money and which are apt, at the same time, to cut the spirit of the music. He is recognized today chiefly as the writer of some of Benny Goodman's most effective orchestrations. Fletcher and his younger brother Horace have turned out many fine, unpretentious scores, thoroughly in the spirit of good improvised jazz. Among them are *King Porter Stomp, Sugar Foot Stomp, Wrappin' It Up, Down South Camp Meetin', Big John Special, Hot and Anxious,* and *When Buddha Smiles.*

But there is a good deal more to be said about Fletcher. His father was a schoolteacher in Cuthbert, Georgia. Fletcher studied chemistry for a while and then played the piano in a road show. Around 1919 he formed his first band for Roseland, where he appeared off and on for the next fifteen years. He was the first hot musician to build a big hot band with full brass, reed and rhythm sections and to orchestrate for sections in the manner now familiar, as may be gathered from his record of *What-Cha-Call-'Em Blues* and *Sugar Foot Stomp* which was made in 1924. The personnel of his band changed frequently but the ensembles were usually excellent, with several top rank soloists. First and last, he has had certainly a good fifty per cent of the finest Negro talent in the country. Back in 1924-25 the band included Louis Armstrong, on from Chicago, and Coleman Hawkins, who has been to the tenor saxophone what Armstrong has to the jazz trumpet, and Charlie "Big" Green, whose comic trombone "comment" is familiar behind the recorded voice of Bessie Smith and who, with Miff Mole, was one of the earliest expressive trombone soloists. In 1927-28 Henderson still had Hawkins, and Buster Bailey on the clarinet, Benny Carter and Don Redman on the alto saxophone, Jimmy Harrison on the trombone, and the superb trumpet team of Joe Smith and Tommy Ladnier.

I first heard the band at this period, at a college party. The dozen pieces were spread in front of a set of Gothic windows and flanked, for a while, by three large, well-corseted hostesses sitting on a divan and determinedly giving the impression that they felt quite at home with *Clarinet Marmalade* being delivered ten feet away with five parts brass. Hawkins sweated out chorus after chorus in his more agitated manner, and Kaiser Marshall sometimes exuberantly threw away the drumsticks, not catching them again, like the trick drummers, but lobbing them out over the heads of the crowd. I think this was the evening when the tuba player was high and kept injecting great haarrrumphing notes where they weren't wanted. When this finally annoyed Fletcher, the tuba player said: "Ah usually only play two three notes, ah'm goin' have some fun this evenin'."

There were alternate trumpet choruses from Smith and Ladnier, Smith's jetting out of the middle range of his horn with those light, slippery rhythms across the pulse of the band which may be heard in the records of *Stockholm Stomp* and *Rocky Mountain Blues*. There were no screams, blasts, or ornate scrambling, however expert, but the most jubilant, singing trumpet passages imaginable, with lovely inflections in the slow numbers (the closest suggestion of Smith I've heard in recent months was from Muggsy Spanier with his small Ragtime Band). And Henderson usually worked up to seething last choruses of full band faking like the end of the *Fidgety Feet* record.

It is hard work to develop large, twelve- to sixteen-piece, jazz combinations, to get ensemble finish, precise intonation, unified attack, the sections phrasing and blending well among themselves and with each other. Many currently popular bands are very musicianly in this sense. They have a polish which Henderson seldom, if ever, had, and for which I imagine he never tried. But his best combinations had a quality beside which a high polish seems a rather routine, if difficult, achievement. It might be called ensemble ease and spontaneity—listen to the records of *Fidgety Feet* or *New King Porter Stomp*. There was a sense of relaxation, lack of strain, reserve strength. This was perhaps largely a matter of individual talent. With a brass team such as Russell and Joe Smith, Ladnier, Green and Harrisson, it would have been too bad to insist on precision. They might have delivered it, but the music would have lost the spirit of these men attacking with their natural enthusiasm. Henderson's best large bands played with the buoyancy of a fine, small, improvising combination. Obviously, few other bands have had such musicians, but, even so, there has recently seemed to be a fetish with regard to precision, and it would seem that, in obtaining it, a lot of the players' gusto is often lost. In the playing of Henderson's *Big John* the premium is on the warm spontaneity, careless in the best sense of the word, which was one of the reasons why, for years, virtually every jazz musician in New York sometimes sat in one of the chairs across the floor from the Roseland bandstand and listened to Fletcher Henderson.

Edward Kennedy Duke Ellington, the son of a Negro worker in the Washington, D. C., Navy Yard, opened with his band at the Cotton Club in Harlem in 1927, when Henderson's band had long since become a byword with other jazz players. Apart from musicians, however, Henderson's music was known mostly to a limited dance hall audience. It had had no effective promotion. Ellington, on the other hand, had Irving Mills' plugging management, a bandstand in the purple glow lamps of the Cotton Club which was a center of the Harlem entertainment vogue, and widespread radio facilities. Also, in addition to being the leader of a remarkable combination, Ellington was a composer of decided interest. In a short time his radio hookups brought him a large, national audience

--his was the first large hot band to attract any such attention.

He has since had all kinds of salutes. Recently it has often been said that Ellington's music has lost the genuineness which characterized it in the late twenties, that it has become overly suave, elaborate, and virtuoso. In a recent appearance at the downtown Cotton Club on Broadway, Ellington's boys wore white jackets, boiled shirts and dress ties, crimson trousers and shoes. Duke himself opened the evening in a light gray coat and black trousers, moved on to full dress, and finished in a henna jacket and the blacks. The trumpets appeared to be made of platinum, heavily embossed, perhaps suitably inscribed and possibly taken out of Tiffany's each day and put back after the night's work. Even the instrument cases were handsomely lettered in metal. The only feature which marred the general splendor was a battered platter which Rex Stewart produced from some hiding place and waved over the bell of his trumpet during the last chorus *tutti* of *The Sheik of Araby*.

These trappings may have little to do with music, but I think they are fitting and proper in this case. If any musician ever earned the right to a dress uniform, Ellington's boys have earned their crimson pants and fancy instrument cases. They have been and are an epitome of a sort. The jazz language, coming out of folk-musical sources, by its own nature bred a lot of remarkable improvising talent. As the players grew more and more interested in the combination of instruments in sections, jazz inevitably acquired considerable orchestral sophistication. Jazz musicians are bound to be more and more experimental *orchestrally*. And it is probably natural that some one organization should most vividly represent *all* the elements of this process in which a folk-music is gradually moving into general musical currents. It seems to me that the band which does this is Ellington's. In it you hear improvising in many spirits, the "low-down" rhythmic playing of trumpeter "Cootie" Williams and trombonist Joe Nanton, the spirited, melodic inventions of the saxophonists Johnny Hodges and

Harry Carney, and the floridity of trumpeter Rex Stewart, trombonist Lawrence Brown, and clarinetist Barney Bigard. Also, this is certainly the most striking *ensemble* in jazz, with a brilliance, finish and ease resulting from long collaboration. Finally, I don't know of any jazz orchestrator as musically fertile as Ellington. His ideas may seldom get sustained development, may often be loosely strung together and over-rich for the thematic material which is carrying them. But in an Ellington performance it is a rare three minutes in which something of *orchestral* fascination doesn't occur. Of how many other bands can the same be said?

The third big band of fine quality developed in New York in the twenties was Luis Russell's, which played at the Saratoga Club in Harlem in 1929. Born in Panama, Russell moved up to New Orleans and on up the Mississippi to Chicago in the middle twenties, and then traveled eastward to Harlem where he assembled a short-lived group whose chief players have recently been heard, with Russell, behind Louis Armstrong. Toward the end of the twenties, under Russell's and Henry Allen's names, this band made some of the finest jazz records, with simple arrangements, a good, rhythmic ensemble, and a trio of superb soloists. These discs were the first to show to advantage the alto saxophone inventions of Charles Holmes, the playing of Jay C. Higginbotham from Georgia, a trombonist who ran the gamut between the muted delicacy of *Biffly Blues* and the explosive strength of *Swing Out*, and the clamorous, lyric trumpeting of Henry Allen, a particularly fine blues player, from Algiers, across from New Orleans.

In the jazz circles of New York, the twenties ended with the arrival of many of the best Chicago players. But with such bands as Henderson's, Ellington's and Russell's already on location, and their members often playing impromptu late hour sessions in the Harlem basements, the city could scarcely be said to lack for syncopation.

X

THE FIVE PENNIES

BY OTIS FERGUSON

NEW YORK in the earliest twenties was shivering in the backwash of the Dixieland noise, so far as jazz was concerned. There seemed to be no particular direction for music to go in; but that is no reason for assuming that directions weren't shaping up under the surface. Musical shows were going on, bands were playing the Palace, people were dancing. "Pure" jazz was not a part of the picture—except for a hole here and a corner there.

But don't forget the phonograph and don't forget the radio. Along with the later development of the sound picture these things were already slated to wipe out the influence of the player piano, sheet music, minstrel shows, and vaudeville itself (I caught my first "jazz" band in a house on the second-run S. Z. Poli wheel at what we might call the turn of the twenties). The important fact is not the mere superseding of older channels, though; these new-fangled devices were about to achieve a perfection of national coverage that was bound to bring everything to their headquarters in the main city of New York (the tug-of-war between New York and Hollywood didn't really start until the thirties). Exciting things were going on in Chicago, and temporarily Chicago was about the only musical place to be. It had to be temporarily though: by the sheer weight of its central resources as a microphone to the nation, New York had already stolen the show.

Chicago is still a good stand, and Victor has a loopy recording studio there; the Palomar in Los Angeles is stronger today than ever, and the West Coast studios are better for bands than those in New York. But everyone knows where bands are booked from and songs are plugged from and where recording contracts are really wangled. The ambition in Chester, Pa., and Kingston, Jamaica, and Panama and Dallas and Honolulu is identical: to get to New York. The Mississippi is no longer the vertebra of music and you could no more imagine a major phonograph company in Richmond, Indiana, than you could fly there under your own power.

It happened in the twenties, but in a hidden sort of way. Jazz was being refined for general consumption by the working of two overlapping processes. I mean the jazz of street bands, né ragtime, né much else besides—Dixieland you might say, though that gives too much prominence to one of many outfits. A hectic brass stridency, with every chorus an all-in chorus and get the hell off my note. One of the processes was the development of the easy-ride quality that had been in the background all along, in the blues, in work songs, and the slower instrumental passages with feeling. When the notes began to hang together and the harmonic structure became a more important means to the effect, the boys would say that it was beginning to swing in there—long before the word swing became a categorical noun for those who need a category before they can tell where they're at. There was the Oliver-Armstrong-Marable-Noone-Dodds brothers influence at work in that; and there was the Friars' Inn line of influence; and between the two (among all of the many tributaries) they polished and developed a Chicago style, a jazz that would jazz and swing too.

The second process of cleaning the raw materials up had small value in itself at the start, but an important place in the eventual result. They called it symphonic jazz long after the fact, and if the truth is known they called it worse names than that during and after. It was a short-cut to the public, essentially. Paul Whiteman was not the first pioneer, but he was the best all-around and all-time showman. Whatever he did, he managed to leave the impression with his audience that when he played it, it stayed played. And what he played was a very modified, musically sophisticated version of what the few people with an ear had been hearing all over the country, the new jazz, the new way to do it.

After the War—and he had been scuffling around plenty before it, legitimate and popular—Whiteman took his new way of doing old things into a hotel job at Atlantic City that began pulling crowds. *Avalon* was in the book even then, and after a while the place was being mobbed and causing comment. Now keep your eye on the ball through here. The phonograph companies, the big companies that were destined to stay right on the ground floor, heard about this fat man with a special jazz band. And they went down to A.C. and fell over each other signing him up.

They signed him up all right and he made records. He had something the public wanted and what the public wanted the phonograph companies wanted even worse. Now what happens in an Atlantic City hotel is nothing I as an average citizen want any part of. So all right, a band is packing them in. But in Worcester, Mass., and Muskegon, Mich., something on a new phonograph record is a different thing. It's national, it's everywhere, it's the kind of fame you can ride on. So Whiteman rode into New York, to an S.R.O. theatre date, to three solid years at the Palais Royal—1920 up to 1923. And to enough recordings of *Meditations from Thaïs* to pave the country. Even Joe Dope and Suzie Cutie in their thousands of home towns all over the country might have found this music strictly pseudo alongside of what was going on at the Friars' Inn, the Sunset Café, the Lincoln Gardens, and the

Rockport Ballroom at the time. The music of these latter spots would probably have been a little hard to take at first, for J. Dope and S. Cutie; but if they'd been fed it with their meals they'd have gone for it just as well, and stayed with it longer. But why they didn't get it with their meals nobody should ask.

Whiteman had a teaser in his dressed-up and, for all I know, symphonic ragtime. He was a showman twenty-four hours a day and forty-eight on Sundays, and he could spot a phony dollar bill as far as you could carry it. But the opening wedge and the hammer behind it was the really "new" thing: the publicity and multiple coverage of modern reproduction. And that, boys and girls, is the whole campus of the New York school of jazz.

It's not a case for one thing or the other, this rising prominence of recording and radio, but a plain and important fact. Anybody who knows can tell you that the present Goodman band was a turkey until the Victor recordings had had time to add their effect to the "Let's Dance" program on the air; and that after the effect had been nationally digested the band came back across the same country through which it had made sad flopping noises working out, and stood them up and turned them away—why? It was the same band with the same high standards. So what went on? Months before the floparoo in Denver, Colo., Mr. G. had signed with Victor and with NBC, both as of New York City. Go back in your swing-band history and you'll see what else poured through the hole this made in the dike—Dorsey, Shaw, Crosby, read all about it in the papers.

But to get back to New York in the early twenties. As it has been in every other art, New York in jazz was mainly a center for outlanders. Its writers and painters have come to live there from somewhere else, dragging most of their creative memory behind them. The few of its accepted legitimate musicians try to appear as though they had come from someplace else, with an air of "Who? Me?" The American stage is centered in New York City and as a tradition is no nearer New York than London. Even Milfred Mole, the trombone man whose achievement was the highest of all achievements in the period we can call the New York twenties, came from Long Island.

There simply is no New York style—which is perhaps just as well, for those who make musical compartments as definite as "Hattie Carnegie, Fall 1938" are always falling over such obstinate angles as the fact that Rappolo, who came up from down river, is more "Chicago" than Benny Goodman, who lived there; that Red Nichols came from Utah and Teagarden from Texas and Beiderbecke from Iowa and the author of *Georgia* from Indiana. New York has always been like the office of Actors Equity: a place to get together, to get news, to swap ideas and gossip.

From the War on, there were bands in New York and plenty coming in, some of them bringing men who were to stay and build names for themselves. Vincent Lopez had been playing at the Pennsylvania roof for five years before he gave his first concert at the Metropolitan in 1924 and next year took a band to Europe; he was one of the first to put slick bandshows on vaudeville tours (remember the plush curtains, the light effects, the plumbing in front of the saxophone section, *The Song of India*, *Nola* and what not?). Paul Specht picked up Arthur Schutt playing piano in a Reading, Pa., movie house, brought him to New York and kept him for a tour to Europe in 1923. The Scranton Sirens got Jimmy Dorsey (who had already organized a band of his own) in 1920; both Jimmy and the younger Tommy came to New York with the band. George Olsen found Red Nichols at the Culver Military Academy in Indiana and took him into his band. Eddie Lang, who had been playing violin in a Philadelphia club, changed over to banjo after he joined Charlie Kerr's orchestra, and then later he too joined the Scranton Sirens.

Jan Garber and Meyer Davis were starting their multiple-band policy. There were the college bands of course, such as Waring's Pencilsharpeners (more music was coming out of Pennsylvania around 1920 than before or since—what, no Pennsylvania style?); and there were more "Varsity Eights" and "University Sixes" than those who got on the records. These titles, incidentally, were used by the California Ramblers, who organized in 1920 although they didn't get to New York until later.

There was a whole forest of bands, but the important thing about their type of music and its influence was the insistence on arrangements and sight-reading and all-around musicianship for the benefit of a dressed-up clientele. Of the men just mentioned I don't believe there is one who didn't have musical training very early and on several different instruments—in fact, the list is almost monotonous in the "mother taught piano" or "father led hometown band" legend. The level of originality and spirit in these big outfits was low in general, but in addition to a certain technical training, the ease of their success did two things: it brought the boys out of the back country into town, and it almost entirely did away with the period of scuffling many better musicians have had to go through. This scuffling might have done them little good, as they were removed by distance from the true musical axis of New Orleans to Chicago, where any punk kid learning his instrument could have the example of the big jazzmen in his ears and over his head where he could look up to it. But much as they derided the empty musicology of the section men they had to work with, they never seemed to lose a sneaking respect for the arranged score, the general polish, and the bright-light kind of achievement that brought them in a steady hundred dollars a week while they were still kids.

Well, there were many bands bringing in many thousands of customers and dollars. All of them have since broken up, or reorganized, or continued intact; but musically there is nothing left of what they did then. They were carriers mainly, and in a way the early New York twenties seems like a gathering of the tribes

Of the Five Pennies group, which under dozens of different names and labels made hundreds of recordings, Miff Mole was about the only one originally on the spot—and when Red Nichols arrived he was playing no nearer to the studios than a Brooklyn restaurant. The two struck up a team that lasted for years and for a while cornered the hot market, recording first in 1922 as an outfit called the Red Heads. Then the two Dorseys showed up, and Eddie Lang. Arthur Schutt came back from Europe. After their return from triumph in England, the Original Dixieland Jazz Band was using Frank Signorelli on piano and Phil Lytell, clarinet, but the original members drifted out of sight fairly soon: they had served their purpose and were already being superseded by a more modified type of the same thing; the ear-music boys were giving over to sight readers and "symphonic" men.

A trumpet player by the name of Phil Napoleon organized with Miff Mole that band which was to be the hot aggregation for the next few years (it recorded from 1923-1928): the Original Memphis Five. They had Signorelli and Lytell and Jack Roth on drums. They played with some of the old Dixieland rip and some of the Dixieland repertoire (Jazz Me Blues), but they toned it down, putting in rehearsed effects—piano, clarinet, trumpet, trombone in chords; brass duet; ensemble modulation; etc. The rhythm element was weak—a characteristic of all the small outfits of this place and period—and Signorelli's piano style was a pumping bass with a scattered right hand, the assumption in those times being if you could play forty notes to the phrase you were really going. I never went much for the Napoleon trumpet, which falls between a good heavy ride and good melodic line, missing both; but it was something for that time. The main difference in this band was the trombone work of Miff Mole, which was quite new then and is still good.

The trombone in jazz had had a pretty checkered career. In the Dixieland style it was used for a halfway bass, for smears, single-note surprise attacks, and laughs. Even in the good Negro bands it had little melodic development—it made a good bottom for a chord, it made a good growl, and it was equipped with a slide, which latter was almost fatal in many cases and worse than fatal in many more. The tendency in early instrumental jazz was always toward the assertiveness of the soprano register. Everybody wanted to play lead (trumpet) or improvise around it (clarinet, soprano, and alto saxes) and if a pianist was to be heard he had to fight it out with the right hand. Even in the drums the steady bass was too often neglected for cymbals, rim shots, wood blocks, and cowbells. The quickest way for a trombone to make itself felt was to jump in with a glissando pick-up. When the band put on paper hats you always got a spot by making it laugh. And after all, even if you went to conservatory instruction, what was there scored for trombone outside of some entrance-cue music in Wagner and a few transposed cello parts?

Milfred Miff Mole was born in Long Island, studied piano and violin through his school days and then learned trombone from A to Z. He heard jazz and wanted to play it, but he patterned his instrument on the work of the trumpet. He was a slight and studious-looking youngster when he first bobbed up in the Manhattan studios in 1922, with a round face and round glasses (he looked as young as the others, though born in 1898). But he could do things on his jazz instrument no one else could do, and so all through the twenties, till the late arrival from Texas of Jack Teagarden—perhaps only until just before that, when Glenn Miller came in with the Pollack band—everybody who thought of organizing a hot band thought of Miff Mole.

He could raise the tension of any band with a four-bar

break, he could swing into the pattern of a trumpet solo with a middle eight bars, he could take thirty-two by himself, and double that, and keep the line of interest clear and free. What is more he was old reliable himself in studio work: he could play straight when he had to and when you wanted something else it was there.

The word that has slipped into the talk about him is "technician," which is short of the fact and a little slighting. Mole is a fine technician of course, but much else besides. His harmonic sense is impeccable; his taste is clean. With everybody else muffing weaknesses with shakes, slurs, repeated phrases, and high notes, he sticks to a rounded phrase of notes struck dead center. His slide is as easy and noiseless as a trumpet valve without sacrificing that typical and exhilarating capacity of the instrument for rolling into a note; more, he knows, as few have discovered, how to use the full lower register to give a phrase an upward spring. He never tries something he can't pull off, and yet there seems to be little he can't pull off—and probably the "technician" stuff comes from the way he will blandly jump five positions or an octave and a third with nothing more of effort between each full note than the slight tonguing effect which cuts each out, with the clarity of good brass work.

He played jazz when jazz was pretty crude; he played on the beat and on the chord and he played with a certain easy bounding zest. He was so far ahead of Brunies and Pecora when he started that there is no telling what a Friars' Inn background would have done for him. He is still so much more interesting in any stretch than all but Jimmy Harrison and Teagarden that I would not guarantee what might now be said of him if he had died ten years ago in rather horrible circumstances. But he is forty-one now, boys, and forty-one is no age for cutting the brash capers of youth. He has settled down to a peaceful and secure middle age in the studios. He might have been greater if he had been pushed around more by more of the right people at the right time and place; but he was one of the first jazz names I knew; he was a lasting influence on an instrument I admire most for its grand depth and brilliance; and I can still put a Miff Mole's Molers on the machine and feel a genuine living interest—which is not to be confused with the scholastic excitement of archaeology. Regardless of influences, I don't imagine Mole ever had what Teagarden has got inside him. For that matter neither has any other trombonist in the world, for my money. But before you follow the crowd in letting him go as merely an expert in plumbing, go listen to ten or twenty good records out of nearly a thousand—perhaps just a couple of casuals he did with his own band, *You're the Cream in My Coffee* or *Moanin' Low*.

All of which is less a digression than it seems. Red Nichols was the number-one man in the New York recording life of the middle twenties. But until he got Teagarden and several of the Chicago men, Miff Mole is always playing just beside and a little over him. Ernest Loring Nichols was no slouch, and it is too bad he took the easy-money way eventually. But his own trumpet playing, even though he worked to bring it to the full perfection of Bix Beiderbecke (never with that jealous selling short or cutting down or astigmatic dismissal of so many others), was more clever than heartfelt, more riding along on top than making everyone else ride.

Red Nichols had been given an early start in Utah, where his father taught music; he was given an early break almost as soon as he had got into military academy (George Olsen put him in his band, as noted above). And he had a respect for the hot style that marked him out from others the minute he got to New York. More than that, for purposes of publicity and success, he had the talent for organizing a band, playing the right tunes at the right time. On the stage, in the pit and for dances he has played with the California Ramblers, the Cotton Pickers, Ross Gorman, Don Voorhees, Sam Lanin, Whiteman, etc. But with Miff Mole he filled the record stores of the country with dozens of sides under at least a dozen names; before 1930 he had taken advantage of the talents of practically every good white musician in the business and played everything from his own compositions to the earliest and latest jazz-band numbers, from *Smiles* and *The Sheik* to *Tea for Two* and *Lady Be Good*. And he had got such a thorough coverage in Europe that M. Panassié was still hotly arguing he was not as great as Louis Armstrong all through a book only a few years ago.

But Mole was not the showman, the shrewd organizer of early jazz and arranger of recording dates. The organizer was Red Nichols, whose trumpet was clever and a bit thin, but whose feeling for jazz was in the right place—as you would find by comparing the general output of the time. Through this part we are up against the fact that men were playing more or less off the top of their heads, that radio and phonograph jazz made the lead instruments the star performers, leaving rhythm in the background—or out the window.

The Five Pennies recording groups were not noticeable for heavy swinging, though music of the time elsewhere was already well developed in that direction. And it wasn't altogether the fault of instrumentalists like Nichols, Mole, Dorsey, Livingston. People as widely assorted as Bix Beiderbecke and Bessie Smith, Rappolo and Fletcher Henderson, Louis and Larry Shields, were playing or singing with a natural ride quality themselves. But that doesn't mean that the groups they played with would swing as a whole. Memory plays strange tricks and the conditions of old acoustic-recording play even stranger. However, if you forget what you've read and go back to some of the actual performances of the Heroic Days, you'll have to admit that the general background of clanging banjos and pumping pianos often wouldn't swing on a rope—by the modern standards on which we're only too willing to condemn some of the non-heroic days.

Even with the shallow rhythmic base (as such) of the fives,

sixes and sevens, most of whose separate men were trying to
be heard most of the time, you could get a general ensemble
feeling of drive. It usually required night after night on the
same stand together though, until even the hall itself seemed
to breathe in unison. In that case the band was its own rhythm
section, the beat was in the mutual understanding and the
constant give and take as between each and all. Here and
there you could find an outfit like this, but not everywhere
by a long shot.

The other way to get rhythmic strength and cohesion was
in the full rhythm section of the full band. And though the
full band was coming into its own in a popular way, the market for good full bands was discouraging: by 1925 Henderson
and Ellington were getting a foothold, but even they weren't
stampeding the country. On the whole it was a transition
period, and the New York boys were caught in it, being so
near the microphone that they couldn't hear what was being
developed in the back country the microphone was addressed
to. Don't forget that even the New Orleans Rhythm Kings
were pioneering in the twenties by the discovery (charmingly
described by Ben Pollack later), made one night when the
M.C. told them to lay off the drum "effects" during the floor
show, that they really got off better on a steady building
rhythm on the bass drum—and they let the cowbells go from
then on. Don't forget that Ellington's band even in its present
size has a haphazard rhythm section and that the left-hand
drive of a man like Stacy is head and shoulders above anything the great Duke himself could give in rhythm if he had
eight hands. The world is full of odd matters that will not fit
into categories.

Anyway, the rhythm element in the music of these men for-
gathering in the phonograph studios during the twenties was
their biggest weakness. They had plenty of talent otherwise—
not only the technical command already mentioned, but a
good collective feeling for high-jinks, tearing through the old

Dixieland numbers or variations of that style in numbers of their own, any pop tunes that were around, semi-comedy numbers. They didn't have a complete style of playing, but each knew what the other was about, and the same few men played so much together that arranging a coda or a trick chorus was easy and more spontaneous than some would have you think.

But while Nichols, Mole, the Dorseys and so forth kept on stacking up piles of records through the middle and late twenties, theirs was a recording rather than a working nucleus. Bands would come into town, reorganize, pick up a few of the men for a while; bands would be formed to play in Roseland or go on the road, or play pit jobs for musical shows. By 1925 the personnels of some working bands were changing so fast you couldn't keep up with them. Sam Lanin had Mole and Nichols at Roseland; Ray Miller had them; Ross Gorman left Whiteman to form a pit band for Earl Carroll's "Vanities," and he had them too. Don Voorhees had them in his band the same year. Then Roger Wolfe Kahn took over the scene more or less, for he had the kind of money that would make anyone jump, and he wanted the best. By the time late in 1925 when he was playing at the Biltmore he had Nichols and Mole, Venuti and Lang, Leo McConville, Arthur Schutt and Vic Berton.

But before that in 1925 something else had happened that gave the boys in the steadily enlarging recording group a taste of what was going to overtake them. Overriding the more cautious heads in their small group, the Wolverines decided to come to town and came, bringing Bix Beiderbecke. Bix played trumpet (cornet) a way they'd never heard and while he didn't stay long at the Cinderella Ballroom, he stayed around long enough before going back to Chicago so that Red Nichols received an impression he never got over. No matter how famous he might get, he wanted to play that kind of trumpet—and this, I should say, is a typical meeting of the two kinds of things that were going on in the country.

The Wolverines flopped in New York, in spite of Bix, be-cause they were in the old ear-music tradition, with a lot of steam but a limited repertory and little or no arrangement. The manager had tried to get them to vary things with a few straight numbers, but they found every time that rehearsal would start with the best of intentions, and then someone would just have to stick in a hot note at the end of his chorus, or take a break, and they'd be off after him hell for. leather, first one, then the next. New York by then was a tough place to break into, because the New York men had worked up a pretty high standard of all-around musicianship, and already had themselves pretty big names. Nick La Rocca wouldn't have taken the town by storm in 1925. Still and all, here were these men playing all the time and in demand everywhere, and they could record twenty different numbers to the Wol-verines' one; but they could no more cut this kid from the sweet-water circuit than they could slice a cobble-stone. They had almost forgotten that music might be that way, for they had been long from home. (Fletcher Henderson had his jump-ing band at Roseland, of course, and little Louis had come to New York with some awe and trembling to join him; but the recording groups just assumed that colored musicians naturally played another kind of music.)

It was rather a shock to them, and each reacted in his own way. Some, like Nichols, couldn't admire Bix enough; others burned with envy and started their tireless campaign to cut him down—but that's another chapter. Music wasn't to be the same after that, or not quite the same, for beginnings are always gradual and nebulous things.

The Five Pennies and like studio groups kept on recording and using larger combinations. Adrian Rollini had come in with the California Ramblers and had somewhere learned to play bass sax, which Nichols and everybody else began to use as a flexible and lyric but not very solid bass. Dudley Fosdick came in with a mellophone. Now and then a man from the well-developed Chicago group would get restless for the big town and come in on his own, sit in and record, and maybe hold a job for some time until he got homesick. However, the ideal for jazz was still felt to be the pattern of the small band.

But just as New York was becoming more and more the key city of music, through the natural pull of its studios and publishing houses and fat contracts, New York was opening up to new influences in jazz: one of them was the individual style of men who had already learned to play good jazz, from Texas to Chicago. The other was the big hot band, with full rhythm section and elbow-room for improvisation. The first really successful orchestra of this type was of course Henderson's. Duke Ellington opened at the Kentucky Club in 1926 and played his first show at the Harlem Cotton Club late in 1927. But colored bands were still restricted in their general influence. Their bookings were limited partly through racial discrimination and partly through the inflexibility of the programs they themselves played. (And the first operates on the second, for it was the tradition of playing everything everywhere that built up the fund of New York musicians, and made it possible for so many different men to gather in the same place, exchanging ideas and complementing each other.)

The first big hot band to rock the East generally was Jean Goldkette's. Goldkette himself had little command of the form, but he liked it and liked to have men around him playing it. He had Bill Rank and Don Murray and Ray Ludwig; he got Frank Trumbauer and Bix Beiderbecke and Steve Brown. When he was playing in Detroit the Chicago boys would come down to hear his men. In New York the band played in town and around the best one-night stands. And indirectly it upset the Nichols-Mole-Dorsey-etc. applecart, for Beiderbecke and Trumbauer took their own small bands into the studios and broke the monopoly wide open. Hoagy Carmichael had given his *Riverboat Shuffle* composition for jazz band to Bix back in 1925 in Indiana; Carmichael's tunes were already getting around and others had played this one; but when the Beiderbecke-Trumbauer aggregation made it for Okeh it simply stayed made, once and for all.

That was the beginning. Goldkette wanted bigger things than one good band and the outfit gradually went to pieces. But he had set old Mister Paul, the pied piper's son, thinking; it wasn't long before Whiteman had Bix and Trumbauer and Rank in his own band, to see if it would swing. He had already given a concert of course and was going along on the king-of-jazz idea, so that a little cornet man like Bix would come rolling in to take his place in the back and have to walk through half an acre of instruments. But when Bix would get him a little opening and let that horn go, it really did seem as though the band was swinging, all seven acres. So Whiteman had a "hot" band.

Meanwhile Ben Pollack, almost as much a pioneer as Henderson, had been working out the big-band idea from the West Coast, coming back home to Chicago, and then working East. When he came to New York in 1927 he was no surprise to pluggers and music scouts, who used to work all sorts of expense-account angles to get on a train and catch the boys on the stand; but it was something in New York. It was not only a big band—full brasses, reeds, and rhythm, with Harry Goodman already making the change to string bass—but it worked as a unit and enjoyed itself, it jumped and it had good men: Benny Goodman, MacPartland, Glenn Miller, Gil Rodin. It could play dance sets or it could chew the *Tiger Rag* all night. It had a pretty good bookful of arrangements. It could clown naturally and without musical loss because it had a couple of naturals in Harry Goodman and Icky Morgan. That was a band.

And about the same time (1927), along with Iron-head Wingy Mannone, there had blown into town a man from Texas with a trombone under his arm and a fine blues timbre in his voice: a Mr. Jackson, a Mr. T., otherwise Jack Teagarden. Pollack's boys spotted him as soon as they got in (playing with a band called Dexter's, I believe); and when they left for Atlantic City, to which Glenn Miller quite understandably did not wish to go, they took him in the band. Later when Pollack decided to stand in front instead of behind the drums, Teagarden in turn got a man still pretty hot from New Orleans in the band: Ray Bauduc.

They were boom years all along the line, and any good musical show could support a good band in the pit; the radio was going great guns; records were still being stamped out as fast as wheatcakes in Childs; and other boys came to town. People like Joe Sullivan and Frank Teschmaker and Pee Wee Russell and Gene Krupa began to show up on records made in New York. Louis Armstrong and Bix Beiderbecke kept setting an impossible pace on their Okeh recordings, and what with the mixing up of Bix and Lang, Teschmaker and Mole, Nichols and Goodman and Teagarden and all, the recording clique was completely resolved.

The later twenties have been set down as the jazz doldrums. Certainly the honky-tonk tradition of a few men blasting it out to their hearts' content was going definitely underground then. But the days around 1927 and '28 were in another sense the golden days, with the first rise of the big hot band carrying as many good men into New York to get together with other good men as the bands of 1920-3 brought in soloists from the outlands.

But even as a thing like that is not apparent at the start—that is, to the naked contemporary eye—it may be gradually easing onto the downgrade while it still seems at its peak. Individuals here and there knew that there were dark clouds for them, and the clouds were partly the weather, partly their own imagination, restlessness or sheer cussedness.

We know that there were hard days starting with the winter of 1929. But hard days for musicians started well before that. Almost any band has a steady inflow and outlet, like a swimming pool; but when big bands got to be the only thing to play in and make money, the men in them began to lose the close feeling of association and stick with it, thick or thin, that had done a lot to keep them together and satisfied when they were still just five, six, seven kids helling around together. It got so many of them never lived long enough in any one house to call it home. For another thing, the big time and the big money do something to everybody to age him more rapidly; and without the excitement and zest of their youth, which coincided with the youth of jazz itself, there were more and more things to find fault with everywhere, and little mannerisms you hadn't noticed at first became major irritations, and instead of feeling the thrill of doing something of near perfection, whether you yourself did it or the man next you did, you began to concentrate on the annoyance of perfection being missed.

There is no need to emphasize the effects of liquor and a general attitude of irresponsibility; but there is no need to forget that a working jazz musician is on the toughest grind of any artist, physically and nervously. There is no space here to indicate that unreal world of perpetual motion and fitful meals and sleep of men on the road (and expenses have become so high now that a band has to spend time on the road to pay off). Night after night after night, making the bus, the train, the barber's, the tailor's, the hotel, the stand, jump, jump, jump, and then the grind of the show itself, the same old numbers until even the good ones are more automatic than fun and the bad ones a matter of foul language. But the thing goes deeper than this: it is as hard on the nerves and thus general health to sit through something being done wrong as it is to break your heart doing it right every time yourself; it is as hard to follow the score playing a steady background four-fifths of the time as it is to wear the skin off your lip taking every chorus.

So men drink or smoke to take the bad taste out of their mouths and weariness out of their bones, and the more they do either the more they need it.

Bix Beiderbecke, after 1928, had plenty of miseries that he'd done himself and plenty more that others had done him. He had to leave Whiteman for a thorough rest—but even a rest couldn't make up for broken health and general disillusionment. The Pollack band seemed to be going in the wrong direction for some of its people, and they began getting off—Benny Goodman was about the first, and he was followed at intervals by over half the others. Red Nichols hung on with a big band of his own, making good records with an enlarged version of the old Pennies, and then, with the addition of outside men—including Goodman, Sullivan, Krupa, but mainly Teagarden—he made a series that is classic, revamping old pop numbers like *Smiles* and *The Sheik*, heating up new ones, doing blues and standards. These were the best ever done under his name, but presently the name disappears from hot music and bobs up in the income-tax returns only. Actually he went right on and is still going, but a record with Goodman and Teagarden like *Sweet Georgia Brown* is a swan song in retrospect. And Miff Mole, who had made some dandies with Teschmaker and others, withdrew more and more into straight studio work.

I should say that about the time the Ben Pollack band began to go to pieces, things began to go to pieces in general. Success was too much for some and not enough for others and the rate of exchange as between band personnels became so low and easy that music became more business than pleasure—and business at the turn of the thirties was plenty tough. The Chicago boys went back to Chicago, and found a different state of affairs. The others either scuffled or made names for themselves with the less discriminating majorities of the nation. Even Louis Armstrong preferred to do his stuff before an impersonal big band than build one of his own. Fletcher Henderson and Duke Ellington remained, not shaken, not changed; but they were here and there, an unregarded example rather than a leading force.

It wasn't only New York: things got tighter all over the country. To book more jobs you had to put on more show, and somebody had to book a job if you were going to work— and does anyone think a musician can live on high ideals and old clarinet reeds? But I think New York and the influence of New York was an important factor in all this, quite apart from primary economics.

New York made the big band possible—not New York as a city but New York as the center of broadcast over the country. And the successful big band made sudden easy living possible for anyone who could play with it. Now while a man may live and be satisfied on $22.50 a week in Kansas City, it doesn't take long at $100 to $200 a week on the big time to make him perpetually dissatisfied with $22.50 or even in many cases $85. New York's offer was glittering and almost none have been able to withstand it forever. But New York's demands, and the general speed-up on the nerves and the scale of living brought about in fulfilling them, were the kind of thing that must stick in the throat of those who want to play only the best all the time.

And then in giving the big bands a chance to work as such, bringing men from all over into town, it broke down the narrow confines that had held the recording group together. Lots of good men recorded together for a while, and were occasionally doing something even in the darkest days of the early thirties. But the good men had gradually become separate tumbleweeds, and while the Hoagy Carmichael dates for Victor and the Venuti-Lang all-star assembly for Vocalion, Louis Armstrong's *Knockin' a Jug* and Bessie Smith's *Down in the Dumps* used the finest of the finest, the men were never working together except on these sporadic occasions; they had no steady homes. The New York influence first set the Five Pennies up as the rallying point for jazz, and then knocked it down, and never really set up another rallying point until the day of the much more casual Goodman-Teagarden-Wilson-Krupa-Stacy-James-Hampton-Elman-Freeman tie-up. There was no common growing ground left, really; and then the depression came along, followed shortly by repeal and the end of the speakeasy and gangsters' hang-out; and jazz, having dispersed itself, went underground.

Things were still going on, such as Isham Jones, and some new forces were gathering. But it was all pretty quiet. I should say that the big band had got its start as a jazz instrument simply by growing up out of the small-band jazz tradition. It grew up too quickly to get itself reorganized, and it partly went to pieces. I should say that outside of such national phenomena as the depression attitude and the readjustment to wide-open bars, those aforementioned pieces were unconsciously testing out the best way they could get put together in a new kind of whole—the big band as we know it today. Through all this latent period, as in the years before it started, people like Henderson and Ellington in New York, people like Bennie Moten and Andy Kirk outside, were going right along. But the very fact that kept them from blowing up too fast—the color-line bias noted above—also kept them from doing more than indicate the way rather than actually lead it.

Not long after 1930 the casualty list included the names Beiderbecke, Lang, Teschmaker. Bessie Smith was off talking to her bottle; Rappolo was in the asylum forever; Louis Armstrong was first abroad and then under wraps; Fletcher Henderson was letting his band be broken up with his customary helpless good-nature. Jack Teagarden flopped on his own in Chicago and joined Whiteman. Benny Goodman was pretty much underground in New York, resentful and discouraged.

Men he had played with or would play with later were scattered here and there, also resentful and discouraged. There would be a rallying point here or a rallying point there, and some of them would get together, but it didn't last. There didn't seem to be any school because everyone had graduated.

HOT JAZZ TODAY

"The world's jazz crazy, Lawdy, so am I"

YOU WALK down Lenox Avenue in Harlem. The soft purr of motor cars makes a steady ribbon for the voices to dance on and for the pattering footsteps. The Savoy is blazing but it isn't what you want. The Big Apple is closed so forget the crowd pushing against a sidewalk window to hear the blues singer. Down Seventh Avenue to 125th Street.

Look, listen for the right rhythm. Kansas City. Boston. New York. Detroit. St. Louis. Birmingham.

> 52nd Street
> 35th and Calumet
> Basin and Customhouse
> Rampart and Perdido

Bob Lyons says it all happened before the war. You ask him what war and he cocks an eye at you. "Kid Bolden was a tough man. Joe Oliver was a tough man." He chews fast and looks at you again. "Louis came after him and locked him." Did he know Bunk? Bunk? Sure he knew Bunk. Played with him lots of times. "Now you're talkin' about the real jazz," Bob said.

> More than a mere $80.00 is involved in this case. New Orleans is the birthplace of jazz and the Court feels that this band was in accord with the reputation New Orleans has for producing such nationally famous hot jazz artists.

So said Judge William V. Seeber, awarding a decision to Johnny Repack's band against a Carny group that hired them to play for Mardi Gras, 1939.

And if Bob Lyons and Judge Seeber are right maybe we are, too. We've tried to tell a story and now it's just about told. The story of the music that was there before the theory was there, singing in a darkness of its own. Only what we tell is a part of the story, in the hope that the accent will fall right and you'll get the rest. How the music moved slowly in a cargo ship or swiftly in a Yankee clipper, out into a strange daylight and a new darkness that gave Bessie words to sing with:

> I'se bo'n in Georgia
> My ways are underground

The singing throat found a new tongue. New words for old music. New words for new ways. Music changing and shifting as the people themselves were shifted and changed:

> Oh, yuh talk e-bout your trouble, you don' think of mine,
> Yeh, yuh talk e-bout your trouble, you don' think of mine,
> I'm blue 'n I'm blue, say, almost lost my mind.

Words were twisted, bent to a new melodic line:

> Sometimes I wonder, why don't you write to me . . .

So they began to make a new music with the instruments and something of the form of a new world. Snatches of melody from a quadrille, a march, a folk song. Diatonic curving to pentatonic. But all the while the core of the song was in the plantation field, on the levee, on Congo Square, waiting for the right time and place. That was how it was "before the war," when Kid Bolden became King Bolden, first reigning monarch of a people's dynasty.

As the music went northward and finally into New York, it was routed over the country through bands, through networks. The blues words, for the most part, were forgotten. To get by, you dragged the tempo—but the words? No, except for Bessie and one or two others, there were no words to fit the music until they began putting words back. First, the small bands in the little joints (Blue Lou Barker singing New Orleans Blues). Then from writers who had not forgotten (Langston Hughes writing Love Is Like Whiskey for Midge Williams). This was what poets wanted to do, wasn't it—to write songs?

> Love, love, love, makes you walk on air,
> Love, love, love, makes you walk on air,
> Somebody touch you on the shoulder,
> You turn around 'n there ain't nobody there.

Billie Holiday, singing specially written words (Allan-Sacher) in a tempo that was slow, reminding you a little bit of the tempo Bessie sang in:

> Southern trees bear a strange fruit,
> Blood on the leaves and blood on the root . . .

Jazzmen think of what happened after Chicago, how the music they'd tried so hard to build (making mistakes very much like us all) was torn down, sold by the piece. Not that they were always right. But the interpretation of their best fell so far short of it! Jive. Noise. Speed. Play loud. Play hot. Play fast.

TAKE OFF ON ANY TUNE. GO DIXIE. SWING OUT. BE A NAME SOLOIST!

It's something of a joke now, because music, along with words, has gone back to musicians. The inbetweeners are still there but the musician has become an individual. Benny, at the Palomar, proved ten years later what Fletcher proved at Roseland. Commercial swing, as apt a term as it was unflattering, came into vogue. For all of its conventional trappings the new jazz had something of the old spirit. The arrangers, like the musicians themselves, were jazzmen. Suddenly piano players and little bands playing in little joints had a public. Ropes around the Onyx. Colored and white bands playing in public for the first time. People asked what it meant, looking all the time at the jitterbugs who were its froth, shagging in the aisles. George Wettling, who kept his drums tuned to the band's background, compared it with Chicago:

"The kids wouldn't act like they do today. They'd get told."

Well, maybe. Floors took punishment in the twenties. There wasn't so much showing off, perhaps, but perhaps we're more extraverted today. Look at the Gallup poll! As for jazz, you still have to take it where you can find it. If you're lucky, the place will be small. Maybe a joint where Pops is playing tonight but nobody knows him so there isn't a crush, where the bouncer loafs near the bar and nobody does calisthenics.

Listen to the trio, quartet or quintet giving emphasis to this or that instrument. Zutty's trio, with Edmond Hall and Duncan, playing at Nick's. To young kids learning their four-in-a-bar it might be a lesson to watch Zutty. The drums are background, melodic, and ride, yet played with a restraint that might go unnoticed if you weren't listening close to the music. Listen to the tonal quality of a small band playing with one instrument of a kind. The one at Nick's, for instance, featuring Bud Freeman, Eddie Condon, Pee Wee Russell, Max Kaminsky.

And where there isn't a joint, there's the phonograph.

Drop a nickel in the slot and listen to the music of America. Jazz and the river. New Orleans to Natchez. St. Louis to Davenport. Tri-cities to Chicago. Rock Island to Roseland. Ragtime. Honky-tonk. Square set. Shag. Creole. Cajun. French quadrille. Buddy Bolden and Bix Beiderbecke. Slow blues. Deep blues. Church Street Sobbin'. Mama Sweet Daddy. Aunt Hagar's Children. Had a nine pound hammer.

> Hold tight
> Hold tight

The world's jazz crazy, Lawdy, so am I.

C. E. S.

XI

FIFTY-SECOND STREET

BY WILDER HOBSON

FIFTY-SECOND STREET just west of Fifth Avenue and the region thereabouts has been the New York center of the "swing" fad. This venerable brownstone residential section just north of Rockefeller City was a honeycomb of speakeasies during Prohibition and then many of its premises were taken over by jazz traps with gaudy signboards outside and bad air inside. This was the first region in the world where large numbers of people were willing to take the most propulsive dance music and take it sitting down without demanding a dance floor. The United States had had jazz bands in public places for twenty years and suddenly a good-sized portion of the population sat down and listened to them. With the help of liquor, of course.

The reason why all this happened on West Fifty-second Street was presumably the Onyx. During Prohibition the Onyx was a conventional enough second-floor speakeasy whose only distinguishing characteristic was the fact that its clientele was mostly made up of dance and radio musicians, and that its entertainment was intended to please them. You went in a brownstone basement entry and up a dark flight of stairs to the second floor where there was a door painted a dirty mottled silver with the customary Judas hole. Inside there was a shadowy hall and a couple of drinking rooms, the rear room containing a bar, one of those push-ball games, a shabby upright piano, a few tables and some wicker chairs. Many musicians used the place as a club, made telephone calls there and parked their instruments, but nothing very much happened until late in the afternoon and nothing at all like a stampede after that. I don't think there were more than ten small tables in the whole joint, and I'm certain that I never saw more than twenty-five people in the place at any one time.

Along about five in the afternoon Joe Sullivan or Charley Born or Art Tatum would be playing the piano, but it was all so casual that if you hadn't known they were engaged by the management you might have supposed they had just dropped in and sat down. This effect was heightened by the fact that any of the guests could make music if he wished. Red McKenzie sang *Four or Five Times* with Sullivan, and "Del" Staigers got out his trumpet and showed how it was possible to play three notes on the thing at the same time. Joe Sullivan fooled around with popular songs and played a lot of blues like the *Gin Mill* record. Over in Tin Pan Alley now you can hear somebody say, with the defensive truculence of all those boys who are either chiseling or afraid of being chiseled all the time, that of course *Gin Mill Blues* is a "composition" on which "we own the copyright." But of course the record was just Joe improvising blues choruses as he did them every afternoon at the Onyx. Charley Born used to imitate not only the music but the manner of a lot of other pianists and I particularly remember the rather rigid weaving of the body which was a dead ringer for Arthur Schutt. Just before Repeal, the Onyx got in a Negro group called the Five Spirits of Rhythm with Teddy Bunn playing the guitar, Virgil Scroggins drumming with whiskbrooms on a piece of wrapping paper wrapped around a suitcase, and three tipple players (rather like a ukulele, if you don't know), including Leo Watson who also did scat-singing more or less in the manner of Benny Morton's trombone playing. This little group played and sang very light, stringy, exciting music.

After Repeal, the Onyx moved downstairs and across the street into larger quarters, and the Spirits of Rhythm moved with it. Joe Helbock, the manager, didn't get his liquor license for a few days and the place was virtually empty. Tommy Dorsey used to drop into the vacant restaurant and kid Helbock to the effect that he had better put the ropes up before the crowd bulged through the walls. That is just about what was happening within six months. And that was the beginning of West Fifty-second Street as a "swing" center. There also ought to be put in the record the fact that around this time "Wingy" Mannone held forth at the Jam Club in the basement of a near-by hotel for a week or so before the place was closed for disturbing the neighbors or serving booze after hours or some other irrelevancy. There was a dance floor, and you practically had to dance with Mannone, "Matty" Matlock, Eddie Miller, Ray Bauduc, and others. During that week Bud Freeman and Fats Waller sat in a good deal, and it was probably the first time a genuine small jazz band had attracted much attention in midtown New York since the Wolverines' engagement at the Cinderella in 1924. At this point, of course, the "swing" fad was yet to come.

It came quickly enough. There was one year when you could see it coming from week to week with those big loads of prep school and college assurance multiplying and those healthy and handsome young girls who were just so squirmingly eager to hear "Wingy" Mannone or "Stuff" Smith or go skiing or sit up and see the sunrise or whatever People Were Doing.

But there has been a lot of fun and some good music on East Fifty-second Street. I remember Mike Riley playing fiendishly eclectic trombone solos in which everybody else's style came in for a few bars, and right in the middle he would suddenly yell "Hello, Joe!" at an imaginary friend in the back of the house. And Benny Goodman's face wryly following the unpredictable turns of Pee Wee Russell's clarinet line—would he get out of this one all right or wouldn't he? He usually did. And Teddy Wilson telling off a nasty drunk who for the better part of twenty minutes kept yammering for a number which Teddy didn't want to play and finally, with a patronizing leer, stepped up and slapped a dollar on the piano. Wilson said quietly that the drunk had gotten more satisfaction out of giving the dollar than he, Wilson, could possibly obtain from receiving it, and the dollar stayed on the piano top and the tune never was played. I remember Joe Marsala playing the kind of clarinet music which would have delighted Teschmaker to an empty house in the Club McKenzie, and Jonah Jones, the trumpet player with Stuff Smith, who popularized "trucking," which should never have gone beyond his version. And there was trumpeter Charlie Shavers playing a wonderful, elaborate *Basin Street* with John Kirby's little band, and "Count" Basie's fourteen men playing *King Porter* with such steam that the leader's hands dropped off the piano and he sat listening to them with a slight, incredulous smile which reminded me of Fletcher Henderson's in the same kind of situation. And there was Bessie Smith, one Sunday afternoon in the upstairs room of the old Famous Door, singing blues without taking her furs off. There was something pretty fatuous about a couple of hundred people sitting on camp chairs and goggling at Bessie while she sang, but it didn't affect her. The obliviousness of many Negro musicians to circumstances which, considering the nature of their music, are absurd is something to think about. Albert Ammons walked out on the stage of Carnegie Hall as if he were moving into a crowd of friends in a South Side Chicago flat and played the way he might have played for those friends, the only difference being that he had a Steinway concert grand instead of the upright which he would have preferred for its easier action. I suppose as long as there is such a thing as Boogie Woogie piano playing there will be occasions when three thousand people will sit in rows and listen to it. But it is too bad they haven't enough curiosity about the music to find their own way to it until it has become a publicity phenomenon.

One thing, at least, could be said for Fifty-second Street, and that is that not by the wildest stretch of the imagination could any cultural atmosphere be discerned in it. If people appeared who were interested in jazz as a cultural item or in the question, "Has Swing a Social Significance?" they were at once lost in the general yammer and shuffle and the same racket went on whether the music was good, bad, or indifferent. The Street offered at least some of the handicaps against which the music has developed—fetid air and sweat, promiscuous body contact, watered whiskey, etc., etc. After a while they even began to put in postage stamp dance floors and anyone who thought it was disrespectful to dance while Count Basie played the *One O'Clock Jump* had to take it or leave the joint, thank God.

At its best, Fifty-second Street offered just about every conceivable discouragement to those who wanted to hear jazz music for phony reasons—which is more than you can say for a lot of places.

XII

RETURN TO CHICAGO

BY FREDERIC RAMSEY, JR.

CHICAGO DREW jazz up the river, welcomed it and sent it on the way to New York. When the depression and the end of Prohibition saw the end of good times, hot musicians returned to Chicago, because it was their home town and because they felt they could still pick up some sort of job there that would keep them going. .

Yet as late as 1934, most of them were still looking for a place to play their music. Many had given it up in disgust, with the feeling Frank Teschmaker had expressed for all of them: "You can't play hot and make a living out of it." Because this was true, some of them, like Dave North, who used to play with Teschmaker in Husk O'Hare's Wolverines, left music entirely. North got a job that was far from jazz; he tends the ticker tape for Chicago's Board of Trade. Tougher spirits, like Muggsy Spanier, refused to give up. He joined Ted Lewis' Orchestra, where his identity was concealed for a number of years.

In 1935 the Congress Hotel hired Benny Goodman's Orchestra as an experiment, for no band had ever been able to pull in the corners of the spacious Urban Room and make it seem cheerful. The trial was a complete success for Benny and the Congress; what was to have been a six-week stay stretched into a seven-month engagement. The important thing about Benny Goodman's Orchestra was that it played hot music. When that got across, "swing" was on its way.

The Three Deuces, once a speakeasy, re-opened with Zutty Singleton, and Fletcher Henderson came into the Grand Terrace. Fletcher also arranged for Benny, and wrote tunes like *Grand Terrace Swing* and *Christopher Columbus* (the latter with Choo Berry). Count Basie arrived, and the Grand Terrace was first to welcome a new kind of jazz that came in fresh from Kansas City. The "Toddlin' Town" was in ferment once more. Old instruments were dug out of attics, carefully polished, tuned up, and made ready for new work. King Oliver's Creole Jazz Band had been forgotten for a long time: the Dodds brothers, who had played in his band, came up from the South Side and took over the Three Deuces with their music. Others from the Creole Jazz Band began to crop up. Lil Armstrong opened a "Swing Shack" where customers could order a meal guaranteed to be "a solid sender right in the groove" from a menu boasting of "Tisket Biscuits and Tasket Hash, Rug Cutter's Roast and Killer Diller Waffles." Louis Armstrong himself was in and out of Chicago more often than before, riding high on the new wave of popularity that "swing" had piled up for him.

Near the site of Lil's Swing Shack, King Oliver's band used to play from one till four in the morning at the old Pekin Café. The Pekin was tough; gangsters who went there began to fire first, asked their questions later—if there was anyone around to ask. When the police came in, it was too bad. Two of them tried it in 1919, and were shot down on the spot. Go to the scene of this shooting today, and you will discover that this same building is now a police station. The old barroom has been converted into a courtroom, and the back wall of the theatre has been filled in to make a garage for the Black Marias.

Seven blocks from the Pekin the old Dreamland Café runs

under a new name, featuring someone's Aces of Rhythm, a Sweepstakes Band, a handful of impersonators, and a floor show "with stepping chorus girls." They dance on the original dance floor, made of a mirror, but not to the same music.

Excellent Negro bands still play the Savoy, Louis Armstrong's old hangout. The first man you see when you enter the Savoy is the venerable King Jones, who fifteen years ago brought audiences to the point of hilarity when he got up to conduct the King Oliver band, which had always managed to get along very well without either a conductor or a master of ceremonies. No one from New Orleans had heard of a master of ceremonies, nor had the patrons of the Lincoln Gardens, until King Jones came forth, caus'ng a near-riot. His great wide grin is a Chicago landmark. In his new job he can still utilize the grin, if not the baton, for he's doorman at the Savoy.

The New Orleans jazz tradition still counts for a lot in Chicago. At 935 North State Street, there's a place called the "P and M New Orleans Bar-B-Q, Specializing in Spare Ribs, Chicken and Steaks," which is run by Paul Mares, who played trumpet with the New Orleans Rhythm Kings when they first came to Chicago in the early twenties. Every Monday night, with Tuesday morning well on its way, Paul calls a session to order: not a Parliamentary meeting run according to Robert's *Rules of Order*, but a New Orleans jam session attended by some of Chicago's best jazzmen. Members in good standing are the musicians who play with the Bob Crosby Orchestra, New Orleanians such as Ray Bauduc, drummer, Eddie Miller, clarinet and tenor sax, and Fazola, clarinet, who used to play with Abbie Brunies.

The Crosby Orchestra plays long engagements at the Blackhawk Restaurant, drawing huge crowds. It is the only large orchestra that has anything of the tradition of both white and colored New Orleans music behind it. Eddie Miller will tell you that Rappolo was the man who set his style on clarinet;

this interest in New Orleans music typifies that of other members of the orchestra. Playing arrangements by Bob Haggart, some of which are based on transcriptions of old King Oliver and Louis Armstrong records, their concern has been to recapture something of the spirit of the small early jazz bands in their own larger group. Consequently, there's a freedom of feeling in this band when it plays along, an easy, relaxed "ride," with liquid clarinet parts that tie up loose ends and carry the music forward. As in all New Orleans groups, the trombone is used as a hot instrument, playing in a clean fast style rather than contributing sickly-sweet runs. The band has discovered that there are more important qualities than balance, so often achieved at the expense of tonality. Sometimes you'll hear the comment, "There's plenty of brass in that band," and that's a very good way of saying that the Crosby brasses sound like the instruments they are. Refreshing in its interpretation of "standards," this band also plays real blues, which are almost lost in these days of "swing." So when its members jam with the Dodds brothers, Boyce Brown, Jimmy MacPartland, Rod Kless, and Paul Mares, they form a small New Orleans combination which allows the maximum of freedom, and go to it.

Musicians from New Orleans have a way of playing that has stayed good. The music grew out of its surroundings and the technical foundation was thus a part of the expression. Think how utterly ridiculous it would be to ask a man to play New York's 47th Street style of 1925, even if it could be done! The corn grows tall on Broadway! But it's natural to ask musicians from New Orleans to play their style, for with a little brushing up, it's a style that lives.

You can see this when Muggsy Spanier's orchestra plays. George Brunies, of the New Orleans Rhythm Kings, is the trombone player. It is George, with his rough, vigorous Dixieland trombone, who sets the style for the group, while Muggsy, a Chicagoan, clearly demonstrates the vitality of the style which he has assimilated from New Orleans musicians. Muggsy plays a counterpart to Brunies' trombone, with an intense, forceful drive that keeps going straight ahead because he doesn't slur it with any sideshows. Rod Kless, who plays clarinet in Muggsy's Band, was taught not by Rappolo but by Teschmaker. Here is living proof of a hot style that, in its inception, seems almost freakish. Teschmaker himself was subjected to two significant influences, the style of Noone and the style of Dodds. But the latter was already influenced by Armstrong's trumpet style at the time Tesch was himself listening to it. Actually, any suspicion of freakishness is dismissed when one listens to the records of Teschmaker and realizes that he successfully fused these influences. And Rod Kless, who had roomed with Tesch, had absorbed from him the basis for his own original style. Recently he tried to locate Tesch's clarinet. Cracked and no longer capable of being used professionally, it had been sold to a high school clarinet player, ending its days in surroundings similar to those where Tesch began his musical career.

There is still one clarinet that successfully bridges the gap from old to new Chicago. This is the one that belongs to Johnny Dodds. There is still as much fire, as much of the blues, in his instrument as there always was. He played it in the spring of 1939 at a concert, ambitiously titled "Swing Saga," held in the University of Chicago's Mendel Hall. With Johnny was Lil Armstrong, playing piano as she had in the Hot Five days. Completing the little band was Johnny's trumpet player from the 29 Club, a drummer and a guitarist. The audience seemed unaware of his presence until he'd stepped out from behind the piano. Modest and quiet, Johnny fussed with his keys while the applause died down, then raised his clarinet and tore out a chorus of *Dippermouth* with all the vigor and force that went into his playing when he first hit Chicago. After the concert someone noticed Johnny wrapping his clarinet in a newspaper; he's probably never had a case for it, not even when he first came up the river to join King Joe. When he's not showing the young generation of jitterbugs what jazz is all about, Johnny plays at night spots around town, sometimes at the 29 Club. The South Side clubs hear a lot of his clarinet.

Another New Orleans clarinet who may be heard on the South Side is Jimmy Noone. For a while Jimmy had a job at "Swingland," but that place has a way of folding up now and then. Alarming where the musician's security is concerned, it is not allowed to affect the music. The history of the South Side has always been that the places folded, but the music went on. One familiar reaction to a place going out of business was, "Bring yo' stuff on over to my house an' we'll have a party an' sweat, that's all!" Then down by the train yards behind the doors of shanty-tenements there'd be "plenty o' sweatin', that's all." Because music comes naturally out of the lives of these people, it continues to be possible to hear real jazz here, jazz played with energy and feeling. Uptown in Chicago, they glow and may even perspire, but the jazz-men seldom sweat.

To take care of some of its unemployed musicians, members of the colored branch of Local 208, A. F. of M., went into the band business themselves. They rented the old Warwick Hall on East 47th Street, rounded up a couple of bands, hoping to fill the hall with dancers and provide the patrons with some entertainment on the side. They got more than they bargained for. The north section of the hall soon became a jam session for paying customers as well as for musicians. If you arrive there before nine o'clock on Thursday night with the girl friend, twenty cents puts you through the door, no charge for the girl. Even when you arrive early, the place is jammed. Dark faces move about in the glow of the dim dance floor light, or jig furiously as an exhibitionistic couple perform the latest version of a shag that began years before in the South.

The north bandstand is always completely occupied by a hot band and its many friends who clamber about the platform and get in each other's way. Coats are piled on empty chairs, instrument cases lie scattered about. The band is never composed of the same personnel for half an hour at a time. Every musician who is in the hall wants to sit in and do some playing. If a cornetist stands up to take a chorus, half a dozen other cornetists are ready to grab his place and his instrument before he has finished, and to continue the chorus. Sometimes the one chair containing the hats and coats of the band in control gets knocked over, by accident or by design. The whole group throws down bass fiddle, guitar, horns, reeds, and rushes to reclaim its wearing apparel in the mêlée that follows. While this goes on in the northern half of the old dance hall, an atmosphere of sweetness and light pervades the southern half, which is presided over by a large commercial band playing dance arrangements through a loudspeaker system for which, apparently, the hotter band has no need.

On the north side of the hall, players such as Mike McKendrick, guitar, Al Washington, tenor sax, both from Louis Armstrong's recording orchestra of 1931, Israel Crosby, string bass, Jimmy Noone, and many others, can be heard. In the north side orchestra younger talent keeps coming in from the small towns, learning, developing. There are young players here who are already comparable as to talent with older men holding down jobs in large bands. They are obscure now, but it won't take long for talent scouts to search out the good men playing for the minimum in this old dance hall. Sometimes Lee Collins, who has a five-piece band of his own at the Derby Club in Calumet City, can be seen at the Warwick; he was one of the first trumpeters to come up from New Orleans.

The most interesting music that comes out of the South Side is that of the Boogie Woogie pianists. As late as 1936, Boogie Woogie was in a position analogous to that of hot jazz in 1920. It had fully developed, yet not many persons outside the Negroes for whom it was played knew anything about it. You could walk into the South Side cabaret where Ammons was playing, see six men tearing through a set with a fierceness and abandon that obviously worried the customers seated at the front-row tables, and ask the name of the band:

"Ah dunno, Albert Ammons, he plays pianer and calls the numbers, Jimmy Hoskins starts the beat, we don't .call the band nothin'."

The men who played this music couldn't stay hidden forever. Meade Lux Lewis and Albert Ammons have moved on to New York. Older exponents of the rolling bass are to be found in Chicago, until recently unnoticed and unsung. One of these men is Jimmy Yancey, upon whose bass figure Meade Lux Lewis built *Yancey Special*. Another is Cripple Clarence Lofton. Dan Qualey went to Chicago in the summer of 1939 to record these forgotten pianists. Qualey's records, released under the Solo Art label, are proof of how varied the party piano can be.

It is not surprising to find that Chicago is still contributing forcefully to the hot jazz of today. With a past that is most significant in the history of this music, this city has carried into the present the same fresh, vital idea of improvised jazz which the players of New Orleans first brought to the South Side. Chicagoans have made their own adaptations, but have nevertheless stuck closely to the basic idea of a small band that allows each of its players full opportunity for improvisation. That is because the example of New Orleans has always been before them, where they could hear it and benefit through an understanding of what it had to offer.

A further proof of the vitality of jazz in Chicago today is to be had in the development of a "second line" of very young musicians. It is made up of the boys who hang around outside night spots like the 65 Club and play on instruments of their own invention. It doesn't seem to matter what kind of instrument they have; it may be an old cigar-box guitar, a soap-box drum, or a set of tin-can cymbals. Regardless of what they use, they produce lots of rhythm and some lively "novelty" music. If anyone throws a dime at them, they race after it and disappear up the cobbled street; then another young group comes along to take their place. Sometimes they go into the clubs, play a bit, then run out as soon as a few pieces of silver are tossed at them, or the management intervenes. Eventually, these toy instruments will be traded for second-hand clarinets, cornets, drums, and trombones, and a new generation of musicians will be on the way.

To see the enthusiasm of these kids with their toy instruments is to realize why Johnny Dodds still smiles when he talks about the day his father came back from New Orleans to his home in Waverley, Mississippi, with a long, mysterious package in his hands. Johnny and Baby, his young brother, had been pretending that they had a band of their own. Johnny had a toy whistle; Baby had a pile of tin cans, his first set of drums. The penny whistle broke, and Johnny had asked his father to buy him a new one. Johnny undid the package in a hurry; when he saw what was in it, he was so pleased and so glad he could hardly hear his father, who was saying:

"Son, I want you to have a real clarinet."

XIII

LAND OF DREAMS

BY CHARLES EDWARD SMITH

IN A vacant lot on Basin Street, in the city of New Orleans, a palm tree quivers lazily in the warm sunshine, a mangy cat drowses on the cement walk beside the name, set in metal on the walk itself, "Tom Anderson." From these mementos and the name in cut glass in the transom at number 235, "Lulu White," one is supposed to conjure up a picture of Basin Street when it was the flamboyant edge of Storyville, New Orleans' famous red-light district. But no mementos can conjure up the row of houses, so absurdly like a potpourri of the most pretentious architectural styles of the late nineteenth century, or the goings-on that made this Basin Street the pattern for high-hat low-life.

On soft spring evenings, Josie Arlington's palm tree waved languorously while hot music emanated from The Function. Revolutions were traditionally plotted at the Countess Willie Piazza's. But now this is no more. The pretty quadroons at Lulu White's Mahogany Hall, who inspired the *Basin Street Blues*, are gone. It will never again be necessary to stretch the canopy from the cut glass transom to the curb. As for the jazz boys who got their start in the district, playing strings in the sporting houses and the works for the more raucous joints—there's no one to hire them any more, what with Pete Lala on

W.P.A. and Nancy Hanks' old place a dumpy bar with a nickelodeon.

On some of the streets there are still rows of cribs, long-shuttered door and long-shuttered window alternating with business-like regularity. And there are the voices of prostitutes, those voices that have the same flat tonal quality the world over, whether it's an unadorned "hello," or a persuasive, "come on in, honey." Sometimes the invitation is more specific. Coming from behind shutters it's weird and blue, a little bit as though you isolated one trembling note from the low register of a clarinet. The cab driver is not interested in where the bands play. "I know a good place," he tells you. "They'll put on a show. All that French stuff. Fifteen bucks!"

Fifteen bucks! Josie would say you must've forgot to tip somebody. Can you imagine putting up the canopy for that? No, and they don't, either, not any more. It's a business proposition now, just as it would be in any other city in the land. Thumbing through the pages of Tom Anderson's Blue Book, you can laugh at "landladies" and "new arrivals," but if you had ever talked with a New Orleans "landlady" you'd know that what Mae West put on in *Belle of the Nineties* was just a heroic imitation. The real product was cool and smooth and compelling. It had to be, for it was the voice that sold the bill of goods, not the goods themselves. Anyway, that's gone. There are only cribs and the phonographs in bars, grinding out the beat blues.

The cabaret idea took hold quickly in Storyville. It was booming by 1900, at Nancy Hanks' Saloon, where the "girls" induced the guests to come through with handsome tips so that Buddy Bolden's Band would play *Careless Love Blues*. Later on in the night it would be the original payoff blues, 219 *Took My Babe Away*. It was rowdy and nobody pretended it was nice.

But Storyville, to a New Orleans musician, is only part of the picture. If you ask him what killed the music business in that town he'll tell you any one of a number of things—the radio, the talking picture, the filling in of the lake front, poverty. "Why, they used to hire bands for everything," one old-timer said. "If you gave a party you'd get a keg of beer and hire three or four pieces." Besides this, the innumerable societies and fraternal orders were constantly giving balls at which they tried to outdo each other in hiring bands. Each group had its own societies—white, Creole Negro, uptown Negro—and these gave the musicians work. Among the Negroes, whether they were Creole or uptown, the burial societies saw to it that when the hearse started out from Geddis & Moss, there was a brass band with it. The brass band was paid for its services, the dance musicians were paid, the small bands for parties were paid. To gig around meant to play for small parties, week-end engagements, and the like. Often the man who gigged around had another vocation. The members of the Original Dixieland Jazz Band at one time had other jobs. But this had to be true of New Orleans where there were always so many musicians that it was expedient for the younger ones to learn a trade. The union was lenient on this score and to gig around did not necessarily imply a non-union job, as it did in the North.

Nowadays when a big name band leader stops off in the Crescent City, to take in the races, maybe, and have a Ramos gin fizz at the St. Charles bar, it is not at all unusual for him to report that all the musicians have left New Orleans. The town is milked dry. A quick glance around might indicate this. No longer do the skilled Creole Negro musicians have spots like Antoine's or the Roosevelt (Grunewald). No longer can a promoter go down to Storyville, make such an exciting discovery as did Frisco when he heard his first Dixieland combination. No longer will the visitor find bands—uptown Negro, Creole Negro, white—at the lake front, at parties, at dances, so many and so varied as to form an unforgettable impression of a city to which music is even more native than Creole cooking.

But here the justification is pulled up short. The simple truth of the matter is that the people of New Orleans enjoyed and sustained the music without the music itself getting more than a passing nod from the local guardians of culture. The music was judged by where it was played most. It's an old story now how the trade journals ventured to localize jazz (a year after Storyville closed) and the bigwigs of New Orleans music, who knew their operas but not their four-in-a-bar, utterly disowned it. Through it all the people enjoyed their music and the musical tradition stayed very much alive. In 1939 during Carnival week, one parade was given over to the kids. In shorts and bright costumes they came down Canal Street, hundreds of them, with everything from kazoos to baritone horns, playing the traditional march tunes of New Orleans street parades.

Although New Orleans continues to be a musicians' city, with the lessening of jobs there has come an inevitable lessening of young talent. There isn't the economic incentive, for one thing. The youngster knows, or is duly warned by his parents, that choosing music for a profession is a shortcut to poverty. Moreover, he will not hear as much good jazz in New Orleans as formerly. But this isn't because there are no musicians. It's simply because the city can't support them. Around Mardi Gras time you'll find all of them working—even Picou can't resist the requests to play for Carnival—but the rest of the year they will be found filling any number of jobs outside their chosen profession.

Perhaps, therefore, the visiting critics shouldn't be censored too precipitantly. It might well be true that on an ordinary week end New Orleans would offer no more music than any other city its size. And at that some of the bands might be from out of town. But the musicians are there and New Orleans hotels could, if they wished, find plenty of talent at home. Generally speaking, this would be more true of Negro than of white talent. Lacking resources to get away, perhaps in some instances being aware that he would have a difficult time of it elsewhere, the Negro musician keeps to his native environment, taking whatever job he can get to keep alive.

Among the white musicians, Abbie Brunies and Harry Shields are two who have managed, on occasion, to get good bands together. But the bands do not last as to personnel, and do not always mature. Abbie, for instance, had a spot in the French Quarter, playing cabaret shows for the tourist trade. Between shows they tried to play standards but the spirit was missing. The band just couldn't pull together. You could say it was because Ray Bauduc was in Chicago with Crosby or because Fano Rappolo was with Prima, but that would be unfair to Abbie's drummer and clarinet player. Actually, you couldn't expect much inspiration from a band whose members felt dangerously close to economic insecurity. If the good spots in New Orleans went to New Orleans bands as they came up, instead of giving preference to those that had first made the grade in the big cities of the North, the quality of present day white jazz in New Orleans would improve. As it is, the men fret in an environment much less conducive to jazz than that of twenty years ago and at the first opportunity they migrate to other parts of the country.

Except during Mardi Gras, most of the better Negro musicians will be working intermittently, if at all. They will tell you that Big Eye Louis Nelson is down to the Gypsy Tea Room two nights a week. Maybe you'll find him there and maybe not. If you do, it will be an experience.

During Mardi Gras in 1939, he played at a cheap cabaret where the girls screamed "How Am I Doing, Hey, Hey?" and the band played as loud as it felt. If the test of a New Orleans clarinet is its strength in the ensemble, Big Eye Louis was an excellent example. His clarinet soared above the unholy din, somehow unifying it and making it a reasonable performance, the short notes running into each other in the New Orleans manner. That's a real trick, because each note is attacked by itself.

The floor show went off and the band played a series of numbers, on each of which Big Eye Louis improvised choruses. The variations were on the melody, given to sudden imaginative upward thrusts, yet never on the screwball side and never mere notes. His tone was broad and when on *Basin Street Blues* he went into the lower register, he produced an incredibly warm tone. On *Darktown Strutters' Ball* and on *Pine Top's Boogie Woogie* Louis played chorus after chorus, his shoulders hunched forward and his clarinet pointed towards the floor.

For the Mardi Gras crowd he not only played these tunes; he also did *High Society Rag*. Before playing it he explained that to play the real chorus like Picou would be difficult on his instrument, since it was old, repaired in a makeshift way, and especially since the keys were stiff, which would make the fast runs in the upper register next to impossible. "It's a tough chorus," he apologized.

"Bechet told me to ask you to play it. He said you did it all right."

"I'll have to fake it," Louis said. "I'll play you a good chorus but it won't be the real one."

On the first chorus Louis faked it. It wasn't the real one but, as Louis had promised, it was a good chorus. The average clarinetist, on a broken down instrument, would crowd the notes. Louis placed them exactly right in the rhythm. They went through the piece twice. Girls pushed back the portières that separated the cabaret from the bar, stood in the doorway and listened. The dark-complexioned bartender (all the bartenders and managers seemed to be either Sicilians or Creoles) poked his head through the little service window, looking over at one of the girls. Suddenly, on the last chorus, Louis was playing the real one, the one he had learned from

Picou. When he asked afterward if that was all right, there was a gleam of self-satisfaction in his eye. He knew it was all right. He was just making conversation.

Walter Pichon, a Negro pianist who arranges for visiting name bands, has a little band of his own at the Crescent Billiard Hall, a white place frequented by the best shaggers in town. Occasionally in the South you see a shag that's right on the floor, not the bouncing kind that makes a Manhattan dance hall a major hazard. And you can, in places like the Crescent, see dancing that is free from exhibitionism. Sometimes when the trumpet player, John Brunious, plays *Dippermouth* in a clean style, a jitterbug climbs the chandelier but, aside from such lapses, the dancing is equal to the music. Usually when Brunious reaches the third chorus of *Dippermouth* the kids have stopped shagging and have formed a semi-circle around the band platform.

Walter Pichon spoke favorably of a Creole piano player named Steve Lewis. He was found working in a small saloon in the French Quarter, a few blocks below the St. Louis Cathedral. There, on a little red piano with the inevitable sugar can to catch tips, he played sometimes for himself, sometimes according to the whims of the patrons. He was something like Jelly Roll Morton and it was hard to figure out at first. Then one realized it was the way he used chords. Watch a man's left hand and you can see if he is a musician. Jelly Roll said that, and watching Steve brought it back. How he got that half-pint piano to respond to his fingers was a constant puzzle to the customers, who would group about, drinks in hands, asking him to do that last chorus of *St. Louis Blues* over again, so that they could see how it was done. Steve looked up with a leonine and very Latin grin, spoke with a slightly Creole intonation, putting his fingers on the keyboard. "They played this a long time ago," Steve said softly, without looking up again.

Every hall was crowded Carnival Day and every hall had its own band. In the bands themselves there was no distinction between uptown and Creole, though there was in the crowds. At Economy Hall and San Jacinto the sea of faces was noticeably Creole. Uptown in one of the old halls you noticed the darker faces of the uptown Negroes. Joseph Robichaux was playing uptown, near the Garden District. It was impossible to get near enough to the bands to hear them properly, though the impression came through. At San Jacinto Hall, Sidney Desvigne had with him a young trumpet player (from uptown) who had tremendous power. Sidney Desvigne, having studied with Manuel Perez, is a finished musician, the tone quality of his trumpet pure and a little sweet. Two or three people in the rhythm section were related to prominent Negro musicians playing in the rhythm sections of leading bands.

After nightfall, Storyville began to take on a semblance of life, not as a red-light district but because it has, in recent years, become a Negro section. The King of the Zulus, after going down North Claiborne Avenue where he stopped at Steve Schlemmer's bar for refreshment, went on to the Aristocrats' Club, where he was toasted again. He'd been doing that all day but apparently could take it. In the late afternoon the little Creole children in Carnival dress shrieked delightedly as the brass band came up the avenue, followed by the white mules that distinguished his Majesty's entourage. The band struck up on the dance floor within the building, trying to sound like a brass band; outside the brass band tried to sound like a jazz band. There wasn't any question of its being a battle of music. The brass band, with its singing clarinets and its battery of drums, carried off the honors.

Misty darkness came over the city while the dancing and revelry continued. Presently the word came by that a King's duties to his people had not been finished. Once more the white mules were harnessed to the float and once more the King

Duke Ellington's Washingtonians at the Kentucky Club, about 1925
Sonny Greer, Charlie Irvis, Elmer Snowden, Otto Hardwick; *seated,*
Bubber Miley, Duke Ellington

photo from Otto Hardwick

Duke Ellington and his Orchestra at the new Cotton Club
"White jackets, boiled shirts, dress ties."

Ella Fitzgerald

nomy and Mutual Aid Association,
nized 1836

Lulu White's Mahogany Hall,
235 Basin Street

NEW ORLEANS, 1939

Tom
Anderson's

Willie Bunk Johnson

"Night and day I puffed on it and when I did get the slite of it, Oh boy,
I really went."

Jack Teagarden

"I was born down in Texas—raised in Tennessee."

Pete Johnson

"Roll 'em, boy, let 'em jump for joy."

Albert Ammons and Meade Lux Lewis

"I want you to learn my Boogie Woogie."
                                    —PINE TOP

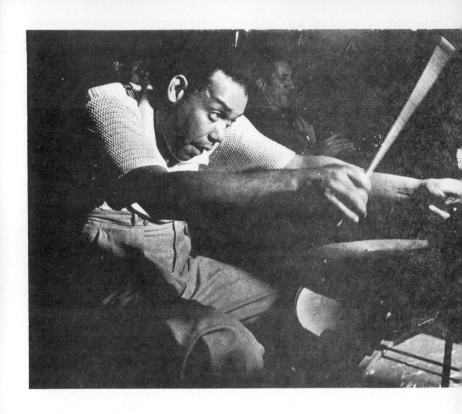

Zutty Singleton (*above*) with Al Gold, Pee Wee Russell, Dickie Wells, Max Kaminsky (*below*) recording for the Hot Record Society. This band includes veterans of New Orleans and Chicago.

took his scepter and climbed amiably to his throne. Torches
lit the way as the parade, now practically taken over by the
"second line" of dancing kids, wound in and out the streets
of the Creole section. As it came into Storyville the procession stopped at each bar. Tomorrow the King would again be
a porter in the Mayor's office but while the night wore on this
Zulu King, with white patches about his eyes and an astounding capacity for liquids of high alcoholic content, surveyed
all that Rex did not survey, and that was plenty.

The procession rumbled on, across Canal Street to Bolden
territory, where the fish-fry wagon was found next morning,
right outside the old Eagle Saloon. It left behind it a flotsam
and jetsam of celebrants who crowded into John Lala's bar,
at what is still the corner of Customhouse and Franklin if
you go by the sidewalk tiles. In the crush at the bar, Big Eye
Louis carefully thrust his hand and arm between two necks,
extracting a bottle of beer and a glass. Viewed through the
thick of the crowd, it looked like a magician's trick. Bumel
Santiago weaved through groups of people. He was dressed in
bright Carnival colors that made his sensitive Latin features
appear even more Latin. He said something in a low voice that
was drowned by a flood of voices, and these in turn were
dominated by a low harsh voice coming from the nickel
phonograph:

Oh when the Saints come marching home . . .

Bumel Santiago nudged Big Eye Louis—was it De Lier or
Nelson? (Big Eye Louis quaffed his beer as though the mere
question of a name were superfluous.) Forming the nucleus of
a small group, they shoved through the crowd to a tiny room
off the ladies' room. There were, in fact, several ladies there
in the ante-room, some with their infants, but the ten square
feet or so could still hold a few more, standing upright like
the piano. They got an old box for Bumel to sit on and he
tried a long run, as though testing the piano. "Too much

noise," he said, indicating with a thrust of his head the partition that only went up about seven feet.

"Play some walking bass, Bumel," Louis said.

Bumel looked around slowly at everyone as he tipped the bottle back. "I know that stuff," he said, "like Mary Lou Williams plays. Willy Forrest is the boy that plays that. Did Steve tell you about him?"

Big Eye Louis put one arm on the piano top, still holding his clarinet case. His brown face looked rather French, what with thick jowls, and bulging heavy-lidded eyes. Bumel had a delicate touch, made you think of Pine Top, the one who was stabbed in the back, but he was nervous, he kept looking back over his shoulder as though the racket out there were something you could see with your eyes. They played low deep blues on the phonograph, the kind you hear in New Orleans a lot, but they'd always come back to that one record, Louis Armstrong singing about the Saints. And Bumel played through it all.

The listeners tightened around the piano as though in that way they could hem in the sound. Nearest the wall stood a gaunt woman with a nursing baby and out in the little room, beyond the circle jammed up against the piano, a young and very stout woman with dark glowing skin tried to accomplish everything from a lindy to a shag, her voice punctuating the music with tiny half-guttural shrieks of delight. The music was dark and deep blue and then suddenly it reminded you of the morning sunlight in front of the Absinthe House where Piron sings Creole songs . . . the three young Creole Negro girls, dressed fine, very cool, and the boy in the white jacket polishing whatever it was that had to be polished:

> Mornin' honey
> Mornin' sweetheart

Buoyant, with a kind of rippling laugh. Big Eye Louis squeezed in against the old upright as someone pushed past him to the ladies' room. He poked Bumel. "That clarinet was beat," he said, "but I played *High Society* anyway!"

And all this time, a few blocks away, Henry (Kid) Rena, who'd learned to play *High Society* on trumpet by listening to Big Eye Louis, was doing his night's work in a taxi-dancehall. That was his job, seven nights a week, and he couldn't stop for Carnival. In at ten, out at four or five in the morning, playing straight through without intermission. The girls sat on a long bench against the wall while the customers lined the rail that cut off the dance floor. Some of the girls didn't bother to sit down between numbers. Two of them stood near a pillar in the center of the floor, a plump brunette in a yellow evening gown of sleazy satin, shoulders cut square, and a blonde with a thin hard face, taffy curls cascading to her shoulders, dressed in low-cut flowering chiffon with tiny pink ribbons. Beyond them, to the left of the orchestra platform, could be seen the inside bar, where the patrons sat dances out with the "hostesses." Kid Rena had only recently resumed work after a long illness and his cheeks looked hollow, especially in the moments when the band rode on and he held his trumpet on his knee.

Kid Rena had been in the "Home" with Louis Armstrong. He spoke gratefully of Captain Jones, who'd taken a bunch of wild kids off Perdido Street and given them a reason for living. Rena, like Louis, was one of three boys who played cornet at the Home. Like Louis, too, he'd hung around the improvising cornet players who took the crown after Buddy Bolden went into the insane asylum, players like Bunk and Joe Oliver. When Louis Armstrong had gone to Chicago, Rena took the latter's place in Kid Ory's band which then consisted of Big Eye Louis on clarinet; Bob Lyons, bass; Lorenzo Stall, banjo; and Joe Lindsay; drums. In 1925 Rena lead a band of his own at the Gypsy Smith Auditorium, winning the Old Gang Best Band trophy against Celestin's Tuxedo Orchestra.

Coming on the dance hall job seven nights a week, it was not surprising that Kid Rena complained of "beat chops." The band had to play all the time, short numbers that didn't seem to last more than a minute or so. Then ticket takers cleared the floor, girls sat down for a split second's rest, and the next number began. On a slow number like *Basin Street* the band had hardly begun when it was time to stop. Stop, begin, stop, begin, that was how it went, all night long.

About eleven o'clock one of the boys left the platform to get a big container of black coffee. The band went right on. When the coffee came, each had a few sips while the others played. Kid Rena said that his lips began to feel the mouthpiece after that first drink of coffee. Around one o'clock he'd have another, and by then he had an embouchure. The whole band felt it. Instead of changing the tune they'd stop, begin, stop, begin,—three or four choruses of the same number with pauses between! For the last chorus of *Royal Garden Blues*, Kid Rena stood up and took it, a clean curving tone held taut, building up the chorus, the band coming up hard with the rhythm. In the semi-darkness you could see the gleam of someone in the band smiling at him. But the dancing went on and the customers hugged the rail and the ticket takers watched out for stuff that would be too tough. A sweet-looking kid tried to break away from her partner and shag; all she managed to do was to throw her head back slightly, so that long brown hair fell back over her shoulders, and her legs squirmed a little, not dancing, just earning the small end of a five-cent ticket.

Outside the dance hall, which was on the edge of the French Quarter, everything was surprisingly quiet. From entrances of other dance halls and saloons came the noise of bands and the rattle of dice. From Canal Street could still be heard the noise of Carnival, subdued to a distant murmur and accented by car horns and drunken whoops. Iberville in the block near Rampart was even less noisy than Bienville. Far ahead you could see the inviting neon of the late joints such as the Round-Up where young white musicians jammed in the early morning hours, and a tireless midget hostess bustled about on the sawdust floor, piping a Texas Guinan line.

But before you came to that neon brightness, there was a comparatively quiet block, with one place still open, a combination sandwich bar and saloon. From outside you caught a tinkly blues piano and a baritone voice. You waited for the record to end and it didn't, it kept right on playing, a left hand rolling the bass. Inside, a come-on girl, who looked a lot like Ginger Rogers, completely forgot the watered Scotch gag. She said with genuine enthusiasm, "Boy, he's got it!"

He had it, too, which only proved that Bumel Santiago and Steve Lewis were prophets in their own country, for this was Willy Forrest, a young uptown Negro who had the stuff. You felt that his fingers were in absolute control of the keys all the time. His face maintained a dignified and somewhat impassive expression so that when he smiled a little it had an almost subtle effect. He said he would play some blues.

Maybe piano players are born, too. You got that impression, seeing the left hand in action, seeing the right find just the desired sequence in the treble, or bear down with clusters. Kids tried to push drinks on him. He didn't like to accept them because he didn't want to drink too much; he was still learning and his life was in that piano. He'd listen politely to their requests. Did he know *They Say?* If he shook his head, smiling a little, the customer would whistle or sing it, Willy chording lightly. When he played it through the second time he might fumble the melody but never the rhythm. The third time he had both and was starting to make the tune over. If he felt right he came in for a fourth, fifth, or sixth chorus, the left hand chording with a sureness that testified to the fact that, as he said, Steve Lewis had taught him the chords.

Several times a night Willy had to play *Tiger Rag*. Because of his superb inventions on this number, the customers had got to like it and ask for it. *St. Louis Blues* was another they kept after him for. He was equally good on several other tunes but these two had become associated with his playing, in the minds of those who came there. He wasn't the least bit flashy. He didn't fake runs and didn't introduce meaningless phrases merely to sound "professional." Each number received from him the interpretation essential to it. He had a good voice and on the blues there were long pauses during which the heavy roll went on, the right hand pounding like mad, the swing exactly right. His playing had both volume and the blue tonal quality that only the best jazz pianists get, that seems right on the strings.

That's the land of dreams, only it doesn't stop in the Delta, not any more. For the jazz strain has spread North, East, and West, stamped here and there with new individual talent. A Negro is born in Johns Hopkins Hospital in Baltimore, apparently destined to go through life crippled, unable to use his legs at all. Before he is twelve he is on the streets of Baltimore, with a little wagon, peddling papers. He has a musical ambition but there isn't much to do with it, because it's for the drums and you need good feet for that. Then Dr. Ralph J. Young, the Negro surgeon, operated on the little newsboy at Johns Hopkins. A miracle happened. After that he would always be little but he could walk.

The boy from Johns Hopkins played the usual collection of tin cans and cheap tom-toms and on the strength of his ability on these makeshift instruments came to New York. Chick Webb was on his way.

Before his untimely death Chick was in the solid booking but success had come too late; illness cheated him of any thorough enjoyment of life. Seen in the flash of the spotlight from fifth row center, hunched over his drums, sticks flying and fingers touching the cymbal rim in what seemed merely a gesture, the showmanship was outside and probably wooed hundreds who could not distinguish between a Gene Krupa, a Zutty Singleton, or a Chick Webb.

It may have been speed and rhythmic performance that won Chick his first job. Certainly there were many in Harlem who smiled at the spectacle of one more drummer in a city already swamped by the influx from Chicago and the South. But Chick got his first job, in a small band with Bobby Stark, Johnny Hodges, Elmer Williams, and Edgar Sampson. They went into Healey's Balconnades, the dance hall at the top of the Great White Way where the Dixieland Band and the Memphis Five had played. They were a success in the Balconnades but they weren't always a success. Even in later years, when they had both Ella Fitzgerald and Taft Jordan in the band they went through months of barnstorming, one-nighters, playing a town cold where no one knew the band or seemed to care. And then the contrast, for the Webb band in time became synonymous with the Savoy Ballroom on Lenox Avenue. You saw them in a dance hall, and you got that steady muffled sound of dancing feet, or you saw them on a riverboat, where moonlight and the boat churning through the water gave an added push to the rhythm.

Ella came to the band in 1934 when she was sixteen years old. On a cold night in January they noticed her hanging around the wings at the old Harlem Opera House on 125th Street. She'd been on the amateur hour and now she was looking for a job. Ella was from an orphanage in Yonkers, had taken up singing in the most natural way: because she liked it. The first time she fronted the band they borrowed a dress from Chick's wife for her to wear and they got a lawyer to clear the way, so that little orphan Ella could be with the band. The first job she did with them was at the Manhattan Casino. Soon after that sixteen-year-old Ella Fitzgerald went up to New Haven with the band for a date at Yale's swank St. Elmo Club. The boys gathered around and that "sent"

Chick a little, too, because Ella was new and no one had written about her in big adjectives.

In arrangements for the big band Tommy Fulford, who plays piano, builds the music around the soloists. The Webb arrangements were not always as satisfying, musically, as those by Mary Lou Williams. This might be because, even when by an Edgar Sampson or a Tommy Fulford, they leaned sometimes too heavily on convention. The arrangements for the small band (Ella's Savoy Eight) have been generally in excellent taste. Those who played behind Ella in this small band, which Chick believed to be the most suitable background for her recorded vocals, were: Chick; Tommy Fulford and Taft Jordan, trumpets; Sandy Williams, trombone; Hilton Jefferson, alto sax; Ted McRae, tenor sax; John Trueheart, guitar; and Bevery Peer, bass.

Before the band played Chick fussed with snare and bass drum, to see that they were tuned to a friendly pitch. Incidentally, the pitch was always a trifle lower than is customary. He played chiefly on open drums, getting gradations in the strength of the beat, and handled cymbals with the utmost delicacy or with overwhelming crescendos, as the score demanded. Listening to the drums, you got a sense of percussive build-up, to the blood as well as to the ear, but you also came to understand that a drummer was, after all, a musician playing tones.

Budem Ali, from Calcutta, handled the baton for Chick Webb and His Orchestra in its stage presentations. From a jazz point of view, this was more satisfactory for the band's morale than the present day convention of hot musicians directing their bands as well as playing in them. Because a baton is on the beat, you also (from fifth row center) got the idea that Chick was the ride man. One of those soft shoe numbers, in which the girls are swathed in organdy, went off. Budem Ali, smiling urbanely, came up front and the audience knew with the first bar, even before Ella came on stage, that this was her number. It was usually a popular song, swung by Ella and hung by Chick. When she sang the first few words in a throaty, halting voice, the audience applauded. Then Ella put her hands together maybe, or tugged at her dress, and put on a serene smile that lit up her face in almost child-like simplicity.

Her irrepressible humor is not loud, but extremely contagious. When Chick was in the hospital in Boston and she was trying to think of something cheerful—weren't they all?—and maybe something to show to Chick when he came out, she got to thinking of childhood games. The little games and rhymes had made a strong impression on her orphaned childhood. It was not at all surprising, then, that in an era of double talk the "tisket tasket" lines began running through her head. Suddenly the words tumbled out, and the pianist put it all down in black and white. (Maybe you didn't know a lot of Mother Goose was originally double talk, anyway?) When Chick got out of the hospital Ella sang it for him, an arrangement was made, and another hit was on the books.

From an excursion boat engagement on June 10, 1939, on the Potomac River at Washington, D. C., Chick was rushed to Johns Hopkins Hospital, to spend the last few days of his life where he was born and where Dr. Young performed the miracle that allowed him to walk.

It had been cold on the river that night. Fleecy clouds obscured the stars above the near-by Virginia hills. While Kaiser Marshall substituted for him in the band, Chick stayed outside with a small group of friends, unnoticed by the hundreds who had jammed the boat to hear him on drums. He stood there, on his face the wistful expression that was characteristic of him, a little hunch-backed figure in a camel's-hair coat. After a while he went in to play the last sets. Ella looked cool, as she always did when watching the band. Chick was already outward bound then but no one knew it, and the whole band was riding. Perhaps that was just as well. At the Little Waters

African Church in Baltimore two weeks later everyone was feeling too bad to "send" him.

Kansas City is next in importance to Chicago in jazz creation. Bennie Moten, Andy Kirk, Count Basie, Pete Johnson, are a few of the musicians who got their start there. A river city with a substantial Negro population, it also boasted that degree of corruption that assured many musicians who played in "joints," of a weekly wage. Andy Kirk's Orchestra, known to hot followers for many years, is today becoming known to the public through records, radio, and that life-line of Negro bands, the colored theatre circuit. The footlights are still on for the stage show and the rows of faces wait, look up expectantly. Footlights fade out the band and a spot comes up on Mary Lou Williams sitting at a grand piano, wearing a cream-colored evening gown with a short bolero jacket. The pleasure of the audience when the tune is announced is something that is perceptible, like a quickening of the breath in two thousand throats at once. The bass rolls, a half smile lights up the high cheekbone nearest the audience, and where the cream-colored evening gown almost touches the floor you see that both feet are well back from the pedals, and that one of them is tapping out the beat. The rhythm section is in, but you keep hearing Mary Lou until the clarinets enter, playing a whimsical duet about Little Joe from Chicago. When the piece has gone through ensemble, vocal, ensemble, clarinets, the lights that had come up on the band begin to fade once more, the spot making a bright circle of Mary Lou and her piano. There's the foot still tapping as the bass rolls, the bolero jacket loose about her throat, the half smile turned now towards the band.

Andy Kirk's Orchestra plays with unbelievable naturalness for such a large band. Mary Lou writes for the band, as she does for many others, including Benny Goodman's, but the Kirk Orchestra reads her arrangements in the most satisfactory manner. They get the feeling first, then build the balance on top of it. The brasses have a harsh quality that is not at all unpleasant. Reedy saxophones and clarinets give a deep complex tonality to the melodic structure and, like Haggart of the Bob Crosby Orchestra, Mary Lou uses clarinets effectively in her arrangements. Oftentimes Floyd Smith, the band's excellent guitar player, takes solos, managing somehow to get music out of an electric guitar.

It would be easier to say what's good about the band's playing if you put it in the vernacular and said that the jive hadn't got them. There is certainly a sincere quality in their work, fused with excellent (technical) balance. Other Negro bands have been encouraged both in the direction of a strident tonality and a strident melodic interpretation that at its worst seems to hang desperately on the background harmonies for its base of operations. In its excesses this strident quality is utterly unlike the tonal excursions of a whacky New Orleans horn as exemplified, say, by Keppard. Like Haggart and a very few other arrangers, Mary Lou Williams has utilized some of the discoveries of the small bands of hot improvisers.

Even today the significance of the small band is not very widely appreciated. After a Carnegie Hall concert Sidney Bechet said, "I didn't feel quite right. I wanted the band with me. They put the rhythm section up on the platform." And he was right, for that's the secret of New Orleans music. Or maybe it's only one of the secrets, since so few composers and arrangers seem to have learned them yet. Listening to Mary Lou Williams and listening to Bechet is listening to music from way down yonder. There's limitless room for individuality in what so many critics, measuring in bars, think of as a cramped framework.

Bechet was born on St. Anthony Street in New Orleans, brought up in an era when Creole kids went to the French Opera, if they were good children. Sidney got to the Opera now and then, but his real interest was in a clarinet that his brother Leonard had picked up somewhere as a bargain. When he came home from school Sidney deliberately put his books on the window sill, took up his brother's clarinet, and blew into it. He had to practice secretly because Leonard had intended to sell the instrument or trade it for a new trombone.

Listening to Bunk Johnson (on cornet) and to Big Eye Louis Nelson (on clarinet) he learned that to play in a swing rhythm with a throbbing vibrato was part of the lesson, too. He learned to hold his hand just so, to be able to finger the fast passages and to shift effortlessly from throaty fullness to the singing thrush notes of the upper register. Whenever he could sneak away or get permission, he watched Big Eye Louis. Maybe for half an hour, an hour, two hours, Louis played around, Sidney watching him with a slightly puzzled expression. What changed the spirit would be hard to say. Suddenly it wasn't early evening and he wasn't feeling a little lazy. Big Eye Louis got off. The tone was as broad as the river from The City to Algiers. The notes tumbled out liquid clear, spaced in a rhythm that kept you waiting, then hit hard with a sweeping power.

The day came when Sidney's mother decided that it was time she let Leonard in on the secret. She told him of Sidney's habit of practicing afternoons, explained how rapidly he had progressed, and begged him to listen to one piece. Leonard said he would. Sidney picked up the clarinet and played *I Don't Know Where I'm Going but I'm on My Way*. When it was over Leonard gave him the clarinet.

After that, Sidney played clarinet and soprano sax around the joints in Storyville, played in Chicago in several bands, including Cook's Dreamland Orchestra, and he was one of the first to introduce jazz abroad. There followed a period of comparative idleness, then his comeback with Noble Sissle and after that a small band in a New York night club, in which Sidney was featured. In the little joints in Storyville, Sidney put on an act they're still talking about down there. It was vaudeville, but it was music, too, a sort of clarinet strip-tease. He took off one part of the clarinet, then another, until finally he was playing on the mouthpiece. It was a trick, but it was probably good training. He plays as though nothing could stop him. His improvisations are as creative as those of anyone in jazz, yet they are extremely personal. If he's down it's crying blues and if he's high it's up there talking about it.

One of the best bands he ever played in was when he was sharing the spotlight at Nick's with Zutty Singleton. That the little combination didn't survive was one of those minor tragedies of the music business. Zutty gave exhibitions of fast, complicated, melodic drumming. When he played behind Sidney you got the packed rhythm of Zutty's traps, then the tone of that powerful sweet soprano sax. Shaggers stopped shagging and dropped back toward the edge of the dance floor, while flash-bulbs of the candid camera addicts exploded blossoms of light around the blossoms of sound.

Does he read music? Jelly Roll Morton, veteran New Orleans pianist and one of the finest composers in jazz, said, "He plays more music than you can put on paper."

XIV

HOT COLLECTING

BY STEPHEN W. SMITH

THE VERY dirty and dusty young fellow who had driven his car all the way from the West Coast drew up in front of a second-hand store in a small Middle Western town. He surveyed its drab exterior with a discerning eye and entered. Carefully treading his way through the maze of stoves, bureaus, and bric-a-brac, he found the proprietor and asked:

"Have you any phonograph records?"

The proprietor moved listlessly behind the counter and rummaged down behind some piles of junk that had not been moved in years. He brought forth a stack of fifty old records. As he placed them on the counter, the young fellow's eyes took on a feverish gleam. He reached eagerly for them and began to turn them over carefully, one by one, as though looking for hidden treasure. When he was about halfway through the pile, the proprietor, who had been watching him, moved forward:

"So you're looking for special ones, eh? Well," he said, snatching them all from before the young fellow's eyes, "we ain't got none."

This very individualistic hill-billy, furious at not selling the entire pile, had evidently never before seen in action that strange species, today quite common, the *hot collector.*

287

That collecting hot is today a recognized hobby, with books dedicated to the subject, is not a matter of chance. It has been a gradual development in which collectors themselves have played a leading part.

How it all began nobody knows. It is fairly safe to say, however, that in the beginning, hot records were collected mainly by musicians and their small-sized brethren, the so-called amateur or non-union musicians. They had various reasons for buying these records, besides a pathological urge to collect something. They recognized the potentialities of the music and had the added interest of studying it technically for their own uses. Of course, they did not go to the trouble that the latter day collectors do to procure records, for they simply bought them as they came out.

Three Princeton Uinversity students and one faculty member were the first known collectors who followed this hobby for appreciation and enjoyment only. Their mutual interest in jazz had them storing up collections of prized items against the day when the music they liked would no longer be played. These four, Albion Patterson, Albert McVitty, "Squirrel" Ashcraft, and Augusto Centeno, are responsible for sending the rest of the collecting gentry into junk shops and Negro districts in search of recorded jazz. It was Patterson and Centeno, who, about 1927, wrote what was probably the first jazz play, "Boy in a Tuxedo," a rather surrealistic drama in which each character was introduced by a hot theme supplied by a phonograph record off stage. The lines were spoken in a seemingly disjointed fashion, with one character leading off and another coming on in a complementary manner, without following the line of thought expressed by the first character. In other words, it was similar to an arranged jam session, except that words took the place of notes. The play was turned down by the *Theatre Intime* in preference to one by Shakespeare.

Meanwhile, Yale had its collectors, Wilder Hobson, John Henry Hammond, Jr., and others, but the two groups didn't get together for years. If a Yale man and a Princeton man entered a junk shop simultaneously in those days there was no danger of collision. The Yale man would almost invariably collect Ellingtonia and a smattering of Fletcher Henderson, and the Princetonian would burrow through the dust for the Red Heads, Bix, especially Bix, and Rappolo on Gennett records. One of the aforementioned Princeton gang felt that the Wolverine Gennetts were so rare and valuable that he kept each one packed in a box of cotton batting.

A year or so later, the jinx was broken. Fred Mangold, then a student at Princeton, found the first records of Louis Armstrong, compared his collection with that of Langston Hughes, and supplemented it accordingly. Thereafter collecting became something of an art and, because of the lack of publicity attending it, an esoteric one.

Among the people that came under the influence of the Princeton group was Charles Edward Smith. Patterson initiated him into the fascinations of hot music and urged him to use his talents for the cause. Esquire printed Smith's article, "Collecting Hot," in February, 1934; the stampede was on. It served notice to widely scattered individuals that there were others who liked the same kind of music, and extended to the public at large the invitation to take up a hobby which was relatively cheap sport. Cheap, because when the radio displaced the phonograph as the beautiful piece of furniture in the front rooms of the nation, the second-hand dealer always bought the records along with the phonograph. Thus, all second-hand stores were over-supplied with records which they considered a poor investment and which they were anxious to sell, the prices ranging from one to five cents, top price.

Collecting hot, while it refers to the collecting of hot records, has many ramifications and its devotees have split into many factions. These fall mainly into four groups.

There are those who will have nothing but the original label, and who will turn down a clean copy of a record in preference to one in bad condition because the latter has what is known to be an earlier label. They spend most of their time checking and re-checking master numbers, personnels, dates of recording, and dates of issue on all makes of records. When two of this type get together, it is not long before the entire conversation is revolving around such label, master, and personnel data, no matter where the conversation happens to be taking place, whether in a night club, restaurant, or private residence. Out come their little black books. Soon they are oblivious to everything except the information they may have to exchange. I know of one collector who has a roomful of charts, showing all sorts of record data in historical sequence, and who keeps these all in order, when he is not making up catalogues of records he has or wishes he had. All this, of course, is done when he is not looking in out-of-the-way places for more records. I sometimes wonder when there is time for listening to the music.

While this group must be given credit for the advance that has been made in the knowledge of the subject, at the same time it is responsible for all the misinformation and erroneous rumors which are spread due to their hasty and enthusiastic judgment. The collectors in this group collect everything that has the faintest resemblance to hot music, keeping records which are of no importance other than the fact that Louis Armstrong was in the studio at the time and can be heard to play a two bar coda as the needle clicks off at the end of the record.

At the opposite extreme are those who will have only records by one man or band. Some want nothing but Bix, or Ellington, or Armstrong, or Nichols, or Venuti. The strangest and most frightening experience of my career was when one of these maniacs burst into my house, walked to the center of the room, and interrupting Pee Wee Russell who was talking to several other collectors, announced in a determined voice: "I am a Joe Venuti collector. What have you got by him?" Just to keep him quiet, we played him a record which had several fine choruses by others than Joe, but of course he was completely bored until Venuti took his little break in the middle of the record. Then he went wild. *He was sent.* It is not safe to get into a conversation with this violent type, because to him everything revolves around his pet. These fanatics are the loneliest people in the world, shunned by other collectors who regard them as not fit to talk to.

The majority of hot collectors are quite normal human beings who do not go to extremes. They look mainly for the classics of hot, for the thrill of possession and enjoyment. They, too, keep up the search for rare records, but solely in the hope of finding something·satisfying to the ear, as well as something they consider to be of historical significance.

A small group which raises a lot of hell are those collectors who have heard that the value of hot records is steadily mounting. They profess an interest in the music and in the records, only hoping that in the end they can sell the records they found at enormous profits. That they never do this is some retribution for the trouble they cause all concerned.

The beginner-collector is the deadliest of the lot, even outdoing the common garden variety of jitterbug in his enthusiasm. There is some peculiar fascination in the collecting of hot which causes the beginner to become violently excited about the whole thing. I have never met a beginner who was not going out immediately to educate the public to the benefits of a music which he himself knew nothing about, and to warn it against the greatly overrated musicians who were "too commercial." The novice is usually introduced to music by way of Bix Beiderbecke. Beiderbecke has probably received more publicity than any other jazzman living or dead; since the beginner is so enthusiastic, this keeps the ball rolling. There is something about the music of Bix which appeals to the initiate. His purity of tone, his evasion of *dirty* notes, the logic of his phrasing, all this is more easily comprehended than that of other hot players. Duke Ellington is also largely responsible for starting people on the road to hot appreciation. It may be a strange paradox that they appreciate Bix because he is a white man, playing in a *white* style for white people, and Ellington because he plays a highly sophisticated jungle style of music which has its fascination in its strangeness to them.

The second-hand dealers were the first to become aware that more and more people were listening to old jazz music. When early collectors started out on their rounds of these places, prices for these records were as low as one cent each. More often than not, the dealer tried to sell the whole lot at a sum resembling an even figure, like one dollar. At present the dealers are aware that they are cheating themselves to go below fifteen cents and usually ask more. With the influx of the public into the field of hot, the junk shops have dried up as a good source of hot items. But of course, just when it begins to look as though there were no more records to be found, some diligent hunter locates a good stock right under the noses of his fellow seekers.

The latest wrinkle which has been in use by collectors is the canvassing from house to house in the Negro districts of the larger cities. New York, Philadelphia, Chicago, New Orleans, and Kansas City have yielded large hauls for the collectors with the energy and fortitude to try it. One highly enterprising record scout I know of in New York has even refined the house-to-house process to the extent that he simply leaves his calling card with all the janitors in Harlem and they notify him when they have records which he might be interested in. In Chicago there is a dealer who sends out several men on this work. He always has a fine stock of rare records on hand to sell collectors. The condition of the records which are procured in this fashion is not all that could be wished for, however.

It was not purely in the interests of thrift that the early

collectors were wont to frequent such dusty places as the Salvation Army warehouses and the second-hand stores in search of records that they wanted. During the period from 1930 to 1934, there were few music dealers who carried representative stocks of hot records. In the search, of course, music stores were not passed by, but the main source of rarities were the junk shops. The early collector, who had no catalogue to go by or any other information, was forced to buy about five times as many records as he needed, since he was always searching for this trumpet or that clarinet which he could recognize as one of the great, and always hoping that an obscure name would reveal a well-known hot band.

The most frequent question asked by the non-collector is "how do you fellows tell a rare record?" The answer is simple. You either look it up in a book or you find it out from a collector who has more knowledge of the subject than you do. There is no other way.

In the beginning, collectors could not depend on books and other collectors were few and far between. They soon became aware of the shortcomings of recording companies' catalogues, since so many items were continually turning up which were not even listed. This was often caused by the fact that the record could have been released after the issuance of one catalogue and cut out quickly before the next catalogue was published.

One thing that makes records extremely rare is that due to the absence of listing in catalogues, they are not even looked for and it is not until some collector recognizes the artist and passes the word along that the record is known to exist. The rarest Bix record known at the present time, for instance, is the third side of the Chicago Loopers, which through the whim of some recording company official was released under the name of Willard Robison and His Orchestra. Collectors for many years had been searching for this third side of the Chicago Loopers session, which had always existed in rumor.

George Beall, a Detroit collector, was the first to become aware of the fact that the record was labeled Willard Robison. This he discovered simply by listening to the record. For many months he kept this a secret, hoping to find a duplicate copy. Finally William Russell, the David Harum of hot collectors, talked him into divulging the information by pointing out to him that if he kept the information to himself long enough, all the records of Willard Robison might disappear and another copy might never turn up. When Russell got back to New York and told me about it, we immediately made wagers with our friends that by the next afternoon we would have a copy of this rare record, for we realized that sitting on the shelves of the Salvation Army warehouses of New York City were a sufficient quantity by this orchestra which had been passed up by all other collectors to insure us, on the law of averages, that this title was among them—as it was.

My basis for judging the rarity of a record would be the number of copies existing in the hands of collectors today. For instance, if Earl Hines' piano solos on Q.R.S. or the Charles Pierce Paramount records are not to be found in great numbers in the collections of the older members of the collecting fraternity, certainly then they will not appear frequently in the collections of those who take it up in the future. This would indicate then that the records are extremely rare.

The reason why the records of Earl Hines on Q.R.S. are scarce is due to the fact that all four Q.R.S. records were released by the company on the same day, and since piano solos are never in the greatest demand by the public, they were not in the big seller class. When the company went into bankruptcy, the receiver for the company broke up all the existing stock, which helped a great deal to make the records rare, although his intentions, I am sure, were not in that direction.

Naturally, a record is rare if it is rare at the source, like the

Charles Pierce records on Paramount. This company did not press many copies, since it was small, had few dealers' outlets, and the records themselves did not sell well.

The Charles Pierce records became exceedingly rare due to great demand, whereas the W. C. Handy records on Okeh, which could easily become rarities on the basis of supply alone, are not in great demand and therefore do not come under the heading of rare collectors' items.

The rarest copies in existence are those which were never, in the strictest sense of the word, released for the public, the studio test copies, which usually never came into the hands of collectors. Recently three records of this nature have been released for the benefit of hot collectors, two of them featuring Frank Teschmaker playing *Windy City Stomp* and *Jazz Me Blues*, and a third featuring an all-star mixed group under the title of Billy Banks' Rhythmakers playing *Take It Slow and Easy*.

Many of the collectors' items were originally issued purely for Negro consumption and consequently were sold only in sections of the country which had a demand for them. Copies which found their way into private homes were usually not given the best of care since many of the Negroes, for their own reasons, did not care to change the needle frequently enough to save the record surface. Most records were completely worn out in this way. New copies have been available from certain dealers, but they have been very few and far between. Most of the early Armstrong accompaniments, King Oliver, and other Okeh artists of the earlier period fall into this class.

The trouble with most collectors is that they don't know what they want. The unfortunate part of the collecting business is that the dealer in collectors' items dares not help the collector with information on the subject. As a student of the situation, working on it on a full time basis, I have been in the position many times to give collectors information which could be of value to them. Unfortunately, it has not always

been safe to do so, since a little information to certain collectors is enough to set them up in business across the street.
This is merely to explain why information on the subject of
hot collecting is sometimes very hard to obtain from either
the collector or the dealer.

Early record scouts who took it upon themselves to become
dealers in collectors' items, who needed cash and could not
afford to take the time to build up a good reputation, have
caused much hard feeling and taken in many a collector when
it came to stating the true condition of records. This, of
course, will be ironed out in time as the collecting of hot records becomes a more established interest.

The rarity of many items soon made it necessary for such
organizations as the Commodore and the Hot Record Society
to pioneer in the field of reissues. It was only recently that
the older recording companies paid tribute to the efforts of
these organizations and started to reissue many of the old
masters which have come to be regarded as collectors' items.
Armstrong, Beiderbecke, and Bessie Smith have been about as
far as the strictly businesslike companies have really cared to
go. However, the special Bluebird series of RCA-Victor and
the plans of American Record Corporation for a general hot
catalogue are signs of improvement from this direction.

When the first reissue appeared, consternation was rife
among the collectors who had spent a lot of time, energy, and
cash in getting together their collections, because they felt that
this was a threat to the value of the original records. It may
be that the reissue causes a falling off in the demand for the
original, but since the demand for these items has always been
greater than the supply, I doubt if in the end the original
copies will lose in value. I believe that the reissue merely pub-
licizes and acquaints the public with the artist and the quality
of his music and will eventually enhance the value of the
original. Were it not for the reissue, the public, and especially
that portion of the public which will eventually collect hot,

would be unable to hear any of the music whatever, and until heard and liked, there is no demand.

The price of original copies has risen to such a point that it makes the collecting of them a very expensive hobby for the beginner. The reissue serves to keep his interest at a point where he is willing to pay the higher prices demanded for original labels.

The process of dubbing is necessary in most cases in reissuing the rare records, and while there have been great advances made by recording engineers in this technique, it is not as satisfactory as the original record, for both high and low frequencies are lost in the process. This fact alone makes the acquisition of original copies more alluring.

The value of collectors' items in hot music, like everything else, obeys the law of supply and demand. But collectors, in dealing with one another, always place too high a value on what they own and try to get what they need as cheaply as possible. This, while perfectly natural, leads to a great deal of confusion concerning the actual value of hot records. I have had offered to me a copy of an Original Dixieland Jazz Band record by a perfectly serious young gentleman who said it was worth at least one hundred dollars. He was not quite so sure of it when I pointed out to him that I had a box of over a hundred copies of these Dixieland records sitting in my closet. In the book- and stamp-collecting business, values are easily ascertained by the prices for which they sell at auction. The Hot Record Exchange has been running auctions for nearly two years, even so, auctions are not yet a true picture of the value of the records; the majority of collectors prefer to scout around on their own hook and in many cases have been successful in locating the items sought. Time, however, will set up the auction as the true delineator of record values.

A comparison of the various catalogues which are put out by dealers in rare collectors' items shows a trend towards standardization of prices. When the Hot Record Exchange published the first mimeographed list of hot collectors' items ever to be made, the prices asked were based solely on rarity and not on condition of records, and it is surprising, in looking over that original catalogue, to find how accurate, in a relative way, these prices were. Other dealers who followed the example of the Hot Record Exchange in various parts of the country had different ideas of what they thought the records were worth, but slowly these dealers have disappeared and as others have taken their places, with more knowledge of the past to go on, the prices of rare records, as listed in the various catalogues, have become more or less uniform.

The recent swing craze no doubt has many psychological and economical factors behind it, but, nevertheless, the noise that a small handful of hot record collectors were making played a large part in bringing swing to the attention of the public. It was their journals, *Hot Jazz*, *Swing Music*, and later, *Down Beat* and *Tempo*, which continually drummed the subject of swing into the ears of the public. In this process, the hot collecting fraternity, as a whole, has been blamed by the musician for every sin on the calendar. Jitterbugs who think you are a collector if you have all the latest Larry Clinton records (both masters), are lumped into the same class with the serious collector who is making a sincere endeavor to study the history of jazz that has been put on wax. Since the advent of the jitterbug type of music, newspaper feature stories, the *Life* photographic section, people who do not even own phonographs have been bothering musicians on every pretext under the sun. Musicians call them all collectors. It is a well-known fact that all collectors bother musicians. But in the beginning serious collectors had no other source of information, and musicians should realize this. I have heard them griping about collectors when the people they described didn't know one end of a phonograph pick-up from another.

Charles Delaunay's *Hot Discography* has probably been the most useful book on jazz for hot collectors. The first edition appeared in 1936 and was as accurate as was humanly possible at the time, listing all the records made by the hot artists, giving the labels, titles, record and master numbers of the collectors' items. The new edition, put out in 1938, greatly augments the previous work and is far more accurate in its information. However, it is to be hoped that in the future discographies of a more limited nature will be written on the great artists of hot music, in which the pattern follows the book bibliographies, giving a short description of the music, titles, labels, personnels, master numbers, date of recording and issue. Then, my fellow collectors, we will be something.

XV

CONSIDER THE CRITICS

BY ROGER PRYOR DODGE

AS SOON as jazz became disturbingly identifiable as something more than "our popular music," countless uninformed commentators sprang up with something to say about it. In what the era might have called "the spirit of the thing," they made a jocose offering of a great part of the early recognition of jazz.

In general, symphonic jazz was considered a progressive advance upon primitive improvisation, and critics were anxious to see an art form blossom divorced from the dance and comparable to nineteenth century concert music. Even throughout the most sympathetic critical writing we find jazz tackled as a problem-child whose significant development is dependent upon immediate separation from the untutored musician.

Unfortunately, such premature white-collar meddling with jazz not only cut off the music public from following the slow, but determined, development of jazz by jazz musicians themselves, but induced academic-minded composers to leap headlong into vast, pretentious jazz works. Pretentious folk-art extension, in the word's best sense, can never be seriously entertained unless the vital elements of the folk-art have been first seriously considered by the ambitious composer. There is no doubt that changes are in order when a folk-art is taken into an extended form; that is, there are elements which the critic might like to cling to but which the composer is defiantly aware cannot be carried along into his extended form. But, such an admission hardly covers the mayhem perpetrated by the first so-called jazz composers in their course of romantic, rhapsodic, European folk extension. All sensitive development of the form inherent in folk-jazz itself was studiously avoided. Perhaps the difference between folk material and the first advanced work of art, should be no more than that in the one the art is scattered and in the other there is an apt concentration into one composition. For such an advance, significant improvised hot solos were scattered about any number of recordings before 1924. However, a conscientious America, anxious to promote American music and secure in the knowledge that any written art work superseded improvised phonograph recordings, gratefully settled for the *Rhapsody in Blue!*

In this article I have drawn out for extended comment three categories of critics: one, important men in any field; two, men who seem to have said the right thing; and three, men who have taken time and care to write at serious length upon the subject. As regards those contemporary, bright but forgotten music commentators, devoted to consideration of the "jazz age," "jazz morals," and "jazz haircuts," time and space have not been so generous to me for purposes of refutation as they were to the original observers.

One of the first outstanding critics I have been able to discover is the writer, Carl Van Vechten. And this is in spite of the fact that the underlying generalizations he made in 1917 pointed towards something quite different from that which he later particularized upon with evident satisfaction. It is strange how many sincere and sympathetic pioneer discoverers of jazz shied away from their own first premises the moment the "refining" element was introduced and the "major" work appeared! In 1917 we find him saying:

Popular songs, indeed, form as good a basis for the serious composer to work upon as the folk-song. . . . If the American composers with (what they consider) more serious aims, instead of writing symphonies and other worn-out and exhausted forms which belong to another age of composition, would strive to put into their music the rhythms and tunes that dominate the hearts of the people a new form would evolve which might prove to be the child of the Great American Composer we have all been waiting for so anxiously. I do not mean to suggest that Edgar Stillman Kelley should write variations on the theme *Oh, You Beautiful Doll!* Or that Arthur Farnell should compose a symphony utilizing *The Gaby Glide* for the first subject of the allegro and *Everybody's Doing It* for the second with the adagio movement based on *Pretty Baby* in the minor key. It is not my intention to start someone writing a tone-poem called New York. . . . But, if any composer, bearing these tendencies (jazz) in mind, will allow his inspiration to run riot, it will not be necessary to quote or to pour his thought into the mould of the symphony, the string quartet, or any other defunct form, to stir a modern audience.[1]

In 1925 we find him still generalizing in fine terms:

real American music, (*Alexander's Ragtime Band*)—music of such vitality that it made the Grieg-Schumann-Wagner dilutions of McDowell sound a little thin, and the saccharine bars of *Narcissus* and *Ophelia* so much pseudo Chaminade concocted in an American back-parlor, while it completely routed the so-called art music of the professors.[2]

But suddenly we are brought up short by the remark:

February 12th, 1924, a date which many of us will remember henceforth as commemorative of another event of importance besides the birth of our most famous president, George Gershwin's *Rhapsody in Blue* was performed for the first time by Paul Whiteman's orchestra with the composer at the piano.[3]

The *Rhapsody in Blue* probably violated all of Van Vechten's modern art stipulations. His long-awaited "running riot in new

---

[1] Carl Van Vechten, "The Great American Composer," *Vanity Fair*, April, 1917.
[2] Carl Van Vechten, "George Gershwin," *Vanity Fair*, March, 1925.
[3] *Ibid.*

form" was no more than a rhapsodic bastardization of what since the day of Haydn has been called the symphonic sonata form; the sonata form with a subject, counter-subject, development, tempi changes, etc. Curiously enough, five months later we find him saying that the blues [4] deserve, from every point of view, the same serious attention that has been tardily awarded the spirituals. If he found melodic beauty in the blues and looked forward to a new form of music out of the jazz idiom, his enthusiastic recognition of Gershwin was a sad jumbling of theory.

Carl Van Vechten allied himself to the exponent of one of the most decadent and at the same time most trying of forms; a form whose no one part is strong enough to bridle bad taste. Moreover, the hot jazz recordings made prior to February 12, 1924, are concrete witness to the actual new style of variation already in use by the jazz folk themselves. If, today, jazz has shown no more interest than twenty years ago in progressing beyond the basis of a tune played over and over to encourage variation, from one point of view it is presumptuous to consider anything further as *progressive*. Let us consider how securely the mighty *Goldberg Variations* of Bach, or the variations in the last movement of Brahms' *Fourth Symphony* are wedged in the contemporary repertoire! It is the romantics, including Gershwin, who are never satisfied with such a timeless form as the *variation*.

As early as 1918 we find Olin Downes making this statement; " 'Ragtime' in its best estate is for me one of our most precious musical assets." [5] In thus taking cognizance of the raw material of jazz of that date and then not following through with earnest investigation, Downes has distinctly avoided a consistent course as music critic. However, he tried to pierce through the tone of the 1924 Whiteman concert:

[4] Carl Van Vechten, "The Black Blues," *Vanity Fair*, August, 1925.
[5] Olin Downes, "An American Composer," *Musical Quarterly*, January, 1918.

Thus the *Livery Stable Blues* was introduced apologetically as an example of the depraved past from which modern jazz has arisen. The apology is herewith indignantly rejected, for this is a gorgeous piece of impudence, much better in its unbuttoned jocosity and Rabelaisian laughter than other and more polite compositions that came later.[6]

One might suspect that perhaps he was holding himself just a little above all jazz music, but in 1937 such a suspicion is confounded:

He [Gershwin] looked into the promised land, and pointed a way—one way—that a greater musician might follow.[7]

The keenest insight into early jazz coupled with the most sympathetic understanding of the necessarily slow development of folk instrumental music, comes from the eminent European concert conductor, Ernest Ansermet. He wrote as early as 1919:

The first thing that strikes one about the Southern Syncopated Orchestra is the astonishing perfection, the superb taste, and the fervor of its playing. . . . It is only in the field of harmony that the negro hasn't yet created his own distinct means of expression. . . . But, in general, harmony is perhaps a musical element which appears in a scheme of musical evolution only at a stage which the negro art has not yet attained.[8]

It seems Ansermet knew how little to expect, manifested his delight when he got more than he expected and in every way came to his subject with an erudition equal to the solution of, or temporary toleration of, the apparently insuperable obstacles which all new art carries in its wake. When faced with Sidney Bechet's clarinet solos his comment was not only musically sure but esthetically sensitive:

[6] Olin Downes, New York *Times*, February 13, 1924.

[7] Olin Downes, "George Gershwin." Editor, Merle Armitage, Longmans, Green, 1938.

[8] Ernest Ansermet, "On a Negro Orchestra," *Revue Romande*, October 15, 1919. Translated by Walter E. Schaap for *Jazz Hot*, November-December, 1938.

they gave the idea of a style, and their form was gripping, abrupt, harsh, with a brusque and pitiless ending like that of Bach's second *Brandenburg Concerto* . . . what a moving thing it is to meet this very black, fat boy with white teeth and that narrow forehead, who is very glad one likes what he does, but who can say nothing of his art, save that he follows his "own way," and when one thinks that this "own way" is perhaps the highway the whole world will swing along tomorrow.[9]

When we consider that the style of playing in 1919 merely *pointed* the way to significant jazz solos of a later day, our admiration of Ansermet for visualizing the mature style which actually materialized, grows by leaps and bounds.

In this same year, 1919, from George Jean Nathan, editor of the *American Mercury*, we get such an incredible dismissal as:

The negro, with his unusual sense of rhythm, is no more accurately to be called musical than a metronome is to be called a Swiss music-box.[10]

Carl Engel was one of the first American music critics of note to be intelligently receptive to our folk-art of jazz. In 1922 we find him trying to dispel the notion that jazz must be ostracized because it is vulgar:

To a great many minds the word "jazz" implies frivolous or obscene deportment. Let me ask what the word "sarabande" suggests to you? I have no doubt that to most of you it will mean everything that is diametrically opposed to "jazzing." When you hear mention of a "sarabande," you think of Bach's, of Handel's slow and stately airs. . . . Yet the sarabande, when it was first danced in Spain, about 1588, was probably far more shocking to behold than is the most shocking jazz today.[11]

With great sense, Engel warns the twentieth century not to indulge in the sort of eighteenth century criticism which was

[9] Ernest Ansermet, "On a Negro Orchestra," *Revue Romande*, October 15, 1919.
[10] George Jean Nathan, *Comedians All*, Knopf, 1919, p. 133.
[11] Carl Engel, "Jazz," *Atlantic*, August, 1922.

proved so contrary to fact by the subsequent good standing of eighteenth century dance music. He decries, as uninformed, the point of view which denies the use of dance material for what is popularly called "serious art." He pertinently quotes the following comment of Karl Spazier in the *Musikalischer Wochenblatt* in 1791, to show how ridiculous such a stand has always been:

I furthermore hold that minuets are contrary to good effect, because, if they are composed straightforward in that form, they remind us inevitably and painfully of the dance hall and abuses of music, while, if they are caricatured—as is often done by Haydn and Pleyel—they incite laughter.[12]

Unfortunately, Engel stretched his attitude to include any and all popular music, and it must be agreed that he let a laudable generalization lead him into unconsidered particularization when we find him denying that

to borrow material for a piano concerto from Mr. Flo Ziegfeld and the American Beauty Chorus should be thought more incongruous than to ask it of Gregory the Great and the Roman Antiphonary. . . .[13]

It just happens that Flo Ziegfeld and the American Beauty Chorus are pretty poor stuff, not because of their moral level of functioning, but for legitimate art reasons. Much of the strength of his comment is weakened by his unnecessary confusion between what is jazz and what is popular song. Actually, Engel never completely identified jazz for himself. On the other hand, like Ansermet, he recognized the strength of improvisation and said as early as 1922: "For jazz finds its last and supreme glory in the skill for improvization exhibited by the performers." [14] His admiration of European composers for their prompt recognition of jazz did not cloud him from observing that in their practical use of jazz "they do not throw

[12] Carl Engel, "Views and Reviews," *Musical Quarterly*, April, 1926.
[13] *Ibid.*
[14] Carl Engel, "Jazz," *Atlantic*, August, 1922.

me into ecstasies." He rightly felt it was more the "spirit" of jazz that affected Europe than an appreciative desire to write within the music itself.

In 1926 he admired Henry Osgood's book *So This Is Jazz*, devoted to uniform eulogy of Gershwin and Whiteman. But six years later we find him saying:

let us further state that we are by no means an admirer of everything Mr. Gershwin has written. His *Rhapsody in Blue* and his *American in Paris*, except for a few isolated measures leave us cold . . . With M. Goffin's estimate of Paul Whiteman and Jack Hylton we are in full accord.[15]

It can be seen that as soon as Goffin's book appeared (1932) Engel's point of view altered. He should have been able to dispose of Henry Osgood by himself. Perhaps, if Engel, constantly concerned with the published opinion of the early twenties, had had a more extended acquaintanceship with hot jazz itself, he would have quickly and emotionally responded to it. As it is, his contribution to jazz criticism has been more that of the erudite music critic, highly sympathetic to the idea of jazz.

George Antheil, the *enfant terrible* of Paris, in the limelight for some time both by order of his own compositions in jazz and by what he has seen fit to say about it, started off in 1922 with the musically meaningless statement:

Jazz is not a craze—it has existed in America for the last hundred years, and continues to exist each year more potently than the last. And as for its artistic significance, the organization of its line and color, its new dimensions, its new dynamics and mechanics,—its significance is that it is one of the greatest landmarks of modern art.[16]

Such confused statements from a musician discussing music would hardly suggest that when we hear a certain kind of

15 Carl Engel, "Views and Reviews," *Musical Quarterly*, October, 1932.
16 George Antheil, "Jazz," *Der Querschnitt*, Germany, summer, 1922.

music and call it jazz, the word "jazz" stands for that kind of music; that when we hear another kind of music and call it ragtime, the word "ragtime" stands for that kind of music! Antheil's effusion on "the greatest landmark in modern art," would seem to be a sincere enough acknowledgment for the time, but in the light of his subsequent entanglement I am led to believe that this early statement was more in line with the "Paris group" smartness than a sincere presentiment of what was to come. Six years later he seemed to think that the validity of the point of view that jazz had great art value, could be easily tested:—"The development of a great composer out of jazz is the only really clinching argument." [17] This, of course, means anything or nothing, depending upon the terms established for great composers. However, further along in the article the following remark seems clear and sensible:

Jazz is her own way out to the future. But until jazz finds its way a little more clearly, let us [the composers] not take it into the concert hall. [18]

But in further discussion of the concert hall, which he admits has often been the scene of bitter and bloody conflict, he suggests that jazz must quickly attain "a dignity that the mere serving out of a parade of popular and clever melodies in trick orchestra garb can never attain." Has jazz moved Antheil or has he confused the issue? Four months later the secret is out with his published comment:

The works of Vincent Youmans are pure clear, and extremely beautiful examples of jazz that is a pure music. [19] (!)

Two great European composers, Darius Milhaud and Igor Stravinsky, composed music under the influence of jazz. Stra-

[17] George Antheil, "Jazz is Music," *The Forum*, July, 1928.
[18] *Ibid.*
[19] George Antheil, "American Folk Music," a letter to the editor of *The Forum*, December, 1928.

vinsky, speaking of his piece called *Ragtime,* composed in the early twenties, comments:

Its dimensions are modest, but it is indicative of the passion I felt at that time for jazz, which burst into life so suddenly when the war ended. At my request, a whole pile of this music was sent to me, enchanting me by its truly popular appeal, its freshness, and the novel rhythm which so distinctly revealed its negro origin. These impressions suggested the idea of creating a composite portrait of this new dance music, giving the creation the importance of a concert piece, as, in the past, the composers of their periods had done for the minuet, the waltz, the mazurka, etc.[20]

It is ever a pity that Stravinsky, unlike the minuet composers of the past, merely toyed with this new dance form upon slight acquaintanceship; that his material was limited to popular sheet music.

Darius Milhaud was publishing small and large so-called jazz compositions at an early date. In an interview in 1923, he is quoted as saying:

One thing I want to emphasize very particularly and that is the beneficial influence upon all music of jazz. It has been enormous and in my opinion, an influence of good. It is a new idea and has brought in new rhythms and almost, one might say, new forms. Stravinsky owes much to it. It is a pity that it is limited at present, practically to dance music, but that will be remedied.[21]

There was something in the best of jazz—blues singing, hot playing—that stirred the emotions, but such is the fallaciousness of human judgment that the intellectual musicians did no more than meddle with the phenomenon, and the popular song writers no more than wallow in the shallowest imitation!

Although the Whiteman-Gershwin concert was not the first of its kind, it came at the time when fever of musical expectancy was at its height. American critics had been inde-

[20] Stravinsky, *An Autobiography,* Simon & Schuster, 1936.
[21] John Alan Haughton, "Darius Milhaud," *Musical America,* January 13, 1923.

fatigable in building up a case for American music. They insisted that this folk-art, which they had been critically nurturing, respectably arrive via a piano concerto and a symphony orchestra. And for them the Whiteman affair was wholly satisfying. February 12 now stood for two births, that of Abraham Lincoln and the *Rhapsody in Blue*. Critics, whose business was sharp musical observation, succumbed to the reasoning that *something* vital must have occurred since a concert crowd roared. Even those sympathetic to Gershwin's bathos, but trained enough to recognize and comment upon the inept handling of the completely familiar concerto form, followed the line of least resistance to the concert public's will. So as we reach the year 1924, we find more writers voicing their opinion of jazz than at any other time until the advent of the particularizing "swing" critics ten years later.

A popular book of great importance was published in 1924—*Seven Lively Arts* by Gilbert Seldes. In this book, Seldes bravely justified the importance of the so-called *minor* and *lively* arts. He was outspoken in his attack upon those who are ill at ease before great art until it has been approved by great authority. But in the following quotation (the italics are mine) Seldes not only shows he makes no distinction between jazz and popular song but confuses what otherwise would be a fine art attitude:

there is no difference between the great and the lively arts . . . both are opposed in the spirit to the middle or bogus arts. . . . The characteristic of the great arts is high seriousness—it occurs in Mozart and Aristophanes and Rabelais and Molière as surely as in Aeschylus and Racine. And the essence of the minor arts is high levity which existed in the *commedia dell' arte* and exists in Chaplin, which you find in the music of Berlin and Kern (not "funny" in any case). . . . We require, for nourishment, something *fresh* and *transient*. It is this which *makes jazz much the characteristic of our time.*[22]

[22] Gilbert Seldes, *Seven Lively Arts*, Harper, 1924, pp. 348-49.

If we admit that the "high seriousness" of major art, and the "high levity" of minor art, is an excellent distinction to make between that which we acknowledge as major art and the work of Berlin and Kern, the inclusion of the *commedia dell'* arte and jazz, as art forms to be equally and categorically linked with "fresh and transient" Tin Pan Alley, is highly objectionable. Seldes fails to tell us that running along with minor and lively arts, and even nourishing them, we often find the new vital folk-art—in its later metamorphosis to be known as the great art of "high seriousness!" In 1924, jazz had already shown qualities which distinguished it from the "transient" art of popular song. But suddenly his artistic boldness turns fainthearted.

I say the negro is not our salvation because with all my feeling for what he instinctively offers, for his desirable indifference to our set of conventions of emotional decency, I am on the side of civilization. To any one who inherits several thousand centuries of civilization, none of the things the negro offers can matter unless they are apprehended by the mind as well as by the body and the spirit.[23]

The Negro may have been indifferent to our emotional decency, but he was certainly far from indifferent to our harmony and musical form. Into Negro jazz has gone the vital part of our centuries of musical experience. Seldes continues in the same vein:

Nowhere is the failure of the negro to exploit his gifts more obvious than in the use he has made of the jazz orchestra; for although nearly every negro jazz band is better than nearly every white band, no negro band has yet come up to the level of the best white ones, and the leader of the best of all, by a little joke, is called Whiteman.[24]

The concluding remark, admittedly slight in witty intent, will ever strike back at its author as a more humorous error in art

[23] Gilbert Seldes, *Seven Lively Arts*, Harper, 1924, p. 97.
[24] *Ibid.*, p. 99.

judgment! As late as 1934, in an article on George Gershwin, Seldes still has no comment to make on hot jazz solos.

In 1922, Clive Bell wrote an essay entitled *Plus de Jazz*. This famous English art critic found it convenient to express the opinion that art

is a matter of profound emotion and of intense and passionate thought; and that these things are rarely found in dancing-palaces and hotel lounges.[25]

But in 1924 he found it convenient to deplore the similar snobbism which maintains that

the *Last Judgment* by Michelangelo, is something essentially nobler and more important than a picture painted by Watteau.[26] (!)

Again, apparently finding it hard to explain why *I'm Just Wild about Harry* is not as great as the *B Minor Mass*, he hazards the opinion that

maybe the only difference between a comic song by Mr. Irving Berlin and a comic song by Mozart is that one stylishly expresses Mr. Berlin, and the other stylishly expresses Mozart.[27]

But almost immediately he feels constrained to explain some difference in magnitude and reverts to his own brand of snobbism in declaring that those who like Mozart

might have understood and been intimate with Mozart himself, whereas the latter [jazz musicians] could have been for him [Mozart], only objects of curiosity, surprise, amusement, or distaste.[28]

In 1924, the magazine *Etude* published a revealing collection of jazz comment headed by an editorial expatiating exclusively upon the art of Berlin, Confrey, and Gershwin. It concluded with the exclamation:

---

[25] Clive Bell, *Since Cézanne*, Harcourt, Brace, 1922, p. 215.

[26] Clive Bell, "There is an Art in Drinking a Cup of Tea," *Vanity Fair*, July, 1924.   [27] *Ibid.*   [28] *Ibid.*

But who knows, the needs of Jazz may be Burbanked into orchestral symphonies! [29]

This same thought has been advanced time and time again. Art is to be "Burbanked" from Berlin to symphonies! A symphony, apparently, is the purification of what would otherwise be dross—never the culminating synthesis of simple but pure elements!

In this same collection of comment, John Alden Carpenter, composer of the jazz ballet Skyscraper, goes out of the way to make the invidious distinction:

I am convinced that our contemporary popular music (please note that I avoid labelling it "jazz") is by far the most spontaneous, the most personal, the most characteristic, and by virtue of these qualities, the most important musical expression that America has achieved.[30]

Here also, Will Earheart, director of music, Pittsburgh, tersely and amusingly enough disposes of jazz:

Bach fugues, Beethoven's symphonies, . . . are heard in certain places and received by a certain clientele gathered there. They seem appropriate to the places in which they are heard, and to the people who are gathered to hear them. So does "jazz." [31]

Yet Sir C. Hubert Parry, professor of music at the University of Oxford, and director of the Royal College of Music, in a most important contribution to Grove's Dictionary of Music, deplored the aloof attitude of composers towards popular dance hall music and maintained that such an attitude had no basis in reality; that on the contrary, all concert music owes an incalculable debt to dance music. He wrote, in part:

Dance rhythm and dance gestures have exerted the most powerful influence on music from prehistoric times till the present day. . . . The connection between popular songs and dancing led to a state of definiteness in the rhythm and periods of secular music . . .

[29] "Where the Etude Stands," Etude, August, 1924.
[30] Ibid.   [31] Ibid.

and in course of time the tunes so produced were not only actually used by the serious composers of choral music, as the inner thread of their works, but they also exerted a modifying influence upon their style, and led them by degrees to change the unrhythmic vagueness of the early state of things to a regularly definite rhythmic system. . . . In fact, dance rhythm may be securely asserted to have been the *immediate origin of all instrumental music.* [Italics mine.] [32]

However, it is a truism, that when professors are brought upstanding with a new and *living* art fact, only too often their own contemporary moral compulsions force a retreat from their previous art premise so easily arrived at on the basis of historically dead issues!

Let us clear up a little point that still induces much argument and was brought up by George Vail in this same issue of *Etude:*

Mozart, Haydn, and Chopin, were they alive today, would write foxtrots as naturally and inevitably as they once composed gavottes, minuets and mazurkas.[33]

This is not necessarily true. Although the attitude of *their times* towards art was different from ours, the artists themselves could not be expected to hold a different professional point of view—given the same conditions—from that of our own academic composers. It was only the *times* that made them write gavottes and mazurkas—not their better judgment.

In 1924, Lawrence Gilman, a thoughtful yet conservative music critic, put his finger, with rare honesty, on the weakness of the whole business surrounding the Whiteman-Gershwin faddism:

We have before expressed our conviction that the trouble with Jazz—the best Jazz, according to the showing of the Palais Royal-

[32] Sir H. C. Parry, "Dance Rhythm," in *Grove's Dictionary of Music and Musicians.*

[33] George Vail, "Would Mozart Write Foxtrots If He Lived Today?", *Etude,* September, 1924.

ists themselves [Whiteman's band] is its conformity, its conventionality, its lack of daring . . . it seems to us that this music is only half alive. Its gorgeous vitality of rhythm and of instrumental color is impaired by melodic and harmonic anemia of a most pernicious kind. Listen to Mr. Archer's *I Love You* or to Mr. Kern's *Raggedy-Ann*, or to Mr. Gershwin's *Rhapsody in Blue*.[34]

Mr. Gilman's point of view was one of the few examples of contemporary considered American opinion which questioned whether the *Rhapsody in Blue* should be properly termed progressive modern art. He speaks of Gershwin as "lacking daring." He was obviously right. For Mr. Gilman could think in terms of the daring of Stravinsky's *Le Sacre du Printemps*. However, if Gershwin was unbelievably old-fashioned, jazz was *always* daring—but only in its hot solos. For the time, that was enough. Gilman, not seeing as clearly as Ansermet, was oblivious to the great possibilities latent in this new folk music. Moreover, although a large number of hot solos were and are daring, there are also any number of hot solos that are significant, but not startlingly novel. They are no more daring than a melody of Mozart is daring. The whole confused attitude toward Modern Art at that time hung on one hook, and still hangs on it to a degree, that *shock* must prevail: that it is only from him who shocks that we may expect Modern Art!

In 1924, the modern composer, Virgil Thomson, decided that it was impossible to use jazz material for "serious" composition:

[jazz] rhythm shakes but it won't flow. There is no climax. It never gets anywhere emotionally. In the symphony it would either lose its character or wreck the structure. It is exactly analogous to the hoochee-coochee.[35]

Thomson obviously believes that modern music should continue along latter day sonata-symphonic lines rather than make

[34] Lawrence Gilman, "Music," *New York Tribune*, February 13, 1924.
[35] Virgil Thomson, "Jazz," *American Mercury*, August, 1924.

a new beginning on a new dance impulse. In a later article he concludes:

For after all, America is just a collection of individuals. . . . The idea that they can be expressed by a standardized national art is of a piece with the idea that they should be cross-bred into a standardized national character, 100 per cent North American blood.[36]

The year before, Charles Buchanan made much the same comment:

Possibly, the most peculiar and arresting phenomenon that the heterogeneous art activities of this country have brought forth is the wide-spread idea, amounting almost to an obsession, that American painting and music must create and express themselves through the medium of an unmistakeable national idiom . . . to prescribe that the American composer renounce the heritage of four hundred years of musical development . . . is disaster breeding nonsense.[37]

These two similar statements incite equal parts of agreement and disagreement. That is, jazz is not the medium for an American composer to express himself within, if he feels that there is still some vitality to the European art-type handed down to us. But the American, or any other national composer, who believes that the old art feeling has been worn threadbare, who feels that some new folk infusion, such as jazz, has vitality, should be urged to study jazz. Buchanan, in further expressing the opinion that "art is the expression of an individual, not of a nation" avoids the fact that music direct from the people makes up 75 per cent of the work of our great seventeenth and eighteenth century composers.

B. H. Haggin, an outstanding young music critic, has been occupied with jazz for some years. In 1925 he sympathetically acknowledged it. In 1935 he regularly devoted a portion of

[36] Virgil Thomson, "The Cult of Jazz," Vanity Fair, June, 1925.

[37] Charles Buchanan, "The National Music Fallacy," Arts and Decoration, February, 1924.

his music column to discussing the new manifestation—
"swing." Nevertheless, in 1925 he seriously stated that jazz
was

lacking the most important source of rhythmic variety in serious
music, namely, variation in the length and shape of phrases, with
artistic use of figuration.[38]

This was true of the fox-trot sheet music but most emphati-
cally not so of the improvised hot solos of 1925. In another
article, after stating that if the "pluck-pluck" were dispensed
with there would be little or nothing left of jazz, Haggin
makes plain his distress over the monotonous foundation beat
of modern dance music. He states flatly that this beat is not
emphasized in the old bourrées; that the bar line is only a
"convenience" of notation for musicians.[39] It may be truth-
fully said that the bar line can be forgotten in, say, a Wag-
nerian opera. But, if the simple beating out of a bourrée inevitably makes one out of every four beats very strong, then I
maintain that not convenience of notation, but a very good
musical reason marks a bar line before this strong beat. Of
course, this foundation beat of the bar is not to be confused
with an accented counter melodic cadence which may cross it
at any time. Haggin goes on to state that because of the monotony of rhythmic folk music, such material is never used
save for the lighter movements of symphony. But any discussion of former folk music and its extension, in relation to possibilities for extension latent in jazz, obviously demands a
skip of the nineteenth century attitude and a return to at
least that of the eighteenth—if not previous centuries. Moreover, his remark that jazz, in the light of modern academic
composition, cannot be characterized as syncopated, seems
unconsidered.

There are many ways of writing technically syncopated

[38] B. H. Haggin, "The Pedant Looks at Jazz," The Nation, December 9,
1925.
[39] B. H. Haggin, "Music, Two Parodies," The Nation, January 13, 1926.

music, but it is not always a profusion of these different ways that leads the listener to identify the result as syncopation. In *Sacre du Printemps*, Stravinsky has been able to make the listener definitely conscious of syncopation; whereas Antheil, in his *Aeroplane Sonata*, although running the gamut of tempi changes from 17—8 time to 1—8 in order to transfer the rhythmic accents, merely leaves the listener with a vague feeling of slightly syncopated music. Obviously, on paper, we may show what is technically known as syncopation, but the music, as heard, may lack that peculiar displacement of expected rhythm we identify as syncopation. The exaggerated syncopation found in many a symphonic score may make transcribed jazz recordings appear comparatively uncomplicated, but a glance at the melody line of hot jazz solos gives evidence of intrinsically syncopated melodies. If we grant that Stravinsky can far outstrip the jazz orchestrator (or arranger) in the clever disposition of mass, rhythmic, chordal shocks of accompaniment, nevertheless such calculated effect does not deny the actuality of the syncopated melodic line of hot jazz solos.

So This Is Jazz, by Henry C. Osgood, already mentioned as occupying the attention of Carl Engel, was a widely read book in 1926. It went into the worst aspects of popular music with obvious admiration. At one point Osgood approvingly quotes a reported interview with a Negro boatman to illustrate how a completely new tune is introduced:

Some good sperichils are started jess out o' curiosity. I been a-raise a sing myself once. We boys went for tote some rice and de nigger-driver, he keep a-callin on us, and I say, "O, de ole nigger-driver!" Den anudder said, "Fust ting my mammy tole me was, 'Nothin' so bad as nigger-drivers.'" Den I made a sing, jess puttin' a word and den anudder word.[40]

I quote this as an example of a false but common assumption. The story may be quite correct insofar as the *lyrics* are concerned but it is doubtful whether any folk remember the

[40] Henry C. Osgood, *So This Is Jazz*, Little, Brown, 1926, p. 56.

circumstance of spontaneous creation of melody. When a Negro sings the blues, he may for the occasion make up the words in entirety. But the melody he sings is never solely his creation; his individual musical contribution is no more than a slight variation on the already familiar form. Only through a slow metamorphic process does one folk tune, in time, become a definite new tune.

Although Osgood in championing Zez Confrey's *Kitten on the Keys* definitely felt that "You can't compare Confrey with Beethoven . . . And you don't need to argue with me that the 'Fifth Symphony' is better music and more important to you and me than anything Confrey ever wrote or may write," [41] he nevertheless identified *Kitten on the Keys* as a masterpiece in jazz! How often have we found this confused championing of the wrong thing under the right name—with the actual circumstance of hot jazz making such patronage laughable!

In 1926 there appeared the very important book *Blues*, by W. C. Handy with an introduction by Abbe Niles. In his foreword, Niles is by far most competent when analyzing the actual blues. His incorporation of the music of Gershwin, accompanied by such comment as, ". . . the *Rhapsody in Blue* without doubt conveys . . . a rowdy, troubled humor as marked as that of the best of the old blues," [42] demonstrates the usual confusion of a critic when faced with the first extension of a new folk form. Niles continues with the absurd statement (absurd in the light of the rhythmical background of much so-called "serious" music) that there is

One valid objection to the idea that jazz is timber for serious writing . . . that of rhythm, especially, of an unvarying tom-tom beat which after a time, must become intolerably monotonous. [43]

---

[41] Henry C. Osgood, *So This Is Jazz*, Little, Brown, 1926, p. 80.
[42] W. C. Handy, *Blues*, A. and C. Boni, 1926, p. 23.
[43] *Ibid.*, p. 47.

Niles is familiar with his subject, but the esthetic conclusions he draws are the weakness of what is otherwise an excellent treatise.

In 1927, Aaron Copland, the well-known composer, expressed the opinion that jazz should become basic material for modern composers and that it was not as outmoded as Darius Milhaud, having finished his *Création du Monde*, now seemed to think. Copland appeared to believe that if only jazz were adequately defined, such definition would be of aid in composition. I doubt whether musicians in the past depended upon adequate verbal definition of their medium in order to compose within it! He expressed great annoyance with jazz musicians who merely·

can tell jazz, from what isn't jazz and let it go at that. Such vagueness will do nothing toward a real understanding of it.[44]

He attributes to Don Knowlton, the author of an innocuous enough little article,[45] the ridiculous statement that the written rhythm:

is a deceptive notation for a far more complicated polyrhythmic performance, i.e.,

Actually, Knowlton said nothing of the kind, merely confining himself to the general remark that publishers have left out polyrhythmic effects in their printed sheet music. But Copland presses the point into such a false sequitur as:

[44] Aaron Copland, "Jazz Structure and Influence," *Modern Music*, January-February, 1927.
[45] Don Knowlton, "The Anatomy of Jazz," *Harper's*, April, 1926.

He [Knowlton] was the first to show that this jazz rhythm is in reality much subtler than in its printed form. . . . Therefore it [jazz] contains no syncopation.[46]

Once more we meet with a theory limiting the amount of syncopation in jazz! But this time it is buttressed by inexcusable misquotation. Copland's flimsily built-up theory that the foregoing rhythm is not syncopated is absurd. There is no basis for the assumption that the jazz player thinks in such polyrhythmic terms; that he consciously alters a normal syncopated 4—4 time into 3—8 plus 5—8 time. Moreover, Knowlton's article was too slight in content—too patently deficient in critical acumen, to hazard erecting a theory upon it.

Jazz, written in 1926 by Paul Whiteman and Margaret McBride, is amazingly naïve; it lets us in on the ground floor of Whiteman's esthetics:

I still believe that Livery Stable Blues and A Rhapsody in Blue, played at the concert by its talented composer, George Gershwin, are so many million miles apart, that to speak of them both as jazz needlessly confuses the person who is trying to understand modern American music. . . . When they laughed and seemed pleased with Livery Stable Blues, the crude jazz of the past, I had for a moment, the panicky feeling that they hadn't realized the attempt at burlesque—that they were ignorantly applauding the thing on its merits.[47]

That panicky feeling has been ultimately justified, for the Livery Stable Blues, burlesqued as it was in spots, contained the style which encourages musicians to improvise in jazz; it has outlived the symphonic jazz orchestra. What is now known as a "swing band" is a continuation of what Whiteman failed to explain away!

In 1927, we find a book written by an Englishman, Robert Mendl, titled The Appeal of Jazz. Mendl, explaining how

[46] Copland, loc. cit.
[47] Paul Whiteman and Margaret McBride, Jazz, J. H. Sears & Co., Inc., 1926.

dance movements were incorporated into suites during the eighteenth century, similarly tried to justify the continued use of jazz. But he slipped only too often into such curious comment as:

You cannot play jazz music as a pianoforte solo: if you perform syncopated dance music on the pianoforte it is ragtime, not jazz. It only becomes jazz when it is played on a jazz orchestra.[48]

Although admiring Paul Whiteman and Jack Hylton for their "refining" influences, at the same time he decried the current attitude that the jazz musician should be rebuked for using other tunes than his own. He justly observed:

"The greatest genius is the most-indebted man," and it is the use which he makes of his legacy that counts.[49]

In 1927, André Levinson, the well-known European dance critic, made an observation on rhythm that should be taken to heart by the jitterbugs:

We should not, however, jump to the conclusion that because of his extraordinary rhythmic gift alone the Negro dancer and musician should be taken seriously as an artist. Rhythm is not, after all, an art in itself [50]

This I feel is a timely rebuke to those whom we find exclusively in the thrall of "swing" rhythm for its own sake—regardless of the value of the melodic line.

Ernest Newman, England's eminent music critic, writes in 1927 as though he were commenting on jazz in 1922. He occupies himself unnecessarily with the jazzing of the classics. However objectionable such jazzing may be, it certainly is a minor phenomenon. It becomes very clear that Newman's well-known antagonism towards jazz is based on no real knowledge of jazz. Newman probably has in mind such ineffectual

[48] Robert Mendl, The Appeal of Jazz, P. Allen & Co., Ltd., London, 1927.
[49] Ibid., p. 134.
[50] André Levinson, "The Negro Dance Under European Eyes," Theatre Arts Monthly, January-June, 1927.

pieces as Paul Whiteman arranges for a concert, when he says:

The jazzsmiths, however, speaking generally, are not clever enough to make their manipulations of the classics tolerable.[51]

This is very true but very unimportant. Another time, he states flatly that:

There is not, and never can be, a specifically jazz technique of music, apart from orchestration.[52]

This is followed by the astounding comment:

Jazz is not a "form" like, let us say, the waltz or the fugue, that leaves the composer's imagination free within the form; it is a bundle of tricks—of syncopation and so on.[53]

A waltz is hardly a "form." It is primarily a rhythm with a certain style of melody superimposed. A fugue is a form, likewise a sonata—but not a waltz. Jazz is a style in which forms are developing. However, Newman immediately detected in the music of Gershwin what should have been more generally observed:

when he launches out into "straight" piano concerto music we begin to ask ourselves what all this has to do with jazz. The work was, in fact, though Mr. Gershwin may not have known it at the time, a commendable effort to shake himself jazz-free.[54]

It is unfortunate that so keen and knowledgeable a critic as Newman is ever bound to the discussion of the tricked-out banalities of "popular music." Possibly he has never heard any jazz of value. But this should not excuse him from searching it out. In a still later article we find the bitter conclusion that

(America is) a purveyor of the most dreary, the most brainless, the most offensive form of music that the earth has ever known.[55]

[51] Ernest Newman, "Summing Up Music's Case Against Jazz," London; printed in New York *Times Magazine,* March 6, 1927.
[52] *Ibid.*   [53] *Ibid.*   [54] *Ibid.*
[55] Ernest Newman, "Music and International Amity," *Vanity Fair,* April, 1930.

In an article written in 1928, Sigmund Spaeth praises Gershwin and Whiteman, but definitely concludes that jazz is not music.[56] Later, he brings up the matter in detail:

Jazz is not a musical form; it is a method of treatment. It is possible to take any conventional piece of music, and "jazz it." The actual process is one of distorting, of rebellion against normalcy.[57]

If he means that the treatment is part of a process that results in an actual music called jazz, he would be correct, but it is only too apparent he means that jazz is a tricky attitude we apply to something of value—resulting in nothing. Moreover, it should be obvious that any style, applied to another style, is a distortion. For instance, a current theme is fitted into fugue by way of distortion—the result, however, is a new normalcy. The same is true of the treatment of tunes by dance movement. We can make a minuet, a waltz, a tango, a sarabande, a rhumba, out of any tune and most composers have done so since the sixteenth century! The musician who employs such comment to put jazz in a derogatory light is extending a weak hand to the layman anxious for something technical with which to disqualify jazz.

Further along he remarks that: "Jazz melodies have been mostly simple and obvious, easily remembered after one or two hearings." [58] If there are blues and popular tunes—and for that matter classic tunes—which are easy to remember, in point of fact a hot jazz solo is as comparatively difficult to re-render as a Bach invention. But when he says that "Stravinsky's *Ragtime* and the jazz movement of his piano concerto cannot compare (as music) with the work of Gershwin, Souvanie, or Grofé," [59] Spaeth has left the platform where there is possible room for argument. On no academic platform of standing would such a statement be offered in evidence. No

[56] Sigmund Spaeth, "Jazz Is Not Music," *The Forum*, August, 1928.
[57] Sigmund Spaeth, "They Still Sing of Love," H. Liveright, 1929, p. 140.
[58] *Ibid.*   [59] *Ibid.*

one of these musicians wrote significant jazz; but Stravinsky, unlike our enterprising popular song purveyors, made a most significant contribution to the Modern Academy.

Spaeth's conception of melody is best stated in his own words:

Melody is the sticky sweetness of music, the cloying jazz which needs a background of nourishing bread before it becomes really palatable.[60]

Quite the contrary is true. A poor melody is unpalatable no matter how lavish the background. More good melodies have been spoiled by sugar arrangements than sugar melodies noticeably fortified by superior background.

As late as 1929 we find a typical literary patronage of jazz expressed by the English author, Aldous Huxley. Speaking of a jazz band featured in one of the first moving pictures with sound (*The Jazz Singer*), Huxley says:

The jazz players were forced upon me; I regarded them with a fascinated horror. It was the first time, I suddenly realized, that I had ever clearly seen a jazz band. The spectacle was positively terrifying.[61]

There is never such "hay-wire" comment found to describe a new phenomenon of music as that utilized by those in the strictly literary field! However, perhaps it is no more amusing than that of the group of so-called music Modernists in America, who are no less oblivious to the qualities of jazz than are their own special *bêtes noires*, the old fogies of the Academy! Paul Rosenfeld is a fair example of this sort of critic.

But the greatest fullness of power and prophecy yet come to music in America, lodges in the orchestral compositions of Edgar Varèse. . . . His high tension and elevated pitch, excessive velocity, telegraph-style compression, shrill and subtle coloration, new sonorities and metallic and eerie effects are merely the result of

[60] Sigmund Spaeth, "They Still Sing of Love," H. Liveright, 1929, p. 140.
[61] Aldous Huxley, *Do What You Will*, Doubleday, Doran, 1929, p. 58.

his development of the search-and-discovery principle in the twentieth century world.[62]

Rosenfeld is continually bathed in a mysticism that must definitely hinder him from listening to any music in terms of music. His identification of great music resolves into the following: a music spelling the space of the planets, digging deep into humanity, sounding the struggle of masses, rushing on with the immensity of it all. A so-informed public in Mozart's age would have expected a music quite different from that which it got in the G Minor Symphony; or in Bach's age, in the D Major Suite for orchestra! In fact, upon being given such a definition, only to be faced with a pure example of musical art, every age would have retreated in puzzled disappointment. Truly, if we were convinced that this was the avowed purpose of the composer and an indication of what to look for in the major works issuing from him, how naturally we would hold in contempt any such pure melodic manifestation as jazz! Rosenfeld, like many another critic, thinking in terms of the complex rhythms of Stravinsky and Varèse, is dogged in his search for the bizarre. Let us conclude with his firm statement:

American music is not jazz. Jazz is not music.[63]

Among the last of the non-jazz critics we find the late Isaac Goldberg.

The Anglo-Saxon American has no more talent for writing or playing jazz than Europeans. Both of them are bungling at it.[64]

This is a curious statement to find in a book written as late as 1930—an American book which purports to go deeply into the history of popular music; such a statement merely adds to the confusion between popular song and jazz and is of no

[62] Paul Rosenfeld, An Hour with American Music, J. B. Lippincott, 1929, pp. 160-66.
[63] Ibid., p. 11.
[64] Isaac Goldberg, Tin Pan Alley, John Day, New York, 1930, p. 15.

help at all in the understanding of folk-art. If white folk musicians do not push jazz conspicuously ahead, they most certainly have availed themselves of the medium with great distinction. On one page we read that "at first the jazz band was a crude nuisance, with the emphasis on noise," and on the next, we find him assailing the academic jazz musician as a ". . . decent white lady in her parlor trying to sing a hot jazz number that literally cries for a wild black mamma." [65] However, one thing always stands out in such books as this one: the heated discussion never commences until the jazz chapter is reached!

The year 1930 closes the chapter on early critics who, for one reason or another, felt something should be said about jazz. And jazz, it would seem, was as much a problem child for the music critics as it was for less specialized attention. We rarely hear names other than those of Whiteman, Gershwin, Lopez, Lewis, or Confrey mentioned. Ansermet is really outstanding for his expressed interest in the hot solo playing of Sidney Bechet.

We now approach the era of the Jazz Critic—he who is to jazz, what the concert critic is to classical, academic music. It is no longer the exception to find a jazz critic on familiar ground when discussing his subject. He knows all of the heretofore anonymous players by name and handles the subject turned over to him in the same sublimated *shop talk* manner as his established, classical *confrères* handle the Academy! Just as the concert critic, well acquainted with the seventeenth and eighteenth century music and full of well-bred enthusiasm, will, however, find no terms enthusiastic enough for Wagner or Debussy, so will the jazz critic talk seriously on Boogie Woogie piano and then proceed with obvious satisfaction to consider a Teddy Wilson!

To my knowledge, Charles Edward Smith published the first article in which separate, improvising players were men-

[65] Isaac Goldberg, *Tin Pan Alley*, John Day, New York, 1930, p. 15.

tioned by name and detached from the group as a whole, and the symphonic orchestra relegated to the background. In 1930 he wrote:

It may be said, almost without qualification, that jazz is universally misunderstood, that the men of jazz, those of the authentic minority, have remained obscure to the last. . . . Paul Whiteman developed a symphonic jazz band, for concert jazz, Gershwin composed a clever tour de force known as Rhapsody in Blue, and the grand misconception was off to a glorious start, generously footnoted by writers none too sure of their material, such as the author of The Seven Lively Arts.[66]

He made three distinctions which more or less hold true today:

To the connoisseur there are three classes of dance music. First of all there is jazz which is called hot—though all that is hot is not jazz. Secondly, there is popular, which the musicians call sweet; when ordered to play a sweet piece as written they play upon the words in, "Come on, boys, play this one as rotten!" Last of all there is that which imitates or plagiarizes real jazz and this brand of stuff is termed corny, the last word in disparagement.[67]

In a footnote Smith says—

My contention is that when hot bands turn corny they are much, much worse than sweet bands could be. There is nothing so disgusting to a musical palate as a simulated ad lib. chorus.

I feel, however, that there is something healthier, in spite of itself, in the attitude of the corny players, than in the saccharine politeness of the "sweet" bands. Eight years later we find Smith saying even more pointedly:

Technical embellishment as an end in itself is so closely identified with improvisation against background harmonies (as distinguished from variation on theme) that the two tendencies are sometimes confused. . . . It is unadulterated corn whether the guilty party is an accomplished musician playing games with his unsuspecting

[66] Charles Edward Smith, "Jazz, Some Little Known Aspects," The Symposium, October, 1930.   [67] Ibid.

public or a tyro trying to sneak out of the long underwear gang
. . . If it seems to have musicianship on its side it is a spurious
musicianship, for this word should connote integration of form
and substance, not merely a mastery of one's instrument from a
technical point of view.[68]

Generally speaking, I find myself in agreement; but I think
Smith overlooks how hard it is to create notable melody.
Irving Berlin is one of the few who can consistently do so, if
only on the popular song level. Mozart could do it. Clementi
could not. Bach presented a much longer line of hits than
Scarlatti, and Beethoven could turn out more than Brahms.
Outstandingly musical jazz solos might be said to be equally
rare phenomena also. To call all other solos corn is a mis-
placed use of the word.

In view of the fact Panassié feels jazz cannot be notated, it
is interesting to observe that Smith feels some musicians have
"a technical equipment that *gives to almost any kind of chorus
an air of authority,* sometimes convincing the musician himself that what he is doing is the real thing." [69] (Italics mine)
Such a remark as the "real thing" must mean: music that
stands up notated.

One of the most popular books on jazz, and deservedly so,
was *Le Jazz Hot*, by Hugues Panassié. Published in Paris in
1934, it not only went into the hot jazz question soberly and
authoritatively, but also managed to catch the attention of
the "swing" public by way of the numerous Swing Societies.
Panassié takes up point by point every feature of jazz; the
player, the orchestra, the orchestrator, the different instruments, etc., etc. The breadth of the book is what counts in its
favor, and it is only through serious reading in its entirety that
its full scope is brought to the fore. However, without meaning to lessen its general importance, there is no doubt it
brings out a number of false attitudes towards jazz and art.

[68] Charles Edward Smith, "Two Ways of Improvising on a Tune," *Down
Beat*, May, 1938.   [69] *Ibid.*

Panassié tries to establish the difference between jazz and other music by saying:

in most music the composer creates ᵗhe musical idea, and the performers recreate these ideas as nearly as possible. . . . They [jazz players] are *creators*, as well.[70]

This is an all-embracing distinction prevalent amongst even the best of jazz critics. It certainly would be a poor way to differentiate jazz from any but nineteenth century music. Although Panassié spends much time stressing the thought that jazz must have "swing," this whole section is weak because he cannot give a musical definition of swing.

Panassié insists on simply maintaining a disc preservation of jazz. He seems to believe that, although "in classical music, a few sheets of paper are enough to note down a work to preserve it with all its values. In jazz, on the contrary, even when there is no improvisation, the actual performance is itself most important." [71] Even if he insists upon believing that for the first time in history a *playing style* is significant, it is strange he does not see that jazz is also significant on paper, and in this way far more susceptible to considered investigation.

Panassié also seems to believe that merely one or two musicians freed jazz from its early inhibitions. King Oliver and Louis Armstrong were not indispensable to the growth of jazz. However, this should not be taken to mean that they did not exercise great influence. It has always been difficult justly to place the great man in the great school. It is proper that the works of an outstanding individual be segregated for special comment as the best examples of the period, not only for their originality but for the high consistency maintained. Our mistake is in attributing to the individual the entire art phenomenon. This is not his due. A school of art is based on a

[70] Hugues Panassié, *Hot Jazz*, Witmark, 1936, p. 1. Translated by Lyle and Eleanor Dowling.   [71] *Ibid.*, p. 20.

rank and file, and out of this rank and file rises the outstanding individual. The relation of their respective contributions is one of degree; the waters of genius rise higher, but they are part of the same fountain produced by the rank and file. From this point of view, the degree of his contribution, if he is working within a strong school, is never as great as it seems in isolation. Thus, outstanding as Oliver and Armstrong were in the early days, the school of jazz playing had in it, even then, all those characteristics which these two artists were able to point up so well. If hot solos were shorter, and did not reach the recording studio, nevertheless, they were all about, and full of the extraordinary variation of jazz.

What is his attitude to the actual music of either jazz or Bach? If he has said that jazz cannot be notated, that there are things in the playing of it that are impossible to divorce from the player, why does he quote with evident satisfaction:

One day I was playing the first measures of his [Teschmaker's] solo in *I Found a New Baby* with one finger at the piano. "Is that Bach?" a composer who was listening, asked me.[72]

Yet here he shows how inventive Teschmaker was, on the basis of the melodic line itself!

It is very evident that Panassié thinks in terms of performance. Although he speaks well of Meade Lux Lewis' *Honky Tonk Train Blues* and of Joe Sullivan's *Gin Mill Blues*, he no more than lists these composers along with all the other pianists; apparently judging them by the amount of swing they have to their playing style. But he picks out Bix Beiderbecke's published piano solo, *In a Mist*, as the great piano solo contribution to jazz music. Panassié clearly retroverts to the French school of modern music when he picks this superficially mannered music as an example of the best piano jazz. Further along, Panassié seems to contradict himself and ac-

[72] Hugues Panassié, *Hot Jazz*, Witmark, 1936, p. 91.

knowledge that jazz may be advancing towards an important notated stage when he says:

In *Panama*, Lewis Russell has written several ensemble choruses with such hot elaborations that a soloist has only to play the written melodic line to sound as if he were improvising.[73]

It seems to me that such a statement from an author denying the possibility of significant, written jazz, gives cause for reflection.

Panassié dismisses the music of Gershwin as though it were music of foreign origin, having no connection with jazz. As much as we may dislike Gershwin's attempt, no critic should avoid discussion of such development, with its precedent in all art—in all classic music. In 'fact the suspicion cannot be avoided, that all the classic music we now have notated is rooted in just such a spontaneous music as jazz, and that sooner or later jazz, in spite of all the vital qualities of performance we now link to it, will also take its place in notated form, alongside our great classical music. But, whatever the disagreement with Panassié on these and other points, his book is a landmark in jazz criticism.

One very well-known critic, whose name has become synonymous with hot jazz, is John Henry Hammond, Jr. Otis Ferguson sums him up as follows:

John Henry Hammond (Junior) is known to practically every one who ever mounted a band stand, or plugged a song, or got on the free list for records and wrote articles using such phrases as gutbucket and out of this world and dig that stomp-box. He is known as The Critic, the Little Father, the Guardian Angel and the Big Bringdown, of dance music. But the point is he is known.[74]

John Hammond occasionally gives evidence of being a critic definitely detached from such musicians' shop talk, but for the most part he seems to be deeply embroiled in the com-

[73] *Ibid.*, p. 211.
[74] Otis Ferguson, "John Hammond," Hot Record Society's *Society Rag*, September, 1938.

mercial ambitions of a band—its desire for smoothness, or for more personality in its singers, etc., etc. All of this is purely the business of a publicity agent—not of a hot jazz critic. But Hammond has said:

> To my way of thinking Bessie Smith was the greatest artist American jazz ever produced; in fact, I am not sure that her art did not reach far beyond the limits of the term "jazz." [75]

This is not the talk of the usual up-to-the-minute hot jazz gossip purveyor. And again we find him saying:

> nobody would be more incredulous upon hearing that this [jazz] is art than the throngs of jitterbugs and the hot musicians themselves. Perhaps this is the spirit of the early Renaissance art movement in Italy, of the stone carvers on Romanesque cathedrals, because it is the thing taken for granted and warmly participated in by the people. [76]

Another time he states:

> The hysterical roars of the crowd which once had been sweet music to his [Goodman's] ears, first perplexed, then irked him. He wanted his music to be appreciated for its essential worth and not because of its fortissimo volume and crazy antics. . . . Benny likes good, simple, relaxed music, whether it is by Fletcher Henderson or Mozart. [77]

The remark "simple, relaxed music, . . . by Fletcher Henderson or Mozart" is very interesting. The sympathetic way Hammond handles this interpretation of Goodman's thoughts leads me to believe that Hammond is quite in agreement. Moreover, the way Benny Goodman actually plays his clarinet, his excursions into Mozart, all point to a musician who feels a need for a more refined form of swing; what he might call a higher type of swing; something nobler to be sought

[75] "John Hammond Says," *Tempo*, November, 1937.
[76] John Hammond, "The Music Nobody Knows," Program Notes for the concert *From Spirituals to Swing*, December 23, 1938, Carnegie Hall.
[77] John Hammond, "Hysterical Public Split Goodman and Krupa," *Down Beat*, April, 1938.

after than "fortissimo volume and crazy antics." But does that side of jazz, considered analogous to Mozart by both Hammond and Goodman, really consist of the noble, relaxed simplicity we encounter in Mozart? Some of us who accept hot jazz as we do the sterner kind of classic music, cannot accept Benny Goodman's refined jazz on the same basis as Mozart. In classic music our good taste is varied, and within certain limits we like to hear more than one kind of music, but it does not follow that the large "swing" public which enthusiastically approves genteel "swing" along with hot jazz, is exemplary of a similar good taste.

Let us think back on the long history of occidental music and observe the invading sweetness that comes sooner or later over each new form of music. It is a sort of decadence which creeps over all art. The strongest academic composers are always fighting it; but in spite of their fight, if their music holds any elements of melodic lyricism, the school becomes sweeter and sweeter with each succeeding generation. The result of such a decadence is our present day American popular music, sweet to the point of puerility. On the other hand, the American Negro jazz phenomenon is a new beginning; and being new it has the earthy quality we find in all new art. America, subjected to both schools, accepts both with equal intensity. We make no real distinction in caliber, and when the two are mixed, even the swing addicts are apparently fooled.

For good jazz, good musicians still have to play at white heat; hence the term "hot jazz." Hot players who cool off in their playing, generally become either sweet or disturbingly banal. This is the way of a folk. Only when the full significance of this jazz material has become apparent to them, will they be able to play their material with a relaxed, simple sweetness comparable to the classic sweetness of a Mozart. The later Goodman clarinet, the Wilson piano, much of the Dorsey and Teagarden trombone work, not to mention the recent Duke Ellington arrangements, are not representative of the best of jazz played with refined distinction but are, rather, an unfortunate demonstration of a superimposed, cheap, classical experience. Neither this experience, nor its derivative, the popular-song-infected mind, can aid us in arriving at "refined, relaxed and simple."

In *Jazz: Hot and Hybrid*, by Winthrop Sargeant, we find an academic book that successfully breaks down the structure of jazz. In rhythmic, scalar and harmonic analysis of jazz, and consideration of both Negro and European background, this book is by far the best to date. But, Sargeant's final and uncomplimentary estimate of jazz is a familiar example of the old truism, that full knowledge of the inner workings of an art form does not necessarily lead to a sensitive awareness of its position in art history.

It is curious to find him dismayed, as the following quotation indicates, because Negro spirituals have been taken into the concert hall:

This, to the superficial observer, has given them [the spirituals] the status of "compositions," that is, of fixed musical creations designed to be "interpreted" according to the conventions of our concert art. This notion, as has often been pointed out by those familiar at first hand with Negro musical expression, is an essential misunderstanding of their nature and function.[78]

When we reverse the thought and consider how often bawdy, secular tunes have been used for religious purposes, prohibition on such a basis as this seems childish. The original intent of folk music is always lost when it is used in concert—whether religious or dance.

But if we agree with his statement that the "jazz musician has a remarkable sense of sub-divided and subordinated accents in what he is playing, even if it be the slowest sort of jazz," it is difficult to understand why he believes that this is "*quite foreign* to European music." (Italics mine.) If it is

[78] Winthrop Sargeant, *Jazz: Hot and Hybrid*, Arrow Editions, 1939, p. 18.

true enough of the playing style of the average, contemporary concert artist, nevertheless the recapture of past dance styles by Wanda Landowska (on the harpsichord) shows us that seventeenth and eighteenth century music, at least, was intended to be played with as much awareness of small metrical units as is contemporary jazz. This is the big mistake Sargeant makes. He gives the impression that European music is intrinsically devoid of this rhythmic quality, whereas it is only a lost school of playing that has given us the unrhythmic, lifeless, classical attitude we are now used to.

Moreover, much as we may be interested in what Sargeant can academically analyze for us, in his concluding chapter titled, "Jazz in Its Proper Place," he not only brings up a point of view esthetically repudiating all that which he has previously intimated, but he leaves us in this disconcerting position without one word of explanation. Let us consider the following statement:

It is not surprising that a society which has evolved the skyscraper, the baseball game and the "happy ending" movie, should find its most characteristic musical expression in an art like jazz. Contrast a skyscraper with a Greek temple or a mediaeval cathedral. . . . Like the jazz "composition" it is an impermanent link in a continuous process. And, like jazz, skyscraper architecture lacks the restraint of the older forms. The skyscraper has a beginning, and perhaps a middle. But its end is an indefinite upward thrust. A jazz performance ends, not because of the demands of musical logic, but because the performers or listeners are tired, or wish to turn to something else for a change. As far as form is concerned it might end equally well at the finish of almost any of its eight-bar phrases. A skyscraper ends its upward thrust in precisely the same way. It might be stopped at almost any point in its towering series of floors. It must, of course, stop somewhere. But the stop is not made primarily for reasons of proportion. Nor does it carry that sense of inevitableness that attaches to the height of the Greek temple.[79]

[79] Ibid., p. 214.

When Sargeant contrasts the skyscraper with the Greek temple and medieval cathedral, I might ask how the medieval cathedral can be categorically linked with the Greek temple! The medieval extravagance of design, its riot of graphic description for what was once a simple device of architecture, might have outraged the ancient Greek if as academic-minded as Sargeant! As far as simplicity is concerned, the skyscraper is the only architectural counterpart of the Greek temple. Moreover, if it is the *undetermined* upward thrust of the skyscraper which limits its art significance, let us not forget that the large Greek temple adhered to no particular length of construction. When he ties up this supposedly pertinent architectural analogy to its musical counterpart of *undetermined* termination in jazz performance, we realize that he is simply observing that jazz is based on the variation form—and that sometimes we know when the end is coming and sometimes we do not. But—do Haydn's 64 variations on a theme give any more notice? The same adjective flung at jazz for its uncultured and so-called "formless" state, can be flung at all pre-Bach music.

One thing keeps intruding throughout the classic references Sargeant enjoys making, and that is, he never refers to past art in terms of great *art form*. For instance he will say that the arts of America

all lack the element of "form" that is so essential, for example, to tragedy, to the symphony, to the great novel or the great opera, to monumental architecture, and to a large amount of Europe's less pretentious expression.[80]

Here, he refers to art in its period of almost sententious importance. Jazz is not at the grandiose stage. The art stuff out of which a Bach passion is tied together *ideologically*, in its original form, had none of the identifying qualities of the great *Passion*. Sargeant has already admitted this himself.

[80] Winthrop Sargeant, *Jazz: Hot and Hybrid*, Arrow Editions, 1939, p. 216.

Why then, such a conclusive, lofty dismissal of a new art stuff for *that* reason? The following reasons seem hardly satisfactory:

The attendant weakness of jazz is that it is an art without positive moral values, an art that evades those attitudes of restraint and intellectual poise upon which complex civilizations are built. At best it offers civilized man a temporary escape into drunken self-hypnotism. . . . It is a far cry from the jazz state of mind to that psychology of human perfectability, of aspiration, that lies, for example, behind the symphonies of a Beethoven or the music dramas of a Wagner.[81]

Unfortunately for such a theory—and scratch every academic critic hard enough and you will find it—jazz is no different in spirit from any other folk music in the heyday of creation. In fact, as Engel pointed out, the liveliness and the ribald atmosphere surrounding most of the early classic music, was far more at odds with the more refined culture of the day than is jazz contemporaneously.

American Jazz Music, by Wilder Hobson, is a book seeking to make us more intimately acquainted with the best in jazz. We find on the jacket the following well-expressed comment:

. . . [Hobson's purpose] has been, not to prove that jazz is "better than Bach" . . . but simply to tell its story and to make its complex, unprecedented rhythms more understandable and hence a greater source of enjoyment.

This, Hobson does well. Occasionally he feels constrained to point out that jazz is different from *all* other music, but at the same time he admits the circumstances surrounding jazz appear familiar.

It is often said that jazz cannot be notated. It cannot; and, strictly speaking, of course, *neither can any other music.* Any music is played with a "translation" of the written note values according

[81] *Ibid.*, p. 217.

to tradition for that particular kind of music and the instincts of the performer. [Italics mine.] [82]

Hobson truly observes that no music is written without a special school of playing in mind. His comment upon the "steady beat" so many critics find objectionable, is well taken and straight to the point:

The very regularity of the beat, of course, facilitates the improvising of rhythms, as does the fact that the beat is unaccented. In other words, movements may be planned around a certain base, whereas an uncertain base allows only uncertainty and the constant likelihood of getting lost—or, in this case, of rhythmic confusion.[83]

The importance of this observation can never be overstressed. Altogether this book is highly satisfying: a sensitive approach to the music the author likes.

In 1938 William Russell presented an extremely interesting analysis and review of Boogie Woogie piano records. With great sensitivity he points out that:

One of the most important developments in hot jazz, the last few years, has been the rediscovery of the Chicago school of Boogie Woogie pianists. . . . In making full use of the resources of the instrument, the Boogie Woogie is the most pianistic of all styles. The piano is treated as a percussion instrument rather than an imitation of the voice or a substitute for an orchestra.[84]

In conclusion, let us say that the early critics occupied themselves with the *extension* of jazz but entertained little consideration for jazz itself. On the other hand the recent critics have concentrated upon the living recording as an end in itself. Without doubt the disc is a priceless innovation towards the preservation of music; it would be a great loss to jazz history and early jazz music had recording not existed.

[82] Wilder Hobson, *American Jazz Music*, Norton, 1939, p. 29.
[83] *Ibid.*, p. 48.
[84] William Russell, "Boogie Woogie," *Hot Jazz* Nos. 25 and 26, June-September, Paris, France, 1938.

Nevertheless, if the musicians themselves are becoming conscious of written music with constant recourse to their own records, such awareness, *built* on the past, will be more lastingly significant than taking off from scratch every day.

My personal attitude might be expressed by the hope that jazz will continue along the path the best of it has taken so far. Inevitably there will be an academy. But the ultimate significance of this academy will be wholly dependent upon the continuance of this virile school of improvisation until such time as the academy materializes. Moreover, the longer we can postpone the arrival of the academy the more profitably will a vigorous school prepare itself for the event. A forced academy, compelled by composers removed from the jazz field, will not do! The jazzmen themselves must crystallize their school of playing. So far, the jazz school is a brilliantly improvisatory one. It is the group of arrangers who set, augment, and redistribute this living art, which has not distinguished itself. The fast "killer-diller" arrangement, the suave hot arrangement, the nostalgic arrangement, although commendable in their effort to break away from the banal, express a tendency to break away from the dance also. It is the dance-inciting, hot, but loosely organized arrangement, that seems safest for the present. As Ezra Pound has so well said:

The author's conviction on this day of New Year is that music begins to atrophy when it departs too far from the dance. . . . Bach and Mozart are never too far from physical movement.[85]

So let us hope that as jazz crystallizes, one portion will be dance music of the best kind, and the other, music of a caliber worthy of intensified listening in concert. There need be no antagonism between the two nor any distinct separation. A quotation from Mozart helps to make me feel this is possible:

[85] Ezra Pound, A B C of Reading, Yale University Press, 1934, p. xii.

I saw, however, with the greatest pleasure, all these people flying with such delight to the music of my "Figaro," transformed into quadrilles and waltzes; for here nothing is talked of but "Figaro," nothing played but "Figaro," nothing whistled or sung but "Figaro,"—very flattering to me, certainly.[86]

By this of course I do not mean to suggest the jazzing of another school's concert music, but the happy balance of a unified folk and academy fastidiously giving and taking from one another.[87]

[86] *Mozart's Letters* (Vol. II) to Herr Gottfried von Jacquin, Prague, Jan. 15, 1787. Oliver Ditson & Co., Boston.

[87] *Editors' Note:* Earlier articles by Mr. Dodge are: "Negro Jazz," London *Dancing Times,* October, 1929, and "Harpsichords and Jazz Trumpets," *Hound & Horn,* July-September, 1934.

Index

Aberdeen Brothers Cabaret, 62
Abraham, Morton, 41, 43-44
Abrams, Bridge, 149
Aeolian-Vocalion, 48
Aeschylus, 311
Algiers and Pacific Brass Band, 16
Ali, Budem, 280
Allen, Jr., Henry, 82, 179, 219
Allen, Sr., Henry, 16, 30, 82, 122
Allen, Wad, 149
American Jazz Music, 339
American Record Corporation, 296
Ammons, Albert, 113, 187-190, 192, 195, 204, 252, 262
Anderson, Tom, 25, 31-32, 47, 52, 62, 124, 265
Ansermet, Ernest, 305, 306, 307, 316, 328
Antheil, George, 308, 309, 319
Antoine's, 25, 29, 267
Apex Club, 116, 167
Appeal of Jazz, The, 322
Arcadia Ballroom, 153
Archer, Harry, 316
Aristophanes, 311
Arlington Annex, 31 (see Anderson, Tom)
Arlington, Josie, 3, 32, 58
Armstrong, Beatrice, 121
Armstrong, Lillian, see Hardin, Lil
Armstrong, Louis, 4, 34, 52, 69-72, 74-75, 84-85, 99-100, 116, 119-42, 146-48, 152, 167, 169, 177, 181, 212, 215, 219, 222, 231, 234, 237, 239, 240-41, 256-58, 261, 275, 289-90, 295-96, 331-32
Asbury, Herbert, 11
Ash, Paul, 127
Ashcraft, E. M., 288
Atkins, 36
Auburn Theatre, 138
Austin High School, 161 et seq.

Bach, J. S., 306, 314, 325, 327, 330, 332, 338, 339, 341
Bailey, Buster, 79, 213, 215
Baltimore, Henry "Zino," 17, 33, 36, 63
Bamboula, 3, 8-9
Banks, Billy, 295
Banks, Louis, 190
Baquet, Achille, 41-44
Baquet, George, 21-22, 33, 99
Barbarin, Paul, 64, 76-77, 83
Barker, Lou, 246
Basie, Count, 252-3, 256, 282
Bauduc, Ray, 237, 251, 257, 269
Beall, George, 294
Beaux Arts (Atlantic City café), 176
Bechet, Joe, 26
Bechet, Leonard, 26, 284
Bechet, Sidney, 19, 25-26, 33, 36, 64-65, 99, 128, 270, 283-84, 305, 328
Beers, Sam (Chicago club), 157
Beethoven, Ludwig van, 314, 320, 330, 339
Beiderbecke, Leon Bismarck "Bix," 50, 98, 137, 164-67, 170-71, 176, 180, 225, 230-31, 233-37, 239, 241, 248, 289-91, 293, 296
Bell, Clive, 313
Benny, Black, 30, 120
Benrod, Emile "Whiskey," 53
Berlin, Irving, 311, 312, 313, 314, 330
Berry, Choo, 256
Berton, Vic, 149-50, 166, 233
Bestor, Don, 151
Big Apple (Chicago), 196
Big Apple (New York), 245
Bigard, Barney, 76-77, 124, 213, 219
Big Easy Hall, 16
Big 4 Hall, 16
Black, Lew, 56
Blackhawk Restaurant, 257

Blake, Blind, 200
Bland, Jack, 176
Bloom, Rube, 184
Bluebird, 296
Blue Blowers, 176
Blue Book, 31, 47, 130
Blue Friars, 164-66
Blue Lantern Inn, 155
Blue Note, 191
Blues diagram, 108
Blythe, Jimmy, 191
Bocage, Peter, 29
Bogalusa, 3
Bolden, Charles Buddy, 3-6, 9-12, 15, 18-21, 23-25, 45, 59, 62, 120, 246, 248, 266, 275
Bonnano, Sharkey, 166
Boogie Woogie, 112, 183 *et seq.*, 328, 340
Born, Charley, 250
"Boy in a Tuxedo," 288
Brahms, Johannes, 304, 330
Bratton's Rendezvous, 192
Braud, Wellman, 36, 138
Briggs, Romeo, 199
Bright, Dalbert, 190
Brown, Boyce, 258
Brown, Henry, 201
Brown, Lawrence, 219
Brown, Steve, 56, 98, 235
Brown, Tom, 45-46, 48, 97
Brundy, Walter, 60, 84
Brunies, Abbie, 43, 50, 53, 55-57, 257, 269
Brunies, George, 43, 50, 55-57, 258-59
Brunies, Richard, 43
Brunious, John, 271
Brunswick, 83, 166, 176, 178
Brunswick, English, 57
Buchanan, Charles, 317
Bucktown, 28
Bulls' Club, 17
"Bunk," see Johnson, Willie G.
Bunn, Teddy, 250
Busse, Henry, 157
Bussey, Willie "Cajun," 52-53
Butterbeans and Susie, 134
Buzzards, The, 12

Café Society, 190, 195
California Ramblers, 226, 230, 234
Callahan, Albert, 52, 57-58
Capitol (steamboat), 147
Carey, Charles "Dolly," 53
Carey, Harry "Sweet Potato," 53
Carey, Mutt, 36
Carlin, Herb, 177
Carmichael, Hoagy, 144, 149, 154, 159, 225, 235, 240
Carnegie Hall, 117, 187, 190, 195, 252, 283
Carney, Harry, 213, 219
Carpenter, John Alden, 314
Carrel, Al, 32
Carrie, Professor, 54
Carter, Benny, 213, 215
Casa Loma Orchestra, 158
Cascades Ballroom, 56
Casino Gardens, 150
Casoff, Jules, 43
Castle Farms, 155
Cauldwell, "Happy," 179
Celestin, Oscar "Papa," 34, 275
Cellar, The (Chicago), 171
Centeno, Augusto, 288
Century Theatre, 48
Challis, Bill, 148, 155-56, 159
Chambers, Tig, 36
Chaminade, C., 303
Chandler, Deedee, 62
Chaplin, Charles, 311
Chauvin, Louis, 114
Cherie, Eddie, 55
Chicago Defender, 68, 72, 75, 77-79, 85, 95, 127-28
Chicago Loopers, the, 293
Chicago's Booster Club, 47
Chopin, F., 184, 315
Christian, Buddy, 34, 63, 75
Christian, Emil, 51
Cinderella Ballroom, 233
Claremont Club, 190
Clarence, Blind, 46-47
Clem, Edward, 17-18
Clementi, 330
Clinton, Larry, 298
Cobb, Cobb Bertrium, 77
Coleman, Emil, 151
Coliseum, 134

College Inn (Chicago), 177
Collins, Lee, 85, 261
Columbia, 74, 158
Columbia Hall, 169
Columbus Brass Band, the Old, 16
Come Clean Hall, 16
Commedia dell' arte, 311, 312
Commodore, 296
Condon, Eddie, 157, 171, 177-78, 248
Confrey, Zez, 313, 328
Congo Dances, 7-9
Congo Square, 3, 5, 7, 14-15, 246
Congress Hotel, 137, 255
Connie's Inn, 138, 210
Conzelman, Bob, 149
Cook, Charlie, 76, 134, 284
Cooperative Hall, 99
Copland, Aaron, 194, 321-22
Cornish, Willy, 6, 13-15
Cottage Grove, 135
Cotton Club, 82, 214, 217, 235
Cotton Pickers, the, 230
Cottrelle, Louis, 20, 36
Cox, Ida, 115
Craven, Cleve "Warm Gravy," 53
Creath, Charlie, 36, 114, 175
Crescent Billiard Hall, 271
Cricket, The, 11
Crosby, Bing, 157
Crosby, Bob (Orchestra), 80, 224, 257, 283
Crosby, Israel, 190, 261
Cutchey, Wallace, 24

Dablayes, Charlie, 16
Dago and Russell, 95
Davenport, Cow Cow, 198, 201
Davenport High School, 148
Davis, Meyer, 226
Davis, Peter, 122
Debussy, Claude, 154, 159, 180, 328
Decca, 192, 194
De Faut, Volly, 170, 176
Delaunay, Charles, 179, 298
De Lisa, Club, 190, 192
De Luxe Café, 97
Derby Club (Calumet City, Ill.), 261
Desvigne, Sidney, 26, 272

Dewey, Lawrence, 34, 36, 64-65
Dexter Park, 83, 211
Diamond Stone Brass Band, 16, 120
Dickerson, Carroll, 134, 135, 137
"Dixieland" music, 39
Dixie Syncopators (King Oliver's), 77, 99
Doc Higgins' Tavern, 192
Dodds, Baby, 68, 70, 75, 99, 123, 131, 256, 258, 263
Dodds, Johnny, 19, 34, 68, 71, 75, 99, 131-32, 167, 170-71, 180, 186, 256, 258, 263
Dominique, Nat, 36, 186
Dorsey, Jimmy, 157, 160, 225, 227, 233
Dorsey, Maddy, 187
Dorsey, Tommy, 157-58, 160, 225, 227, 233, 251, 335
Down Beat, 298, 330, 334
Downes, Olin, 304
Doyle's Pavilion (Cincinnati), 149
D'Pree, Reese, 117-18
Dreamland Café, 64-67, 127-28, 256
Duchin, Eddie, 196
Duncan, Hank, 248
Dunn, Johnny, 147
Dusen, Frank, 16-18, 23, 25, 60
Dutrey, Honoré, 67-68, 72, 75
Dutrey, Sam, 17, 123

Eagle Band, 23, 25-26, 28-30, 60-61, 120-23
Eagle Saloon, 4, 5, 17, 273
Earheart, Will, 314
Early, Frank, 34
East Louisiana State Hospital, 18
Economy Hall, 16, 62, 272
Edwards, Eddie, 43, 44, 47-51
Elite Café, 95
Ellington, Duke, 75, 80, 82, 138, 177, 210, 213-14, 217, 232, 235, 240-41, 290, 292, 335
Ellis Building, 99
Elman, Ziggy, 241
Engel, Carl, 306, 307, 308, 319, 339
Entertainers' Cabaret, 99
Esquire, 289
Etude, 313, 315
Everleigh Club, 95

Excelsior Band, 30
Excelsior Brass Band, the Old, 16
Ezell, Will, 200-01

Faggen, I. H., 77, 81
Fair Ground Dance Hall, 16
Famous Door, The, 252
Farnell, Arthur, 303
Farrar, Fred, 156
Fazola, Irving, 257
Ferguson, Otis, 333
Fewclothes's Dance Hall, 62
Fio Rito, Ted, 152
Fischer, Johnny, 45, 50
Fitzgerald, Ella, 279, 280-81
Five Rubes, 48
Five Spirits of Rhythm, 250
Forrest, Willy, 274, 277
Fosdick, Dudley, 234
Foster, George "Pop," 33, 37, 82,
 123
Fourth District Carnival Club, 12
Fowler, Lem, 191
Frank, Alcide, 60
Frank, Bob, 34
Freeman, Bud, 145, 149, 155, 157,
 159-61, 163, 167-70, 174, 177,
 241, 248, 251
French Quarter, The, 11
Friars' Inn, 50, 56, 71, 97-99, 163-64,
 176-77, 222-23
Frisco & McDermott (vaudeville),
 46; Frisco, 267
"Fron-zi-me" Hall, 16
Fulford, Tommy, 280
Function, The (New Orleans), 52,
 265

Gallaty, Bill, 45
Galloway, Charlie, 17
Gande, Al, 149
Garber, Jan, 180, 226
Garland, Edward, 67-68
Gary Municipal Beach Pavilion, 150-
 51
Geddis & Moss (Buddy Bolden's un-
 dertaker), 267
Gennett, 73-74, 98, 144, 150, 164,
 289
Georgians, the, 210

Gershwin, George, 112, 116, 303,
 304, 305, 308, 310, 311, 313, 315,
 316, 320, 322, 324, 325, 328, 329,
 333
Giardina, Ernest, 41, 43-44
Gifford, Gene, 158
Gillette, Bob, 56, 149
Gilman, Lawrence, 315, 316
Gilmore, Patrick Sarsfield, 40
Glaser, Joe, 135
Globe Hall, 18
Goffin, Robert, 308
Goldberg, Isaac, 327
Goldfield, Harry, 157
Goldkette, Jean, 146, 148, 153-57,
 167, 235-36
Goldkette, Orchestras and Attrac-
 tions, Inc., Jean, 81
Goodman, Benny, 159, 162, 165,
 175, 178, 215, 224-25, 236-37,
 239, 241, 247, 252, 255-56, 282,
 334-35
Goodman, Harry, 236
Gorman, Ross, 230, 233
Grand Terrace, 256
Grand Theatre, 96
Green, Charlie "Big," 213, 215, 217
Gregory the Great, 307
Greystone Ballroom, 155-56
Grieg, Edvard, 303
Grociele, Eddie, 34
Grofé, Ferde, 156, 325
Grove's *Dictionary of Music and
 Musicians*, 314
Grunewald, the (now the Roose-
 velt), 25, 267
Guitar, Willy, 41, 44
Guriffe, Professor Sonta, 55
Gustat, Joe, 146
Gypsy Smith Auditorium, 275
Gypsy Tea Room (New Orleans),
 269
"Gyp the Blood," 47

Haggart, Bob, 177, 258, 283
Haggin, B. H., 317, 318
Halfway House, 33, 53, 55-57
Hall, Edmond, 248
Hall, Minor, 67, 68
Hall, "Tubby," 36, 186

Hammond, Jr., John Henry, 192, 288, 333, 334, 335
Hampton, Lionel, 241
Handel, G. F., 306
Handy, W. C., 295, 320
Hanks, Nancy (New Orleans saloon), 14, 266
"Happy," 119
Hardin, Lil, 36, 67-68, 70, 74, 79, 96, 125-128, 131, 133, 140, 256, 259
Hardy, Emmett, 50, 147
Harlem Opera House, 279
Harmon's Dreamland Casino, 76
Harney, Benjamin, 95   [229
Harrison, Jimmy, 138, 213, 216-217,
Hartwell, Jimmy, 149, 166, 229
Hassler, Bud, 154
Hawkins, Coleman, 167, 179, 213, 215-16
Haydn, Joseph, 307, 315, 338
Healey's Balconnades, 279
Helbock, Joe, 251
Henderson, Fletcher, 114, 127, 137, 177, 210, 213-14, 216-17, 231-32, 234-36, 240-41, 247, 252, 256, 289, 334
Henderson, Horace, 215
Higginbotham, Jay C., 213, 219
Hill, Bertha, 131
Hines, Earl, 99, 116, 134, 136-38, 173, 184, 294
Hobson, Wilder, 288, 339-40
Hodges, Johnny, 213, 218, 279
Holiday, Billie, 247
Hollywood Bard (Chicago club), 177
Holmes, Charles, 219
Holst, 180
Holt, Nora, 116
Honegger, Arthur, 201
Hope Hall, 16, 62
Hoskins, Jimmy, 190, 262
"Hot Chocolates," 138
Hot Discography, 298
Hot Jazz (book), 331
Hot Jazz (journal), 298
Hot Record Exchange, 297-98
Hot Record Society, 57, 199, 296, 333
Howard, Darnell, 79

Howard, Joe, 122
Hughes, Langston, 246-47, 289
Huxley, Aldous, 326
Hylton, Jack, 308, 323

Imperial Band, 29
Imperial Theatre, 195
Indiana University, 153-54
Indians, Oumas, 7
It Club, 190

Jackson, Rudy, 75, 79-80
Jackson, Tony, 24, 32-33, 95, 111
Jacobsen, Bud, 174
James, Harry (booker), 47
James, Harry (trumpet), 241
James Lake, 98
Jazz (book), 322
Jazz: Hot and Hybrid, 336
Jazz Hot, Le, 103, 330
Jazz Singer, The, 326
Jefferson, Hilton, 280
Johnny, "Sugar," 36, 64, 96-97
Johnson, Al, 162
Johnson, Buddie, 29
Johnson, Dink, 20, 36
Johnson, George, 98, 149
Johnson, James, 14, 25
Johnson Park, 13, 16
Johnson, Pete, 195, 202-03, 282
Johnson, Victoria Davis, 59, 82, 89-91
Johnson, Willie G. "Bunk," 4-6, 16, 23, 26, 36, 59-62, 84-85, 91, 120-21, 123, 126, 139-41, 245, 275, 284
Johnson, W. M. (Bill), 20, 64, 70
John the Baptist (piano player), 32
Jones, Captain Joseph, 120-22, 275
Jones, Dave, 123, 125
Jones, Isham, 176, 241
Jones, Jonah, 252
Jones, King, 257   [127
Jones, Maggie, 37 (Lizzie Green),
Jones, Richard M., 32, 62, 66, 134, 142
Joplin, Scott, 15, 22, 30, 42, 96, 114
Jordan, Taft, 279-80

Kahn, Roger Wolfe, 233
Kaminsky, Max, 248

Kassel, Art, 170, 177
Keelin, Jr., Johnny, 120
Kelly, Bert (Orchestra), 47
Kelly, E. S., 303
Kelly, Guy, 84, 190
Kelly, Peck, 175
Kelly's Stable (Chicago), 75, 99, 167
Kenchen, Walter, 59-60
Kentucky Club, the, 82, 235
Keppard, Freddie, 18, 20-22, 30, 34, 62, 65-66, 95, 99, 116, 134, 283
Keppard, Louis, 36
Kern, Jerome, 311, 312, 316
Kerr, Charlie, 225
Kimbal Hall, 125
Kimball, A. W., 85
Kirby, John, 252
Kirk, Andy, 241, 282
Kless, Rod, 174, 180, 258-59
Knowlton, Don, 321, 322
Korn, Monty, 45
Kramer's lot, 40
Krupa, Gene, 113, 159-60, 177-78, 237, 239, 241, 279

Lacoume, Sr., Emile August "Stale Bread," 43, 52
Lacoume, Jimmy "Dude," 53
Ladnier, Tommy, 37, 213, 216-17
Laine, Alfred, 43, 51, 210
Laine, Jack "Papa," 39, 40-45, 49, 57, 175, 210
Lake Forest Academy, 148-49
Lala, John, 43, 273
Lala, Peter, 33, 62, 63, 69, 130, 265
Lambert, William, 46
Lamb's Café, 46
Landowska, Wanda, 337
Lang, Eddie, 156, 158, 176, 225, 227, 233, 237, 240-41
Lanin, Sam, 151, 230, 233
Lannigan, Jim, 155, 161-62, 165, 169-70, 177, 180
La Rocca, D. J. "Nick," 22, 48-51, 97, 146-148, 234
Lee, "Sonny," 155
Levinson, André, 323
Lewis, Frank, 14, 60
Lewis, Meade Lux, 113, 187, 189-92, 196, 199, 204, 262, 332

Lewis, Steve, 271, 277
Lewis, Ted, 127, 180, 225, 328
Lincoln, Abraham, 311
Lincoln Gardens Café, 69, 70, 72, 74-76, 124-25, 127, 132, 195, 223, 257
Lincoln Park, 6, 13-14, 16
Lindsay, Herbert, 36
Lindsay, Joe, 123, 275
Lindsay, John, 75
Liston, Virginia, 115
Livingston, Fud, 167, 231
Local 802, A. F. of M., 151
Local 208, A. F. of M., 260
Lofton, Cripple Clarence, 191, 196, 200, 262
Lone Star, the (Kansas City night club), 203
Longshoremen's Hall, 15
Lopez, Ray, 46
Lopez, Vincent, 225, 328
Loral, P. G., 25
Lord, Jimmy, 166
Louisiana Five, the, 51, 210
Louisiana Six, the, 36
Love and Charity Hall, 16
Loyocano, Arnold J., 46, 50-51, 56, 170, 175
Ludwig, Ray, 155, 235
Lusher, Irving, 43
Lyons, Bob, 17, 23, 60, 245, 275
Lytell, Paul, 227

MacDowell, 154, 303
MacPartland, Dick, 161-63, 169
MacPartland, Jimmy, 155, 161-63, 165-66, 169-70, 177, 180, 236, 258
Madame John's legacy, 3
Mahogany Hall, 3, 32, 265
Malneck, Matt, 157
Malney, Doc, 53
Mangold, Fred, 289
Mannone, Joe "Wingy," 171, 236, 251
Marable, Fate, 36, 99, 114, 116-17, 123, 147, 175, 222
Mardi Gras, 14, 268-70 et seq.
Mares, Paul, 50, 56, 124, 147, 257-58
Margulies, Charlie, 157

Marlow, Manuel, 43
Marrero, Billie, 84
Marrero, John, 84
Marsala, Joe, 171, 173, 180, 252
Marsala, Marty, 173
Marshall, Kaiser, 216, 281
Martin, Chink, 56, 165
Martin, Sara, 115, 134
Martinique, 151
Masonic Hall, 4, 17-18, 25-26, 120-21
Massarini (band leader), 45
Matlock, "Matty," 251
McBride, Margaret, 322
McConville, Leo, 233
McCullons, George (brass band), 16
McKendrick, Mike, 261
McKenzie and Condon's Chicagoans, 176
McKenzie, Club, 252
McKenzie, Red, 147, 176, 178, 250
McKinney's Cotton Pickers, 137
McMurray (drummer), 14
McRae, Ted, 280
McVitty, Albert, 288
Melrose, Walter, 55, 136
Memphis Five, see Original Memphis Five
Mendel, John, 174
Mendl, Robert, 322
Metropolitan Theatre (Chicago), 136
Mezzrow, Milton, 80, 151, 155, 167, 178, 181
Michelangelo (Last Judgment), 313
Midway Garden, 136, 170, 173; Orchestra, 172, 178
Miles, Lizzie, 84
Miley, Bubber, 80, 159
Milhaud, Darius, 309, 310, 321
Miller, Eddie, 251, 257
Miller, Glenn, 228, 236-37
Miller, Ray, 233
Mills, Irving, 217
Milneburg, 28, 40, 42, 57-58
Miss Cole's Lawn Parties, 11
Mole, Milfred Miff, 210, 213, 215, 225, 227-28, 230-31, 233, 235, 237, 239

Molière, 311
Montluzin, Albert "Slew-foot Pete," 53
Moore, Pony (Chicago club), 95
Moore, Vic, 149, 166
Moorehouse, Chauncey, 156
Morgan, Icky, 236
Morris, Paul, 143
Morton, Benny, 250
Morton, Ferdinand "Jelly Roll," 31-32, 68, 71, 95, 96, 100, 114, 271, 285
Moten, Bennie, 114, 241, 282
Mozart, Wolfgang, 311, 313, 315, 316, 327, 330, 334, 335, 341
Mueller, Gus, 46-47
Mumford, Brock, 17, 23, 25, 60
Mumford, Jeff, 14
Mundy, Jimmy, 177
Murray, Don, 56-57, 235
Mustache, 17
Myers, Sig, 169, 170
Mysterious Babies (club), 12

Nanton, Joe "Tricky Sam," 213, 218
Napoleon, Phil, 227
Nathan, George Jean, 306
Nelson, "Big Eye" Louis, 19, 34, 62, 269-70, 273-75, 284
Nelson, Romeo, 198-200
Nest, The (Chicago), 116, 135, 167
Nest, The (New York), 83, 210
Nevin, Ethelbert, 184
New Hall, 16
Newman, Ernest, 323, 324
New Orleans City Guide (Federal Writers' Project), 132
New Orleans Jazz Band, 65, 96 (see Johnny, "Sugar")
New Orleans Rhythm Kings, 33, 41, 43, 50-51, 56-57, 97-98, 149, 163-65, 168-69, 232, 257-58
Nicholas, Albert, 75-77, 79, 124
Nichols, Red, 151, 178, 225, 227, 230-31, 233-35, 237, 239, 290
Nick's Café, 195, 248, 285
Nicodemus, 120
Niles, Abbe, 320, 321
Noone, Jimmy, 19, 22, 34, 64, 67,

99, 116, 135, 152, 167, 170-71, 179-80, 222, 259-61
North, Dave, 155, 165, 167, 169, 255
Number 12 Hall, 16
Nunez, Alcide "Yellow," 42-45, 47-48, 51, 210

O'Brien, Floyd, 155, 165, 167, 169-70, 181
Odd Fellows' Hall, 16-17, 25, 62
O'Hare, Husk, 166-69, 255
O'Hare's Red Dragons, 167
Okeh, 73-74, 80, 130, 134, 159, 174, 176-78, 236-37, 295
Oliver, Joe "King," 4, 30, 33-34, 57, 59-91, 96, 99, 116, 124, 126, 131-32, 134-35, 146-48, 152, 169, 195, 210-12, 222, 245, 256, 258, 260, 275, 295, 331-32; his Creole Jazz Band, 66, 68, 71, 77, 80, 91, 96, 124-25, 164, 256
Olivier, Adam, 24
Olsen, George, 225, 230
Olympia Band, 19-21
101 Ranch, 33-34, 62
102 Ranch, 47
Onward Brass Band, 30, 61
Onyx Club, 247, 249-52
Orchard Cabaret, 123-24
Original Creole Band, 20-23, 36, 64, 95, 209
Original Dixieland Jazz Band, 22, 33, 42, 48-49, 97, 114, 149, 209, 213, 227, 267, 269, 279, 297
Original Memphis Five, 227, 279
Orpheum Circuit, 55
Ory, Edward "Kid," 33, 77, 83, 99, 123, 130, 133, 275; Ory's Brown Skinned Jazz Band, 36
Osgood, Henry, 308, 319

Palace (theatre), 176, 221
Palais Royal, 214, 223, 315
Palao, Jimmie, 17, 21, 68
Palmer, Bee (vaudeville), 55
Palmer, Roy, 33, 36
Palomar, 222, 247
Panassié, Hugues, 103, 179, 231, 330-33

P and M New Orleans Bar-B-Q (Chicago), 257
Panico, Louis, 147
Paramount, 72-73, 172, 176, 192, 200-01, 294-95
Parker, Daisy, 122
Parker's (New Orleans), 62
Parlophone, 192
Parry, Sir C. Hubert, 314
Patterson, Albion, 288
Peer, Bevery, 280
Pekin Café, 67-68, 256
Pennsylvania roof (New York), 225
"Pepper Boys, The," 152
Perez, Emanuel, 29, 33-34, 36, 61-62, 95, 272
Perfect, 212
Pergola Dancing Pavilion, 68
Perkins, Dave, 41-45, 55
Perseverance Hall, 12, 16
Pete, Black, 34
Peterson, Harold, 53
Petit, Buddy, 30, 34, 77, 96
Petit, Joseph, 20
Petrone, George, 170
Pettis, Jack, 56
Peyton, Dave, 77-79, 81, 83
Philip, James, 60
Phillips, Billy, 33-34, 47
Piazza, Countess Willie, 32, 36, 265
Pichon, Walter, 271
Picilli, Bob, 170
Picou, A. J., 19, 29, 50, 55, 96, 123, 270-71
Pierce, Charles, 171-72, 294-95
Piron, J. A., 29, 34, 83, 124, 274
Plantation Café, 76-77, 79-82, 134, 144
Pleyel, 307
Plus de Jazz, 313
Poli, S. Z. (vaudeville circuit), 221
Pollack, Ben, 28, 56, 157, 167, 180, 232, 236-37, 239
Pontchartrain, Lake, 5, 13, 28, 56, 58, 98
Porter, King (pianist), 32
Pound, Ezra, 341
Powers, Ollie, 75
Prima, Leon, 175

Prima, Louis, 269
Princeton University, 288

Q.R.S., 294
Qualey, Dan, 262
Quarella's Pavilion (New Orleans), 44
Quartel, Frank, 152

"Rabbit" (drummer), 99
Rabelais, 311
Racine, 311
Ragas, Henry, 43-44, 47, 49, 51
Ragtime, origin of, 114
Rainey, Ma, 99, 101-03
Rank, Bill, 156, 235-36
Rappolo, Fano, 55, 269
Rappolo, Leon Joseph, 41, 43, 50, 52-57, 98, 165, 175, 225, 231, 241, 257, 259, 289
Ravel, Maurice, 154
Real Thing, The (New Orleans cabaret), 124
Record companies, 223 (see under trade name of record label)
Red Heads, 227, 289
Redman, Don, 137, 215
Red Onion Jazz Babies, 127-28
Reisenweber's, 48, 51
Reliance Brass Band, 43, 57
Rena, Henry "Kid," 119-20, 275-76
Rena, Joe, 120
Repack, Johnny, 245
Rice's Hall, 34, 61
Riley, Mike, 251
Riskin, "Itzy," 155
Riverview Park (Des Moines), 174
Riviera Theatre (Chicago), 152
Robbins (music publisher), 159
Robichaux, John, 6, 13, 25, 29
Robinson, J. Russell, 51
Robinson, Zue, 20, 33, 63
Robison, Willard, 293-94
Rockport Ballroom, 224
Rodemich, Gene, 176
Rodin, Gil, 236
Rolfe, B. A., 158
Rollini, Adrian, 156, 234
Roman Antiphonary, 307

Roosevelt (New Orleans), the, 25, 267
Roseland Ballroom, 127-28, 156, 214, 217, 233-34, 247-48
Rosemont Dance Hall (Brooklyn), 77
Rosenfeld, Paul, 326
Roth, Jack, 227
Round-Up (New Orleans), 277
Royal Gardens Café, 64-67, 69 (see Lincoln Gardens Café)
Russell, Bob, Band, 25
Russell, Luis, 76-78, 83, 124, 210, 213, 217, 219, 333
Russell, Pee Wee, 149, 155, 160, 167, 170, 174-75, 237, 248, 252, 290
Russell, William, 294, 340
Ruth, Babe, 83, 89, 159

St. Cyr, Buddy, 131
St. Paul (steamboat), 68, 116
Salvin, Sam, 48
Sampson, Edgar, 279
San Jacinto Hall (New Orleans), 272
Santiago, Burnel, 273-74, 277
Saratoga Club, 210, 219
Sargeant, Winthrop, 336, 337, 338
Savoy Ballroom (Chicago), 136-38, 257
Savoy Ballroom (New York), 81-82, 245, 279
Saxbe, Marvin, 170
Sbarbaro, Tony, 44, 47, 49-50
Scarlatti, Domenico, 330
Schiller's Café, 98
Schilling, George "Happy," 45, 50 51
Schoebel, Elmer, 56, 176
Schoenberg, Arnold, 10
Schoffner, Bob, 78
Schumann, Robert, 303
Schutt, Arthur, 225, 227, 233, 250
Scott, Bud, 77
Scranton Sirens, 225
Scroggins, Virgil, 250
Seldes, Gilbert, 311, 312, 313
Seven Lively Arts, 311, 329
Shavers, Charlie, 252
Shaw, Art, 224
Sherman, Morris, 177

Shields, Harry, 269
Shields, Larry, 47-50, 231
"Shots," 119
Signorelli, Frank, 156, 227
Silver Bell Band, 26
Simeon, Omer, 99, 100
Singleton, Zutty, 27, 37, 113, 123, 136-38, 179, 248, 256, 279, 285
Sissle, Noble, 284
Skyscraper (jazz ballet), 314
Slevins, Dick, 176
Small's Paradise, 210
Smith, Bessie, 35, 114-15, 127, 148, 152, 195, 212, 215, 231, 240-41, 246-47, 252, 296, 334
Smith, Charles Edward, 147, 289, 328-30
Smith, Chris, 99
Smith, Clara, 114, 126
Smith, Floyd, 283
Smith, Joe, 213, 216-17
Smith, Laura, 114
Smith, Mamie, 114-15
Smith, Pine Top, 113, 187-88, 196, 201
Smith, "Stuff," 251
Smith, Trixie, 114
Snyder, Frank, 56
Solo Art, 191, 262
So This Is Jazz, 308, 319
Sousa, J. P., 30
Southern Syncopated Orchestra, 305
Souvanie, 325
Spaeth, Sigmund, 325-26
Spand, Charlie, 200
Spanier, Muggsy, 98, 135-36, 169-72, 178, 180, 216, 255, 258-59
Spazier, Karl, 307
Specht, Paul, 225
Speckled Red (Rufus Perryman), 200
Spikes Brothers, 73
Stacy, Jess, 135-36, 159, 170-71, 174, 232, 241
Staigers, "Del," 250
"Stale Bread," see Lacoume, Sr., Emile August
Stall, Lorenzo, 275
Stark, Bobby, 279
Starr Piano Company, see Gennett

Stein, Johnny, 47
Stevens, Mike, 43
Stewart, Rex, 218-19
Stitzel, Mel, 56
Stockton Club (Hamilton, Ohio), 149
Stork Club (London), 176
Storyville, 5, 31, 33, 57-58, 61, 63, 119, 123, 130, 139, 187, 266-67, 272-73, 284
Straight, Charlie, 143, 152
Stravinsky, Igor, 154, 184, 309, 310, 316, 319, 325, 326, 327
Strekfus Line, 56, 99, 123, 147
Sugar Cane Club (New York), 210
"Sugar" Johnny, see Johnny, "Sugar"
Suggs, Doug, 201
Sullivan, Joe, 157, 160, 165, 173, 177-78, 237, 239, 250, 332
Sunset Café, 78, 99, 134-36, 167, 203, 223
"Swing Shack" (Lil Armstrong's, Chicago), 256
Swing Music (journal), 298
Symphonic Syncopators (Peyton's), 76

Tanner, Lucy (New Orleans resort), 40
Tate, Erskine, 128-29, 134
Tatum, Art, 250
Taylor, Eva, 115
Taylor, Lottie, 64
Taylor, Montana, 199
Teagarden, Jack, 174, 212, 225, 228-30, 236-37, 239, 241, 335
Teamsters and Loaders Hall, 15
Teao Brass Band, the Old, 16
Tempo (journal), 298
Teschmaker, Frank, 135, 143, 149, 155, 157, 161-63, 165, 167-72, 175, 177-78, 180, 237, 239, 241, 252, 255, 259, 295, 332
Theard, Sam, 198
Theatre Intime (Princeton), 288
Theatrical Owners' Booking Agency, 187, 198
Thomas, Hersal, 189
Thomson, Virgil, 316

Three Deuces (Chicago night club), 171, 256
Tillman, Cornelius, 14, 25
Tin Pan Alley, 96, 140, 312
Tin Type Hall, 11-12
Tio, Lorenzo, 30, 33, 36, 63, 85
Tio, Louis, 30
Tonti Social Club (New Orleans), 44
Tony, Dago (New Orleans honkytonk), 120
Toro's (New Orleans), 53
Tough, Dave, 149, 165, 167, 169
Town, Floyd, 170
Trapiana, Ernest, 20
Triangle Club (Chicago), 172
Trueheart, John, 280
Trumbauer, Frank, 153-55, 167, 176, 235-36
Turner, Joe, 203
Turpin, Tom, 114
Tuxedo Band, 30, 69, 124
Tuxedo Dance Hall, 16
28 Club, 34-35
25 Club, 33
29 Club, 186-87, 259-60

Usonia (Chicago), 136

Vail, George, 315
Van Vechten, Carl, 104, 302-04
Varèse, Edgar, 184, 327
Vaudreuil, Marquis de, 3
Vean, John, 19
Vega, Lawrence, 41, 43-44, 50, 53
Vendome Theatre (Chicago), 99, 116, 128-29, 135-36, 140
Venson, Eddie, 21, 64-65
Venuti, Joe, 156, 158, 233, 240, 290-91
Victor, 22, 83, 86, 158, 192, 222, 224, 240
Villani, Pip, 97
Vocalion, 77-78, 188, 191, 200, 240
Voorhees, Don, 230, 233
Voynow, Dick, 149, 166

Wagner, Richard, 303, 328, 339
Waifs' Home (New Orleans), 120-21

Wallace, Wesley, 201
Waller, Thomas "Fats," 184, 189, 213, 251
Waring's Pencilsharpeners, 226
Warner, William, 14, 25
Warwick Hall, 116, 136-37, 260
Washington, Al, 261
Washington, Buck, 135
Washingtonians (Duke Ellington's), 82
Washington Park, 28
Waters, Ethel, 115, 148
Watson, Leo, 250
Watteau, 313
Wayside Park (Los Angeles), 68
Weatherford, Teddy, 79, 116
Webb, Chick, 113, 278-81
Welsh, Frank (brass band), 16
Wettling, George, 98, 135, 169-73, 248
White City, 98, 155, 157, 167-70
White, Jack, 34
White, Lulu, 3, 32, 52, 265
Whiteman, Paul, 127, 144, 148, 151, 156-59, 177, 214, 223-24, 230, 233, 236, 239, 241, 303-4, 308, 310-12, 315-16, 322-25, 328-29
William, Claiborne, 14
Williams, Albert "Cootie," 213, 218
Williams, Clarence, 32, 36, 96, 109-11, 117-18, 124, 127
Williams, Elmer, 279
Williams, Jabo, 201
Williams, Mary Lou, 177, 274, 280, 282-3
Williams, Mayo, 187-88
Williams, Midge, 247
Williams, Norwood, 20-21
Williams, Sandy, 280
Williams, Spencer, 96
Williamson, Shorty, 170
Wilson, Teddy, 184, 196, 241, 252, 328, 335
Winter Garden (New York), 22, 209
Wolverine Orchestra, 51, 98, 143, 146, 148-54, 164, 166-68, 233-34, 289

Wolverines (Husk O'Hare's), 174, 178

Yale University, 279, 288
Yancey, Alonzo, 185
Yancey, Jimmy, 183-86, 191, 196, 205, 262

Youmans, Vincent, 309

Ziegfeld, Flo, 307
"Zino," see Baltimore, Henry
Zulus, King of the, 132, 272
Zurke, 174

Index of Music

Aeroplane Sonata, 319
Alexander's Ragtime Band, 303
Alligator Crawl, 131
Alligator Flop, 96
Alligator Hop, 19
American in Paris, 112, 308
Angry, 57
Animal Ball, 120
Apologies, 80
Arkansas Blues, 176
Aunt Hagar's Children, 248
Avalon, 223

Baby Won't You Please Come Home, 109
Bach, J. S., B Minor Mass, 313; D. Major Suite, 327; Goldberg Variations, 304; Passion, 338; second Brandenburg Concerto, 306
Backwater Blues, 102, 115
Balling the Jack, 120, 121
Barnacle Bill, 159
Barnyard Blues, 30
Basin Street Blues, 36, 252, 265, 270, 276
Bass Goin' Crazy, 191
Beethoven's Fifth Symphony, 320
Biffly Blues, 219
Big Butter and Egg Man, 136
Big John Special, 215, 217
Black Bottom Stomp, 100
Blue Blues, 176
Boogie Woogie Stomp, 191
Bowery Buck, The, 114
Brahms, J., Fourth Symphony, 304
Buffalo, The, 114

Cake Walkin' Babies, 128
Camp Meeting Blues, 80
Cannon Ball Rag, 30
Careless Love Blues, 13, 266
Celeste Blues, 194-95
Chimes Blues, 73, 198
Christopher Columbus, 256
Church Street Sobbin' Blues, 248
Circus Day, 120
Clarinet Marmalade, 216
Clementine, 155

355

Climax Rag, 30
Coal Cart Blues, 128
Come Back Sweet Papa, 134
Cornet Chop Suey, 134
Court House Blues, 126
Cow Cow Blues, 198
Crazeology, 174
Création du Monde, 321
Creole Love Call, 80

Darktown Strutters' Ball, 178, 270
Deep Morgan Blues, 201
Detroit Rocks, 199
Detroit Special, 199
Didn't He Ramble, He Rambled Round the Town, 27, 120
Dinah, 143
Dippermouth, 61, 80, 126, 259, 271
Dirty Dozen, The, 200
Dixieland Shuffle, 80
Doctor Jazz, 80
Don't Go 'Way Nobody, 12
Down in the Dumps, 240
Down South Camp Meetin', 215
Drop That Sack, 131

Emancipation Day, 13
Empty Bed Blues, 115
Everybody's Doing It, 303

Fanny Lee Blues, 201
Fidgety Feet, 216-17
Fifty Hot Choruses of Armstrong, 136
"Figaro" ("Le Nozze di Figaro," Mozart), 342
Firebird Suite, 154
Five O'Clock Blues, 183
Fives, 183, 186, 189
Four O'Clock Blues, 202
Four or Five Times, 116, 250
Free As a Bird, 27
Friars' Point Shuffle, 176

Gaby Glide, The, 303
Georgia, 225
Get Out of Here and Go On Home, see Tiger Rag
Gettin' Dirty Just Shakin' That Thing, 199
Gimme a Pigfoot, 35
Gin Mill Blues, 250, 332
Good-by Bag, I Know You've Gone, 30
Good Time Flat Blues, 37
Grand Terrace Swing, 256

Gulf Coast Blues, 109
Gully Low Blues, 131
Gut Bucket Blues, The, 130-32

Harlem Rag, The, 114
Hastings Street, 200
Head Rag Hop, 199-200
Heebie Jeebies, 116, 128, 134
Henry Brown Blues, 201
High Society, 19, 27, 50, 270, 275
Hold On—Keep Your Hands on the Plow, 107
Hold Tight, 248
Hometown Skiffle, 200
Honky Tonk Town, 99
Honky Tonk Train Blues, 191-93, 199, 201, 332
Hot and Anxious, 215
How Am I Doing, Hey, Hey?, 269

I Ain't Gonna Give Nobody None of This Jelly Roll, 109
I Can't Dance, I've Got Ants in My Pants, 109
Idaho, 13
I Don't Know, 197
I Don't Know Where I'm Going but I'm on My Way, 284
I Found a New Baby, 332
I'll See You in My Dreams, 152
I Love You, 316
I'm Just Wild about Harry, 313
In a Mist, 159, 332
Indiana Avenue Stomp, 199
I Thought I Heard Buddy Bolden Say, 13
I've Got Elgin Movements in My Hips, 32
I Wish I Could Shimmy Like My Sister Kate, 109, 124

Jabo Blues, 202
Jazzin' Babies Blues, 71
Jazz Me Blues, 150, 165, 179, 227, 295
Jim Jackson's Jamboree, 200
Joyce 76, 13

King of the Zulus, 132-133
King Porter Stomp, 27, 32, 71, 215, 252
Kitten on the Keys, 320
Knockin' a Jug, 240

Lady Be Good, 231
Lazy Daddy, 50, 178
Lift 'Em Up Joe, 30
Little Joe from Chicago, 282
Livery Stable Blues, 42, 305, 322

Lonesome Blues, 131
Love Is Like Whiskey, 247

Mahogany Hall Stomp, 32
Makin' Friends, 212
Mama Sweet Daddy, 248
Maple Leaf Rag, 30, 114
Margie, 51
Marseillaise, La (Tiger Rag), 30
Meat Ball (Tiger Rag), 42
Meditation from Thaïs, 223
Michigan Water Blues, 109
Midnight Dream, 96
Milneburg Joys, 28, 32
Minnie the Moocher, 107
Mr. Freddie Blues, 201
Moanin' Low, 230
Monday Struggle, 191
Mozart, G Minor Symphony, 327
Muskrat Ramble, 19, 131
Mutiny in the Parlor, 181
My Pretty Girl, 155

Narcissus, 303
Nearer My God to Thee, 27, 58
New King Porter Stomp, 217 (see King Porter Stomp)
New Orleans Blues, 246
Nobody's Sweetheart, 177
Nola, 225
Now I Ain't Got Nothin' at All, 188
No. 29, 201
Number Two Rag (Tiger Rag), 30

Oh, How I Miss You Tonight, 81
Oh, You Beautiful Doll!, 303
Olympia Rag, 19
One O'Clock Jump, 253
Ophelia, 303

Pacific 231, 201
Panama, 22, 333
Pee Hole Blues (Milneburg Joys), 32
Pepper Rag, 22, 96
Pine Top's Boogie Woogie, 187-88, 192, 270
Pitchin' Boogie, 200
Poor Little Rich Girl, 171
Potato Head Blues, 131
Praline (Tiger Rag), 42
Pretty Baby, 303
Put 'Em Down Blues, 131

Raggedy-Ann, 316
Ragtime, 310, 325
Rhapsody in Blue, 112, 302, 303, 308, 311, 316, 320, 322, 329
Riverboat Shuffle, 152, 235
Riverside Blues, 80
Rocky Mountain Blues, 216
Roustabout Shuffle, 22, 96
Royal Garden Blues, 65, 109, 276
Rubber Plant, 30

Sacre du Printemps, Le, 316, 319
St. James Infirmary, 107
St. Louis Blues, 109, 138, 271, 278
St. Louis Stomp, 200
Salty Dog, 120
Savoy Blues, 131
Second Hungarian Rhapsody, 145
Sendin' the Vipers, 181
Shadow Rag, 42
Sheik of Araby, The, 218, 231, 239
Shim-me-sha-wobble, 109
Shortnin' Bread, 118
Shout for Joy, 191
Singin' the Blues, 51, 176
Sing On, 61
Smiles, 231, 239
Snag It, 78-79
Snake Rag, 19
Some Day Sweetheart, 211
Song of India, The, 235
Soon This Morning, 200
Souvenir (Drdla), 126
Squeeze Me, 109
Steamboat Blues, 22, 96
Stockholm Stomp, 216
Stomp 'Em Down, 201
Strange Fruit, 247
Streamline Train, 197-98
Strut That Thing, 197
Sugar Blues, 109
Sugar Foot Stomp (Dippermouth), 77, 215
Suitcase Blues, 189
Sweet Georgia Brown, 239
Swing Out, 219
'Swonderful, 116

Take It Away, 120
Take It Slow and Easy, 295
Tea for Two, 231
Texas Moaners Blues, 128

The Old Cow Died and Old Brock Cried, 17
The Planets, 180
There'll Be Some Changes Made, 178
The Rocks, 189
The World Is Waiting for the Sunrise, 136
The world's jazz crazy, Lawdy, so am I, 248
Tiger Rag, 30, 42, 50-51, 99, 147, 173, 236, 277
Tight Like This, 181
Tin Roof Blues (Jazzin' Babies Blues), 71, 163
Toddlin' Blues, 51
Tomcat, 71
219 Took My Babe Away, 13, 266

Wabash Blues, 56
West End Blues, 109
What-Cha-Call-'Em Blues, 215
When Buddha Smiles, 215
When the Saints Go Marching On, 27
Whistling Blues, 195
Who's It, 132
Wildman Blues, 131
Wilkins Street Stomp, 200
Windy City Stomp, 179, 295
Woodland Sketches, 154
Wrappin' It Up, 215

Yancey Special, 191, 193, 262
You Don't Know My Mind, 109
You Rascal You, 198
You're the Cream in My Coffee, 230